UNIVERSITY OF
WOLVERHAMPTON
KNOWLEDGE • INNOVATION • ENTERPRISE

 **Latin American Studies Series**

Series Editors Michael C. Meyer John D. Martz Miguel León-Portilla

University of Nebraska Press   Lincoln and London

Modern Brazil

Elites and Masses in

Historical Perspective

Edited by Michael L. Conniff and Frank D. McCann

First paperback edition: 1991
Most recent printing indicated
by the last digit below:
10   9   8   7   6   5   4   3   2   1

Library of Congress
Cataloging-
in-Publication Data
Modern Brazil: elites and masses in
historical perspective / edited by
Michael L. Conniff and
Frank D. McCann.
—1st pbk. ed.
p.   cm.
Includes bibliographical
references and index.
ISBN 0-8032-6348-1 (pbk.)
1. Social classes—Brazil—History.
2. Elite (Social sciences)—Brazil—
History.   3. Brazil—Social conditions.
I. Conniff, Michael L.   II. McCann,
Frank D.
HN290.Z9S643   1991
305.5'2'0981—dc20
90-49909   CIP

To the memory of Edwin Lieuwin—
mentor, colleague, friend

Contents

Frank D. McCann and Michael L. Conniff

Introduction

Brazil /brǎ zil'/ n. 1. Country in South America occupying 5.3 million square kilometers (5th largest in world). Capital: Brasília. 2. Nation of 140+ million people (6th most populous in world), representing most racial groups and admixtures thereof. 3. South American democracy with some 82 million voters. 4. Capitalist economy partially owned and regulated by the state (in 1987 GNP equaled U.S. $286 billion, making it 8th largest in the world). 5. The largest foreign debt among Third World countries (U.S. $114 billion). 6. Industrial exporter. 7. Future world power?

Brazil is all these things and more. It is complex, fascinating, and deceptive. How do we begin to describe such a country to students? The geographer, historian, sociologist, poet, anthropologist, political scientist, economist, and psychologist all have their particular approaches. They can make Brazil understandable within the context of their disciplines yet may still fail to convey a total vision of the country. All the same, researchers keep trying to portray Brazil to the world, for it is a country that each year grows in importance and will perhaps rank among the world's half-dozen leading nations in the twenty-first century.[1]

This volume looks at Brazil from an interdisciplinary vantage. The historians among us are social scientists who, among other things, synthesize the work of our more specialized colleagues. The non-Brazilian contributors have lived many years in the country. We regard the last hundred years of Brazil's history as a coherent whole, a period when the country achieved true nationhood and made many material and social advances.

We have chosen to examine Brazil's elites and masses as a technique for understanding its complex makeup. We define elites as limited number of people in high positions who manage the affairs of the nation. The masses, in contrast, are the multitudes of poor and working-class persons who individually have little influence in national affairs. We believe that the approach is both analytically coherent and heuristically efficient, in that it provides an integrated view of the society. We have separated the chapters into sections that look at various kinds of elites and masses. As editors, we have avoided imposing rigid definitions, allowing the contributors to explore the subtleties of their material.

Elite Studies

Scholars from Aristotle to C. Wright Mills have studied elites as a way to understand how society operates.[2] Others, as for example Emile Durkheim, Karl Marx, and Max Weber, have examined the masses. In general, these studies divide human behavior into two basic kinds, that of leaders and that of followers. The best researchers have always kept the two patterns in mind while writing about one or the other, since neither can be understood alone.

Observers of Latin America have long used elites and masses as analytical tools. From the nineteenth-century travelers' accounts (e.g. by Alexander von Humboldt and Charles Darwin) to the mid-twentieth-century textbooks (e.g. by Hubert Herring and Donald M. Dozer), authors have portrayed Latin America as having class-based societies primarily defined as elites, masses, and amorphous middle strata. These and other authors portrayed the societies in each country as headed by a small number of landowning families descended from colonial times. Typically, the eldest son inherited the family estate, while the younger sons were groomed for leadership in government, commerce, religion, and the military. The less ambitious might pursue the arts or a life of leisure. Daughters, indeed women, were rarely mentioned in such studies. The elite was tight-knit and integrated by kinship and mutual interest. The masses, in this view, lived at the poverty level on the great estates or in urban slums. They lacked any preparation for leadership and hence depended completely on the elite. The masses were also split internally by ethnic, racial, geographical, and political differences, so that they almost never acted in concert. The only exceptions were the great uprisings, as in Peru (1780), Haiti (1791), and Mexico (1810), when alienated masses rebelled against masters who oppressed and exploited pressed and exploited them. Usually, however, the system was held together by middle strata professionals (priests, soldiers, teachers, bureaucrats, doctors, lawyers) whose welfare depended on serving the elite and preserving the status quo.

The foregoing social portrait of Latin America eventually became outmoded, especially for describing such dynamic twentieth-century countries as Argentina, Brazil, Chile, Colombia, Mexico, Peru, Uruguay, and Venezuela. A few authors in the 1930s (e.g., Frank Tannenbaum, Simon Hanson, and George McBride) discussed attempts by socialist-leaning elites to mobilize the masses. More innovative studies appeared in the 1950s. John J. Johnson's pioneer work on the rise of the "middle sectors" (*Political Change in Latin America*, 1958), for example, suggested that leadership in some of these countries had already shifted from the elites to the middle classes. While some scholars denied that the middle sectors could transform their nations into bourgeois societies, others noted that the various functional elites—e.g., army officers, industrialists, intellectuals—represented institutional and professional interests other than those of the traditional elite. By the time the Cuban revolution was consolidated in 1959, a new generation of scholars within Latin America and abroad had research agendas on which the traditional view of elites and masses no longer fit.

Seymour Martin Lipset and Aldo Solari's *Elites in Latin America* (1967) represented the new approach. It was organized around functional elites, such as industrialists, politicians, the military, and the church. Surprisingly, the editors also included chapters on nonelite groups—e.g., middle strata, labor, peasants, and school teachers — presumably because they had gained recognition as actors on the political stage. No single group monopolized power, according to Robert E. Scott's chapter: "no power elite of the sort envisioned by C. Wright Mills exists in Latin America."[3] This assertion flew in the face of much research and did not gain widespread acceptance. One of the aims of the Lipset and Solari volume was to explore strategies for national development in Latin America. Most participants assumed that both the elites and nonelites had to be committed to modernization goals for development to succeed.

Anthropologists made important contributions to elite studies by applying ethnographic research methods to social, economic, and political leaders. Anthony Leeds's research discussed in Michael Conniff's chapter is a good example, as is Oscar Lewis's portrait of the Castros in *Five Families*.[4] Lewis also made his readers aware that women existed in Latin America. Historian James Wilkie borrowed a page from the anthropologist's journal when he created the term *elitelore* to describe this approach. Drawing on his own experience with oral history, Wilkie proposed that researchers examine elites the way ethnographers look at common people, analyzing their outlook on life, mores, superstitions, values, kinship rituals, and so forth.[5]

Studies of Latin American masses also became popular in the 1960s and 1970s, as researchers tried to view social systems "from the bottom up." Scores of dissertations and monographs were written about peasants, urban laborers, slum dwellers, immigrants, racial and ethnic minorities, and marginal populations in general. Irving Louis Horowitz's *Masses in Latin America* (1970) contained chapters based on a number of these studies. In his rationale for the book, Horowitz argued that the masses figured prominently, and sometimes decisively, in both economic development and major political events. A more recent study of masses is Charles Bergquist's *Labor in Latin America*, which deals with unionism in Chile, Argentina, Venezuela, and Colombia.[6]

Some researchers began to examine the connections between elites and masses. Stanley J. Stein's pioneering work, *Vassouras*, brought elites and masses together in the context of the nineteenth-century coffee plantation society. The book also had the virtue of examining the roles of women. Stein found that the planters' sons were educated to follow in the fathers' footsteps or to enter a profession, while the daughters were prepared for marriage. Love was less a factor in selecting a mate than the quality of the dowry and the marriage's contribution to preserving or extending family wealth. Planters' wives were expected to be passive, to run the household, to bear the children, and to tolerate the husband's extramarital relations with female slaves. Negro women, slave or free, enjoyed greater independence than their planter-class sisters. They did the work of men in the coffee groves and raised foodstuffs whose sale sometimes allowed them to purchase their freedom. In middle age, however, with the death of the planter, the wife sometimes took charge and "administered her plantation with a wisdom and acumen absent in her deceased spouse."[7] In the late 1970s, Thomas Skidmore and E. Bradford Burns sought to link the behavior of elites and masses, the first with a study on urban labor movements and elite responses, and the second with a look at nineteenth-century modernization strategies and their impact on the masses. These studies signaled the growing maturity of historical analysis, for they dealt with both elites and masses and synthesized much monographic research done by others.[8]

Elites and Masses in Brazil

Many scholars of Brazil have used analytical frameworks based on elites and masses. Just after the republican coup of 1889, the French writer Max Leclerc judged that Brazil's elite of businessmen, merchants, industrialists, and planters held absolute power over the country's affairs. He also described the masses as politically inert and without a sense of citizenship. The 220,000 persons permitted to vote in the country amounted to only 1.5 percent of the population, perhaps the lowest share in the world.[9] Not long afterward, Euclides da Cunha made literary history with his *Os sertões* [*Rebellion in the Backlands*], which portrayed the resistance, resilience, and intelligence of the rural masses of the Northeastern interior.[10]

Pedro Calmon's three-volume *História social do Brasil* (1935–39) used an elites and masses approach. Drawing largely on secondary literature and heavily influenced by Gilberto Freyre's *Casa grande e senzala* (1933), Calmon saw a basic continuity in elite composition from the fifteenth to the twentieth century. The masses remained poor and disorganized, a vast lower class of racially mixed people.[11]

At the end of the 1940s, Victor Nunes Leal in *Coronelismo, enxada e voto,* examined the structure of elite-masses relations at the municipal level, focusing on the figure of the political boss, or *coronel,* whose exercise of economic, social, and political hegemony colored the national political system. Curiously, while *coronelismo* (rule by rural strongmen) always preserved the threat of force, the *coroneis* felt compelled to present themselves as champions of local improvements to maintain the loyalty of elite allies and to present a paternal image to the masses.[12] (For these and other specialized terms, see the glossary on pp. 281–87.)

A decade later, Raymundo Faoro, in *Os donos do poder,* took the reader back to medieval Portugal to find the origins of Brazil's political leadership. That legacy, he discovered, was a bureaucratic establishment, secure and self-contained, that preserved the status quo and served as an instrument of authority. In his view, modern elites compete with one another to control the state apparatus, which in some ways is the ultimate arbiter. Meanwhile, "The masses— that is, the disadvantaged—who since 1930 have gained an ever- larger voice in politics, have been restrained by the new Moderating Power, i.e., the army." Faoro's analysis was very influential in the 1970s.[13]

Historian José Honório Rodrigues, in *Conciliação e reforma,* pro- vided another interpretation, one based on elite strategies for an- ticipating and avoiding violence and upheaval by the masses. Why these were necessary for the numerically small elite to maintain its control over the masses can be seen in such studies of rural and urban social movements as those by Duglas Teixeira Monteiro, Maurício Vinhas de Queiroz, Paulo Sérgio Pinheiro, and Maria Is- aura Pereira de Queiroz. As the world capitalist system expanded into Brazil, it restructured socioeconomic relations in the country- side and stimulated industrialization and urbanization, with ac- companying armed revolt and strikes. In the rural areas, the revolts studied used religion as an organizing principle, while nascent labor ideology infused the urban strikes.[14]

João Camillo de Oliveira Tôrres's synthesis on social stratification argued that *coronelismo,* in the early twentieth century, was a symp- tom of a weak national elite, one that had little control over rural areas. Moreover, until 1930, social structure remained remarkably stable. Urbanization was the strongest factor in the emergence of a political elite and of a true bourgeoisie in the mid-twentieth century. Previously what passed for the economic elite was in fact a series of wealthy families or dynasties in the major states that had little in common. Only in the last several decades has a truly national, integrated economic elite emerged.[15]

Luiz Aguiar Costa Pinto's stratification study in 1963 was based on an occupational analysis of the 1940 and 1950 censuses. He suggested that the upper, upper-middle, lower-middle, working, and lower classes made up, respectively, 4, 2, 6, 18, and 70 percent of the population. He found the middle class, a consolidation of intermediate strata, to be the least stable. He also suggested that from time to time new elites arose, coexisted with, and then took leadership from older elites. This usually happened in moments of crisis.[16] In the early 1960s, Fernando Henrique Cardoso examined the industrial elite of Sao Paulo.[17]

Foreign scholars also used elite and mass approaches, especially after 1960. Charles Wagley's chapter on social classes, in *An Introduction to Brazil,* is one of the best syntheses available for the period up to 1964. Thomas Skidmore's *Politics in Brazil* focused on the political elite from 1945 to 1967; Stepan's *The Military in Brazil* looked at the officer corps as a functional elite in the political arena, especially after 1964; Warren Dean, Nathaniel Leff, and John Wirth analyzed the rise or functioning of economic elites. Peter Mc-Donough's *Power and Ideology* examined the attitudes of a large sample of the functional elites of the early 1970s. Linda Lewin's *Politics and Parentela in Paraíba* examined the historical relationship between elite kinship and political organization by analyzing "the central Brazilian institution of the extended family or *parentela.*"[18]

As for the masses, two early studies are representative, Shepard Forman's *The Brazilian Peasantry,* which analyzes the social structure and evolution of the rural poor, especially in the Northeast, and Kenneth Erickson's *The Brazilian Corporative State and Working-Class Politics.* Finally, some authors looked at interaction between the elites and masses, as for example Ralph Della Cava, whose *Miracle at Joaseiro* is discussed in Eul-Soo Pang's chapter.[19]

Drawing upon these and many other studies, we can offer tentative definitions of elites and masses in twentieth-century Brazil. These synthetic remarks should be taken as preliminary to the refinements offered in the various chapters below.

The Elites

Changing elite structures in this century make definition especially problematical. The formal aristocracy of the nineteenth century gradually disappeared in the early twentieth. Persons with titles of nobility continued to enjoy prestige and served in high government posts, yet their power diminished greatly. They were shouldered aside by powerful state oligarchies consisting of families that had grown wealthy through the export of coffee, cotton, beef products, cacao, and other commodities. A recent study hypothesizes that in the period 1889–1937 the economic elite of São Paulo, already Brazil's wealthiest state, overlapped so much with the political elite that it resembled the "power elite" described by C. Wright Mills.[20]

These oligarchies managed to collaborate among themselves

enough to control national political affairs. No integrated national elite emerged, however, due to regional differences and rivalries. Unlike elites in Argentina, Chile, and Peru, for example, which tended to be concentrated in the capital cities, those of Brazil were dispersed among a half-dozen major cities. Moreover, since 1960 more and more members of the political elite have resided in Brasília, a new capital purposely established far from the old regionalist centers. Finally, the unusually sharp economic cycles Brazil has experienced in this century also impeded the coalescence of a ruling class.[21]

Most writers assert that since about World War I the dominant elements in Brazil have formed a shifting set of elites (e.g., merchants, financiers, landowners, industrialists, high-ranking military officers, and church leaders) whose decisions and actions are loosely coordinated by governmental leaders. Membership in the elites depends partly on such ascriptive characteristics as family, race, and inherited wealth. Belonging to a particular elite requires other attributes, however, such as the proper college or professional degree and membership in exclusive clubs, and it implies acceptance of mutually supportive "rules of the game." For example, members of the religious and military elites must endorse the institutional goals of the church and the armed forces. Still, talent and individual achievement are also necessary for admission to the ranks of the elites, for leaders realize that their legitimacy depends in part on accomplishing certain tasks entrusted to them—the economic elite, for example, must achieve productive efficiency and profits.

What prevents the various elites from coalescing into a single, unified power elite or a homogeneous upper class? Not only do some elites disagree with others on important issues, they are often divided internally. This gives rise to what McDonough calls "limited pluralism," in which elites compete over the formulation of public policy.[22] This competition is not as open as that which occurs in the United States or in some western European democracies, and it was not as free during the years of military government (1964–85). Still, the ability of different elites to advocate and promote their interests in the marketplace of public opinion kept Brazil from being a totalitarian society. In this view, the *abertura* or redemocratization begun in the late 1970s gradually permitted nonelites and opponents of the regime to operate in the political arena.

To avoid exaggerating the divisiveness of elites, we should stress that they have certain goals common to all elites: preservation of high status, access to wealth, and exercise of political power. Moreover, elites enjoy many advantages in their pursuit of these goals. They usually come from so-called good families and use kinship ties to further their interests. They attend the best schools and forge lasting friendships with other members of the elite. These friends will influence their social, political, and economic behavior; after family relatives, friendships are a Brazilian's most important social relations. The elite members manage the most powerful organizations in the country. The elites will change composition, but the pattern of elite dominance is apparently unshakable.

In part, elite stability endures because the elites' views of society and their roles in it have become more similar than different. Indeed, the study of the ideology of Brazilian culture and its relationship to national identity and social behavior have become the object of serious social science analysis. Much of the resulting literature is consumed by actual or potential members of one elite or another, thus influencing their perceptions of self and society.[23]

The model of elites competing for political control has been elaborated by Octávio Ianni and Francisco Weffort and was labeled by the latter an *estado de compromisso*. In this view, the 1930 revolution and the Great Depression destroyed the ad hoc collaboration of state oligarchies that had characterized the Old Republic. From then on, no single class or elite had sufficient power to rule the country alone. Those in high office had to balance a variety of different interest groups, keeping them all satisfied by multiple compromises. Getúlio Vargas is thought to have been the chief architect of this *estado de compromisso*. The job became more difficult because of the rise of new power contenders, especially those representing industry and the masses.[24] Such a situation eventually led to the rise of populist politicians in the 1940s and 1950s, persons who could, at least temporarily, balance the competing elites and maintain power by courting the masses. This model, with some modification, seems to describe Brazil of the 1980s.

The Masses

The simplest way to define the masses is to say they are all those who are not in the middle class or the elites. Similarly, following Faoro, we can define them as the disadvantaged, meaning those with insignificant status, wealth, and power. Another approach is to enumerate the sectors that make up the masses: clerical and manual laborers, domestic servants, providers of personal services, factory workers, peasants, rural laborers, marginally self-employed persons, the unemployed, and dependents of these people. We could also use an income test, describing the masses as all those belonging to families that receive less than, say, U.S. $300 per month. By any of these definitions, the masses would account for 60 or 70 percent of the Brazilian population.

The masses can be differentiated from the upper-middle and upper classes in other ways. The elite drinks imported Scotch whiskey in "piano bars," while the masses down *cachaça,* the national drink, in open-air corner establishments (*botiquins*). The elite eats French-style bread and prime cuts of beef, and the masses make do with *farinha de mandioca* and dried meat. Though black beans are the national staple, the elite has ritualized their consumption in a delicious stew (*feijoada*), served during long Saturday afternoon repasts, while black beans and rice make up the daily fare of the masses. The urban elite's late-night suppers contrast sharply with the early meals and bedtimes of workers.

The physical geography of the two is different as well. In large metropolitan areas, such as Rio de Janeiro, São Paulo, and Brasília, elite homes are found in the Zona Sul, Jardim Paulistano, and around Lake Paranoá, while the masses fill the Zona Norte and *subúrbios,* the ABC industrial region, and Ceilandia or Gama. You will find the masses en route to their work places in buses, trucks, or trains, and the elite in private automobiles and air-conditioned "executive" buses. Physically, the elite are generally white, European-looking, perhaps with deep, cultivated tans, and, thanks to orthodontia, gleaming straight teeth. The masses tend to be dark, with traces of Amerindian or African ancestry, and missing teeth are a sure badge of their socioeconomic status. Finally, the masses crowd the interstate bus terminals, while the elites zoom into the sky aboard *VARIG, VASP,* or *Transbrasil* airlines. And no one can doubt which group fills the jets heading north to Disneyland.

Interpretations of the role of the masses have varied with fashion and politics. Are they the driving force that keeps the country moving? Are they the sturdy mixture of bloods that Euclides da Cunha called "the hardy nucleus" of Brazil's future, "the bedrock of our race"? Are they the *povão,* or great unwashed masses that, without disciplined leadership, would lapse into idleness and chaos? Are they a seething mass of discontented persons ready to revolt to satisfy their basest instincts in an anarchist orgy? Are they, finally, just humble folk who struggle to hold onto the small stake fate has dealt them? The chapters in part III of this book offer at least partial answers to these questions. Here we can only offer some tentative generalizations.

The masses were not totally disorganized. The style of association that rural masses adopted was often that of a community where the fruits of their labors were held in common. Communities such as Canudos (1882–97), Joaseiro, Contestado (1912–16), Caldeirão (–1936), and Pau de Colher (1937) were organized around religious principles, but their mere existence as an alternative to rural elite dominance made them dangerous to the existing order. With the exception of Joaseiro, these self-improvement attempts were suppressed with extreme violence. As Rui Facó observed, "Canudos and the Contestado lived like a nightmare in the minds of the men of the dominant classes."[25]

From the early twentieth century on, a number of mass urban associations have been founded and have grown, some formed from the grass roots up, others initiated from the top down.[26] The earliest were mutual benefit societies and labor unions. The former have declined, replaced by social security programs, but the latter have expanded and now encompass a majority of the employed population. Leisure and recreational groups also appeared, foremost among them soccer clubs and samba schools. Political parties penetrated neighborhoods and factories to form associated clubs, and, after 1945, most Brazilians displayed at least some loyalty to parties as well as to leaders.[27]

The fact that most people belong to organizations does not mean that the masses are unified and well-represented. In fact, the masses are far more divided and fragmented than the elites. They share some characteristics—powerlessness, poverty, rudimentary education, lack of status—yet have few means of articulating their common interests. If lower class consciousness is to develop, it must overcome a tremendous inertia encouraged in the past by the overseer's whip, the *capanga*'s knife and pistol, and the policeman's rifle and billy. The political culture, formulated by the elites since colonial times, stresses conciliation, inter-class harmony, gradual material improvement, and respect for hierarchy. The underside of that political culture was repression. Elites on occasion used divide-and-conquer tactics on the masses, but usually they were unnecessary.

The educational system strengthens the elitist character of society in several ways. First, free public schools cannot provide adequate education for the masses, so they produce millions of teenagers who can only perform low-level jobs and who will never move very far up the social ladder. Second, the public schools condition the children of poor people to respect authority and to accept their place in life. Third, far better private school education is reserved for children whose parents can afford it. This selection allows children of well-to-do and elite families to get a head start, regardless of their native talents. It is they who fill the universities. In other words, the school system reinforces ascriptive criteria of upward mobility.

The masses seldom have acted in concert, and when they did the elites became concerned that a revolution was imminent. The following examples make the point: in 1937 demonstrations in Rio helped to create the climate for the *Estado Novo* coup; in 1945 pro-Vargas demonstrations (the *queremista* rallies) led the military to depose him; and in 1964 João Goulart's huge rally on March 13 precipitated the coup that ushered in the decades of military control. And these rather mild actions of the masses were not countrywide but occurred in a single city.

The phenomenal growth of fundamentalist evangelical sects in recent decades throughout Brazil (see Fred Gillette Sturm's chapter) may be an expression of the masses' need for association. The seeming political neutrality of such sects make them appear harmless to the elite, and indeed their emphasis on hard work and thrift gives them an attractiveness that the "fanatics" of Canudos and the Contestado lacked.

Today the masses do influence politics through the ballot box. The growth of effective political participation, although occasionally halted, may be leading to a larger popular role in politics. The franchise has gradually been extended to all Brazilians over the age of sixteen. An elected national assembly has existed, with brief lapses, since the time of independence, and while it has not always been strong, congressional elections have served as weather vanes of public opinion. The twenty-one years of military rule did not dampen Brazilians' aspiration for democracy—indeed, civic-mindedness may have been strengthened by the experience. The massive turnouts in the 1989 presidential elections may have heralded an era of participatory politics.[28]

Popular culture provides the masses with another way to influence the country's affairs. This happens in three ways. First, popular culture holds the masses together in a way no political or intellectual movement has to date. Samba, radio, carnival, soccer, and lately television (especially some of the *novelas* or soap operas) have given virtually every Brazilian a sense of identity with the rest of the population. Second, belonging to a national society builds bonds and tolerance but also gives the right to comment on the directions society and its leaders take. Early examples of this phenomenon were the barbed carnival verses of the 1910s and 1920s, by which the masses criticized their leaders. Popular songs remained a powerful source of protest even in the depths of political repression in 1969–72. Finally, the organizations formed to generate popular culture can play a part in politics. Samba schools helped recruit voters for populists between the 1930s and the 1950s, and Umbanda sects rallied support for their candidates in the 1960s. The political impact of popular culture has barely been explored.

The rural masses also have other means of expression and resistance. For example, pilgrimages to religious shrines always had political implications, from Joaseiro in Ceará to the church of *Senhor do Bom Fim* in Salvador, Bahia. In the Northeastern *sertão*, the literature of *cordel* seems to play a cultural role similar to that of the urban samba.[29] Backland violence and banditry were an early expression of inconformity with the rural social and economic order. Yet in the end, the most telling expression of protest for the rural poor has been migration to the great coastal cities. Everything we have learned about the rural exodus points to the powerful desire of peasants to improve their lives. And living in the cities exposes them to other means of expression: unions, clubs, the press, parties, rallies, and the right to vote as they wish.

We should finally note that, in very rare cases—since they almost always lack the appropriate education—talented persons from the masses may achieve elite standing in the clergy, the military, or politics. For example, several labor leaders won elective office in Rio de Janeiro in the late 1920s and early 1930s, and the 1933–34 constitutional convention included eighteen labor representatives from various states. David Fleischer's analysis of congressmen from

1946 to 1975 uncovered four persons with manual occupations. Frank McCann's chapter shows a growing pattern of lower-class recruitment into the army officer corps. These scattered data, plus the election to congress of a metal worker (Luís Inácio da Silva, nicknamed Lula), an Indian (Juruna), and a black playwright (Abdias Nascimento da Silva) in 1982, and the first's runner-up candidacy for president in 1989, suggest that there may be some substance to the promise of upward mobility.[30]

In sum, the masses of Brazil are neither a unified proletariat poised for class struggle nor an undifferentiated aggregate of people.

Format

A few words about this book's format are warranted. Although most chapters cover Brazil's history in the twentieth century, some adopt different time frames. Several authors delve into the nineteenth century for essential background. The entries by Joseph L. Love and Bert J. Barickman, Thomas Holloway, Sam Adamo, and Eul-Soo Pang end their coverage around 1940, a natural terminal period for their subjects. Joseph Dean Straubhaar's necessarily begins in the 1930s, when electronic media made their debut in Brazil. And the chapter by Eli Diniz picks up roughly where Steven Topik's ends.

In addition, most chapters cover the breadth of Brazil's territory, but in some cases the topics dictated otherwise. Love and Barickman's work looks at three key states, São Paulo, Minas Gerais, and Pernambuco. Pang's study, dealing with rural masses, focuses on the impoverished Northeast, a region that has resisted efforts at economic and social modernization. Holloway's chapter examines rural masses in São Paulo and the South, where millions of immigrants settled. The different regional responses to economic opportunity warrant further study. The Topik and Diniz chapters tend to concentrate on the Southeast, where most of the business elite resides. Finally, the Adamo study looks at Rio de Janeiro alone. Despite these geographical limitations, many of the conclusions, with appropriate caution, can be generalized to the rest of the country.

Part one deals with the political elite of Brazil, seen from several perspectives. Part two looks at the economic elite, especially businessmen and industrialists. Part three examines the masses. The final section searches for relationships between the elites and masses.

Robert M. Levine takes the reader through many of the intellectual exercises by which elites tried to understand (and perhaps manipulate) the masses. Straubhaar seeks to discover how elites and masses both contributed to the development of a unique mass culture that is conveyed by electronic media. And Fred Gillette Sturm sees the various religions as vehicles by which the elites keep in touch with, guide, and ultimately try to regulate the masses.

These various parts and chapters will, we hope, make sense by themselves and yet eventually blend together as well, yielding a coherent vision of modern Brazil.

Notes

1. At the start of the 1980s a former deputy director of the CIA ranked Brazil fourth, behind the United States, the Soviet Union, and China (Ray S. Cline, *World Power Trends and U.S. Foreign Policy for the 1980's* [Boulder: Westview, 1980], p. 87. A more conservative appraisal placed Brazil between tenth and fifteenth (Wayne A. Selcher, "Brazil in the World: A Ranking Analysis of Capability and Status Measures," in *Brazil in the International System: The Rise of a Middle Power,* ed. Selcher [Boulder: Westview, 1981], p. 56).

2. A good, if dated, introduction and guide to the general literature is Suzanne Keller, "Elites," in *International Encyclopedia of the Social Sciences,* 17 vols. (New York: Macmillan and The Free Press, 1968), vol. 5, pp. 26–29. A recent review of the theory and literature is provided in George E. Marcus, ed., *Elites: Ethnographic Issues* (Albuquerque: University of New Mexico Press, 1983), chs. 1–3.

3. Robert E. Scott, "Political Elites and Political Modernization: The Crisis of Transition," in Seymour Martin Lipset and Aldo Solari, eds., *Elites in Latin America* (New York: Oxford University Press, 1967), p. 127.

4. Oscar Lewis, *Five Families* (New York: Basic Books, 1959), pp. 295–350. See also the chapters by Arnold Strickon, Dwight B. Heath, Robert W. Shirley, and Nancie L. Gonzalez in *Structure and Process in Latin America,* ed. Arnold Strickon and Sidney M. Greenfield (Albuquerque: University of New Mexico Press, 1972).

5. *Elitelore* (Los Angeles: UCLA Latin American Center, 1973).

6. Irving Louis Horowitz, ed., *Masses in Latin America* (New York: Oxford University Press, 1970); Charles Bergquist, *Labor in Latin America* (Stanford: Stanford University Press, 1986). Recent Ph.D. dissertations have sharpened the analysis even further; excellent examples are Todd A. Diacon, "Capitalists and Fanatics: Brazil's Contestado Rebellion, 1912–1916," Ph.D. diss., University of Wisconsin, 1987; John D. French, "Industrial Workers and the

Origins of Populist Politics in the ABC Region of Greater São Paulo, Brazil, 1900–1950," Ph.D. diss., Yale University, 1985; and Joel W. Wolfe, "The Rise of Brazil's Industrial Working Class: Community, Work, and Politics in São Paulo, 1900–1955," Ph.D. diss., University of Wisconsin, 1990.

7. Stanley J. Stein, *Vassouras, A Brizilian Coffee Country, 1850–1900: Roles of Planter and Slave in a Plantation Society* (Princeton: Princeton University Press, 1985), p. 151.

8. E. Bradford Burns, "Cultures in Conflict: The Implication of Modernization in Nineteenth-Century Latin America," and Thomas E. Skidmore, "Workers and Soldiers: Urban Labor Movements and Elite Responses in Twentieth-Century Latin America," in *Elites, Masses, and Modernization in Latin America, 1850–1930,* ed. Virginia Bernhard (Austin: University of Texas Press, 1979).

9. Max Leclerc, *Cartas do Brasil,* trans. Sérgio Milliet (São Paulo: Companhia Editora Nacional, 1942), pp. 31, 124, 164–65.

10. Euclides da Cunha, *Rebellion in the Backlands,* trans. Samuel Putnam (Chicago: University of Chicago Press, 1944). See Levine's discussion in his chapter.

11. Pedro Calmon, *História social do Brasil,* 3 vols. (São Paulo: Companhia Editora Nacional, 1935–39); Gilberto Freyre, *The Masters and the Slaves,* trans. Samuel Putnam (New York: Knopf, 1946).

12. Victor Nunes Leal, *Coronelismo, enxada e voto,* 2d ed. (São Paulo: Editora Alfa-Omega, 1976) [1st ed. 1949].

13. Raymundo Faoro, *Os donos do poder: formacão do patronato político brasileiro,* 2nd rev. ed. (Porto Alegre: Editora Globo; São Paulo: Universidade de São Paulo, 1975). The quote is from p. 256 of the 1958 edition.

14. Duglas Teixeira Monteiro, "Um confronto entre Joazeiro, Canudos, e Contestado," *Histfia geral da civilização brasileira,* vol. 9, ed. Boris Fausto, pp. 41–92; Paulo Sérgio Pinheiro, "O proletariado industrial," in ibid., pp. 137–78. Maurício Vinhas de Queiroz, *Messianismo e conflicto social: a guerra sertaneja do contestado, 1912–1916* (São Paulo: Editora Atica, 1977); Maria Isaura Pereira de Queiroz, *Um mandonismo local na vida política brasileira e outros ensaios* (São Paulo: Editora Alfa-Omega, 1976). See also the Diacon, French, and Wolfe dissertations cited in note 6.

15. João Camillo de Oliveira Tôrres, *Estratificação social no Brasil, suas origins e suas relações com a organização politica do pais* (São Paulo: Difusão Européia do Livro e Centro Latino-Americano de Pesquisas em Ciências Sociais, 1965), pp. 131–33, 151–71, 177, 201.

16. Luíz Aguiar Costa Pinto, "As classes sociais no Brasil," *Revista brasileira de ciências sociais,* 3:1 (Mar. 1963): 217–37.

17. Fernando Henrique Cardoso, *Empresário industrial e desenvolvimento econômico* (São Paulo: Difusão Européia do Livro, 1964).

18. Charles Wagley, *An Introduction to Brazil* (New York: Columbia Uni-

versity Press, 1963); Thomas Skidmore, *Politics in Brazil: An Experiment in Democracy, 1930–1964* (New York: Oxford University Press, 1967); Alfred Stepan, *The Military in Politics: Changing Patterns in Brazil* (Princeton: Princeton University Press, 1971); Warren Dean, *The Industrialization of São Paulo, 1880–1945* (Austin: University of Texas Press, 1969); Nathaniel Leff, *The Brazilian Capital Goods Industry, 1929–1964* (Cambridge: Harvard University Press, 1968) and *Economic Policy-Making and Development in Brazil* (London: John Wiley and Sons, 1968); John D. Wirth, *The Politics of Brazilian Development, 1930–1954* (Stanford: Stanford University Press, 1970); Peter McDonough, *Power and Ideology in Brazil* (Princeton: Princeton University Press, 1981); and Linda Lewin, *Politics and Parentela in Paraíba* (Princeton: Princeton University Press, 1987), p. 9.

19. Shepard Forman, *The Brazilian Peasantry* (New York: Columbia University Press, 1975); Kenneth Paul Erickson, *The Brazilian Corporative State and Working-Class Politics* (Berkeley: University of California Press, 1977); Ralph Della Cava, *Miracle at Joaseiro* (New York: Columbia University Press, 1970).

20. Joseph L. Love and Bert J. Barickman, "Rules and Owners: A Brazilian Case Study in Comparative Perspective," *Hispanic American Historical Review* 66, 4 (November 1986); C. Wright Mills, *The Power Elite* (New York: Oxford University Press, 1956). Robert Wesson and David V. Fleischer argue that a power elite may be emerging in the 1980s: *Brazil in Transition* (New York: Praeger and Hoover Institution, 1983), pp. 59–60.

21. Douglas A. Chalmers, "Political Groups and Authority in Brazil: Some Continuities in a Decade of Confusion and Change," in *Brazil in the Sixties*, ed. Riordan Roett (Nashville: Vanderbilt University Press, 1972), pp. 60–61.

22. McDonough, *Power and Ideology*, pp. 11–13.

23. Carlos Guilherme Mota, *Ideologia da cultura brasileira, 1933–1974* (São Paulo: Editora Atica, 1980); Roberto da Matta, *Carnavais, malandros, e heróes: para uma sociologia do dilema brasileiro* (Rio de Janeiro: Zahar, 1979) and *O que faz o brasil, BRASIL?* (Rio de Janeiro: Editora Rocco, 1984); Renato Ortiz, *A cultura brasileira e identidade nacional* (São Paulo: Editora Brasiliense, 1985).

24. Octávio Ianni, *Crisis in Brazil*, trans. Phyllis Eveleth (New York: Columbia University Press, 1970); Francisco C. Weffort, "State and Mass in Brazil," in *Masses in Latin America*, ed. Horowitz, pp. 385–406.

25. Rui Facó, *Cangaceiros e fanáticos* 4th ed. (Rio: Civilização Brasileira, 1976), p. 186. Joaseiro, a town in Ceará, became an important pilgrimage site after Padre Cícero claimed that a miracle occurred there in 1889. See della Cava, *Miracle at Joaseiro*. On the Contestado see Todd A. Diacon, "Capitalists and Fanatics: Brazil's Contestado Rebellion, 1912–1916," Ph.D. diss., University of Wisconsin, 1987. It and Canudos are discussed in Eul-Soo Pang's chapter.

26. Michael L. Conniff, "Voluntary Associations in Rio: 1870–1945; A New Approach to Urban Social Dynamics," *Journal of Inter-American Studies* 17 (1975): 64–81.

27. Francisco Pedro de Coutto, *O voto e o povo* (Rio: Civilização Brasileira, 1966), an especially useful analysis of voter behavior in Rio de Janeiro between 1945 and 1966, makes this point.

28. Thomas Skidmore, *The Politics of Military Rule in Brazil, 1964–85* (New York: Oxford University Press, 1988); Alfred Stepan, ed., *Democratizing Brazil: Problems of Transition and Consolidation* (New York: Oxford University Press, 1989); for the elections see series of reports by Ronald M. Schneider and William Perry, "The 1989 Brazilian Elections" for the Center for Strategic and International Studies, Washington, D.C. (1989). The election symbolized the elites and masses division in the candidacies of Alagoas governor Fernando Collor de Mello and labor leader Luís Inácio da Silva (Lula). Collor's victory reaffirmed elite dominance, but his startling economic measures in early 1990 carried the promise of reform.

29. Joaseiro and Bom Fim are popular pilgrimage sites. See Candace Slater, *Trail of Miracles: Stories from a Pilgrimage in Northeast Brazil* (Berkeley: University of California Press, 1986). *Cordel* is a popular folk poetry put to song by Northeastern troubadours. See Candace Slater, *Stories on a String* (Berkeley: University of California Press, 1981).

30. Michael L. Conniff, *Urban Politics in Brazil: The Rise of Populism, 1925–1945* (Pittsburgh: University of Pittsburgh Press, 1981), pp. 112–13, 31; David V. Fleischer, "Thirty Years of Legislative Recruitment in Brazil," Johns Hopkins, Center of Brazilian Studies, Occasional Papers no. 5, 1976, p. 21, n. 1.

Part I: Political Elites

Joseph L. Love and Bert J. Barickman

Regional Elites

Elite studies have made rapid advances since the advent of the computer, whose analytic and storage capabilities allow researchers to ask new questions of existing data. This chapter builds on three studies by John Wirth, Robert Levine, and Joseph Love, who compiled machine-readable biographies of hundreds of politicians active from the beginning of Brazil's Republic to the Estado Novo, covering the years 1889–1937. Their parallel histories of the states of Minas Gerais, Pernambuco, and São Paulo analyzed these data in an attempt to portray the political elites of the time. The authors defined the elites with respect to a set of formal positions judged relevant to political power and patronage, i.e. they used positional rather than reputational or decision-making criteria.[1]

This chapter goes beyond that effort by (1) making systematic comparisons *among* the three regional elites and analyzing a composite elite; (2) adding and analyzing new data; (3) asking new questions of the old data, with new statistical techniques; and (4) comparing the composite elite with other political elites.

A few words about the three regional data sets are in order: they constitute populations rather than samples of the state elites, and they are fully comparable to each other. Yet they are only a sample of all state elites and the national elite. The states cannot be said to be "typical"—if any are—nor was their selection random. States were chosen whose elites wielded real power in an age when the state-based party was the only cohesive unit of political organization. São Paulo and Minas Gerais, with the largest populations and economies, dominated federal politics. Pernambuco, the most important state in the Northeast, perhaps best represents the many political, social, and economic dilemmas that its region poses for the rest of the country, then as well as now. The original studies went beyond simple biographical comparisons of age, education, and occupation, in order to find out how these politicians acted as elites. Other variables were added, including participation in key political events, social attributes, foreign ties, interstate ties, family linkages, intrastate geographical characteristics (such as urban-rural and sub-regional origins), and generations. Composite variables expanded the analysis, so that altogether some 100 variables were coded or derived.[2]

The populations of 263 (São Paulo), 276 (Pernambuco) and 214 (Minas) may seem small in comparison with some other elite studies, but the three state studies explored a number of dimensions that studies of larger groups have ignored.[3] For example, the books treated family and foreign ties, both of which require close contextual analysis. This greater depth perhaps compensates for limited breadth, allowing a view of relationships that a more inclusive approach might overlook. For example, Love's analysis of São Paulo's elite turned up an intricate network of business and family ties, showing how 97 of the 263 members of the set were interlocked (see figure 1).

Contours of the Composite Elite

With this brief introduction, we turn to elite behavior and background characteristics. One important pattern of behavior is the extent to which elite members remained loyal to the incumbent party (situação) or broke ranks. This matter was addressed by determining how members of the three elites acted at critical moments. First of all, how did politicians stand on slavery a year and a half before abolition? Only 15 percent of the relevant age cohort (N = 322) had favored freeing the slaves, with little regional variation. Second, what were elite members' political affiliations before the coup overturning the monarchy in 1889? Only 42 percent were "Historical" Republicans, i.e., those who had favored a change of regime before the Empire fell (N = 268). The other 58 percent were adesistas, those who converted to republicanism after the Republic was a fact, presumably to continue to qualify for political office. (Regional variation was conspicuous, however, for a majority of the Paulistas were "Historicals," compared with only 23 percent of the Pernambucanos.) By these two measures, then, the composite elite

São Paulo's Elite Networks

Key
b   brother
bl brother-in-law
c   (first) cousin
cl (first) cousin-in-law
g   grandson
gn grandnephew
n   nephew
nl nephew-in-law
s   son
sl son-in-law

The dotted lines link directors of the same firm.

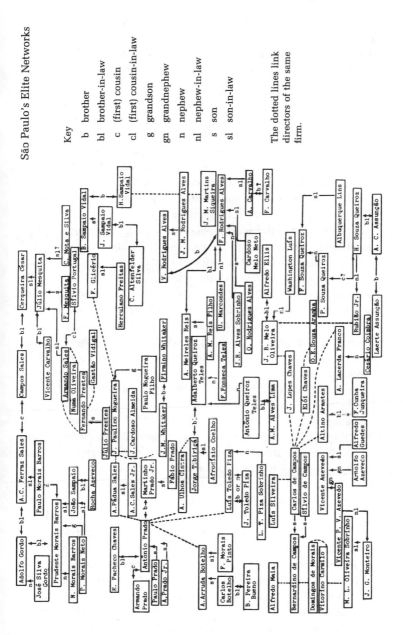

revealed that the Republic would be led by conservatives from the outset.

Other tests confirmed the composite elite's cautious nature. During Deodoro da Fonseca's attempted coup of 1891 and during the only contested presidential elections—those of 1910, 1922, and 1930—*at least* 86 percent of the elite members in each contest adopted the official position of their respective state parties. Likewise, only 8 percent of the composite elite identified with the *tenentes,* or young military radicals, after the revolution of 1930. (Pernambucanos were somewhat less cautious, since 19 percent joined the tenente faction.) Again, these data show the state elites to have been disinclined to break ranks with the dominant groups.

There was relatively little overlap between the political elites and social leaders, though incomplete data might partially account for this finding. Almost no one was associated with the labor movement, and no elite member belonged to the working or peasant classes. Surprisingly, few political leaders held positions in the agricultural, commercial, or bar associations (5, 3, and 4 percent, respectively). Fewer than 20 percent belonged to leading social clubs. This lack of correspondence may be partly due to the late appearance of many such organizations—after World War I—rather than to a lack of social prominence of politicians. Moreover, overlap ranged from a low of 11 percent in Minas to a high of 27 percent in São Paulo, which fact may have been largely a function of greater urbanization in the latter state.

Seventy percent of the composite elite took law degrees, overwhelmingly choosing to study in their own states. Another eight percent earned medical degrees, and almost eight percent held engineering degrees. Only two percent had military training. In all, ninety-three percent of the elites had university-level training, making them the most educated political elites for which we could locate comparative data. (See p. 18 below.) As late as 1940, only one in 370 persons in these three states held university degrees, which meant that members of the composite elite were some 345 times more likely to be college graduates than the average citizen.[4]

The importance of university degrees in Brazilian politics antedates the Republic. The "mandarin" model of the imperial political elite offered by Eul-Soo Pang and Ron Seckinger shows that university education was a virtual requirement for high political office.[5] With the advent of the Republic, however, another imperial requisite for holding high office—transregional political experience—disappeared, but the need for university education remained.

As for occupation, about two-thirds of the political elite were lawyers, including those who were judges. The average politician had 2.5 occupations (and in São Paulo, nearly three), not counting "politician" as an occupation. The small number of university graduates faced too many demands and opportunities to be confined to a single career, so they doubled and tripled their areas of activity.

Engineers and physicians each made up about 10 percent of the elites, while military officers accounted for only 3 percent, and clerics less than 1 percent. In addition, some 28 percent worked as journalists, and 27 percent as secondary school and college teachers. When all these categories are collapsed into a general one, we find that 91 percent of the elites exercised a profession. This made them 285 times more likely to have a profession than the average citizen in the three states as late as 1940.

Turning to the occupations associated with property ownership, we find that a quarter of the composite elite were landowners (*fazendeiros*). This figure seems low, given the predominantly rural character of the economy. Moreover, sharp differences occurred among the states: landowners constituted 38 percent of São Paulo's elite, roughly double their share among the Minas and Pernambuco elites. Industrialists made up 20 percent of the composite, but again São Paulo's share was much larger than those of the other two. Merchants and bankers made up 12 and 14 percent of the whole, respectively. Of the composite elite, 34 percent were businessmen (merchants, industrialists, bankers, commodity brokers, investors in railroads, and mine owners). Regrouping the categories, we find that 28 percent were engaged in the agricultural export sector (rural association leaders, exporters, landowners, and brokers). A composite category called "proprietor," which included all property owners, accounted for a total of 47 percent of all the elites. Again, São Paulo's elite had much more extensive involvement as property owners (56 percent) than the elites of the other states.

Analyzing the occupations of fathers of elite members provides information about the class origins of the elite and about their social mobility (see table 1). Among the 344 persons whose fathers' occupations could be identified (46 percent of the whole), the overwhelming majority were professionals or property owners, or both. Nine or fewer (3 percent) had fathers whose occupations may or may

Table 1   Father's Occupation: São Paulo, Minas Gerais, Pernambuco, and Composite Elite

Father's Occupation	São Paulo Number	%	Minas Gerais Number	%	Pernambuco Number	%	Composite Number	%
Lawyer	45	34.6	17	18.3	22	18.2	84	24.4
Doctor	6	2.3	3	3.2	3	2.5	12	3.5
Journalist	9	6.9	1	1.1	—	—	10	2.9
Fazendeiro	61	46.9	53	57.0	83	68.6	197	57.3
Merchant	10	7.7	7	7.5	10	8.3	27	7.8
Industrialist	8	6.2	2	2.2	—	—	10	2.9
Banker	8	6.2	—	—	1	0.8	9	2.6
Educator	10	7.7	—	—	3	2.5	13	3.8
Engineer	2	1.5	3	3.2	1	0.4	6	1.7
Cleric	—	—	—	—	1	0.8	1	0.3
Mil. Officer	8	6.2	3	3.2	3	2.5	14	4.1
Magistrate	9	6.9	6	6.5	3	2.5	18	5.2
Rural Land-dealer	2	1.5	—	—	—	—	2	0.6
Comissário	4	3.1	—	—	—	—	4	1.2
Manager, Railroad Company	6	4.6	—	—	—	—	6	1.7
Low-level Bureaucrat	4	3.1	2	2.2	2	1.7	8	2.3
High-level Bureaucrat	1	0.8	2	2.2	1	0.8	4	1.2
Tropeiro	3	2.3	—	—	—	—	3	0.9
Pharmacist	1	0.8	—	—	—	—	1	0.3
Other occupation	—	—	—	—	6	5.0	6	1.7
Social Positions								
National Guard officer	7	5.4	42	45.2	—	—	49	14.2
Member of Imperial elite	17	13.1	8	8.6	10	8.3	35	4.6
TOTAL	130		93		121		344	

Note: All percentages are adjusted. Occupations are multiple-coded. See definitions in Love, *São Paulo*, p. 285, except for the following: low-level bureaucrat (local or provincial civil servant); high-level bureaucrat (imperial government official); *tropeiro* (cattle or mule drover). Chi-square goodness-of-fit tests show that this sample of the elite is not biased toward the more successful members of the elite.

not have been lower class (*tropeiro* plus "other"). Thus, as expected in a traditional rural society, members of the political elite derived largely from the uppermost and upper middle strata.

The large proportion of fazendeiros among the fathers deserves special note. An absolute majority (197 out of 344) were estate owners. The second largest group was lawyers. Yet among the sons

Table 2   Elite Members Who Had the Same Occupation as Their Fathers

Occupation	Percent	Chi-square[a]
Fazendeiro	79.0%	0.0000
Military officer	33.3	0.0106
Merchant	27.7	0.0000
Doctor	20.0	0.0001
Industrialist	8.9	0.0018
Engineer	7.5	0.0238

[a]A significance level of 0.05 or lower indicates that chances are at least 19 out of 20 that the relationship is not random.

(i.e., elite members), almost two-thirds were lawyers, and only a quarter landowners. Predictably, because they exercised an "inherit-able" occupation, fazendeiros also "reproduced themselves" in the largest numbers, as table 2 reveals.

The foreign connections of the elite are obviously an important feature, especially in economically dependent countries, yet they are often slighted in elite studies. Our comparison reveals that about a third of the entire group had foreign ties of some sort.[6] In addition, those with foreign connections tended to be the most prominent politicians. One-fifth of the whole had lived abroad at least six months. Of the three states, São Paulo had the export-oriented elite with the most foreign connections, while Minas's had the fewest.

One type of foreign tie is interesting for its low incidence: foreign birth. Less than one percent of the political elite was born abroad, and only four percent had at least one foreign parent. This is striking, given the mass immigration Brazil experienced in this period. Moreover, there was little difference among the states. Despite the fact that São Paulo received half of all Brazil's immigrants for the period studied, its elite contained only one foreign-born member (N = 239)—Miguel Costa, who accompanied his parents to Brazil from Argentina as a child.

Data on interstate connections of the elites revealed many ties. A quarter of the whole group held out-of-state jobs other than posts in the federal government and congressional service. Forty-four per-cent of the Pernambucanos had such connections, compared with 22 and 17 percent of the Mineiros and Paulistas. This finding appar-ently reflects the relatively meager economic opportunities in Pernambuco. Sixteen percent of the composite group had been born in a state other than that where they made their careers, with little difference among the three cases. Almost the same share had out-of-state secondary education. A composite variable comparing all out-of-state links showed that 57 percent had such connections.[7] Mineiros had the highest share—72 percent—and Paulistas had the lowest—39 percent. The latter were apparently not as eager as the former to work in Rio de Janeiro, the most frequent single out-of-state link for Mineiros.

Family ties were an important element binding the elites together. Two-fifths of the total had relatives in the elite of the same state. Surprisingly, tradition-oriented Pernambuco had the lowest share (34 percent), compared with 46 and 43 percent in Minas and São Paulo. In compensation, however, Pernambuco's elite had a higher rate of relatives in other state elites. São Paulo is perhaps surprising for being so much like the other states in this respect and in its lack of penetration by foreigners. A fifth of the whole group belonged to, or was closely related to, the imperial elite, and almost half had some form of kinship with other members of the same elite, other state elites, or the imperial elite.[8] Upper levels of leadership seem to have had greater familial links: 81 percent of the governors had kinship ties to other members of the elite, compared with only 46 percent of the nongovernors.

The sex, race, and religious affiliations of the elite held few surprises. Only one woman turned up among 753 elite members, and her role was minor: Maria Tereza de Azevedo served only one year on the executive committee of São Paulo's Constitutionalist Party. Race was a sensitive issue for the elite of the period, and whiteness was assumed or attributed in the overwhelming majority of the cases. In São Paulo, only two persons were known to be nonwhites, Francisco Glicério and Armando Prado; and in Pernambuco Manoel Lubambo was rumored to have African ancestors. Many more must have had mixed racial origins, but such matters were rarely referred to publicly and did not appear in most biographies. The same was true of religion, for virtually everyone was assumed to be Catholic, or of Catholic tradition, since a number were nonpracticing. We found only a handful of non-Catholics (including a professed atheist), but no Protestants.

An urban-versus-rural classification of political bases shows that three-fifths of the total operated in cities, usually the state capital.

Variation was great, however, ranging from a low of 44 percent in Minas to highs of 67 and 71 percent in São Paulo and Pernambuco. (Belo Horizonte, capital of Minas, was built in the 1890s, so we included Juiz de Fora in the "urban" category.) In general, a member of the elite was eight times more likely than the average citizen of the three states to reside in the cities: 61 percent of the elite, compared with only 8 percent of the general population, lived in the capitals (or Juiz de Fora) in 1920.

Geographical movement was characteristic of at least two of the state elites (data for Pernambuco are not available). Seventy percent of the Mineiro and the Paulista elites had political bases in counties other than those where they were born. This movement, however, was not always to cities: in São Paulo, 63 percent of the elite still in the interior (n = 71) were not situated in their county of birth.

For the elites, as distinguished from the masses, the urban-rural dichotomy was perhaps meaningless. In São Paulo, for example, half of those elite members who were also fazendeiros (n = 89) had their political bases in the state capital. Jorge Tibiriçá, the father of the coffee price-support scheme, twice governor of São Paulo, and the atheist mentioned above, was no less a fazendeiro for having been born in Paris. But the urban connection gave the elites access to information and opportunities denied the rural masses.

The average age at which elite members entered politics was 44.2 years, with little variation among the three states. This seems surprising, when we consider that the vast majority first held office at the state level and that forty-four was the average age at which cabinet ministers in the Empire (1822–89) took office, i.e. at the national level.[9] For the Republican elite considered here, some 35 percent of the composite group held their first political office before the age of forty, though there was a spread among the three states. About 40 percent of the Mineiros and Pernambucanos held office before age 40, compared with some 25 percent of the Paulistas. The latter case might be explained in part by the more formally bureaucratic nature of the political process there.[10]

An analysis of generations reveals other aspects of elite behavior. The three generations were defined as (1) persons born in 1868 and earlier, who reached maturity before the fall of the Empire; (2) those born between 1869 and 1888, who came of age by the middle of the Old Republic and witnessed the first contested presidential race of 1910; and (3) those born during the Republic (1889 and after). Almost half of the entire elite fell into the first generation, about a third into the second, and a fifth into the third. Table 3 classifies the composite elite by generations and lists variable scores that were significant when cross-tabulated by generation (chi-square test at the 0.05 level).

The first two columns show that across the generations a decreasing share of the elite belonged to the Republican party leadership, and an increasing share to opposition party leadership. In São Paulo the third generation was completely excluded from Republican leadership before 1930. This fact was probably significant in the discontent that led to the founding of the Democratic Party in 1926.[11]

The next three columns show predictable results: members of the third generation were more than three times more likely to break with the establishment party than the first; legislative experience declined across the generations, but a majority of the third still had served at state or federal levels; and entry into the elite before age forty rose sharply with the third generation, who tended to push aside their elders after the Revolution of 1930.

The next three columns demonstrate that businessmen, fazendeiros, and others connected to the export trade, plus all those with foreign ties, bulked largest in the second generation. This seems to parallel the experience of Argentina: the generation of 1880—roughly corresponding to our first generation—studied at home, but their sons studied and traveled abroad. Among the professions, the majority of cross-tabulations by generation did not reach statistical significance. Of the three that did, the share of judges declined over the generations, while those of educators rose by half and engineers more than doubled their share.

The elite that emerged from Getúlio Vargas's Revolution of 1930 merits separate treatment, since that event was a watershed. About a quarter of the whole elite entered the group after the coup. Sharp differences separated the three states' experiences. São Paulo had the highest proportion of newcomers, 37 percent. This pattern owed as much to the formation of new political parties as it did to federal intervention. Minas did not suffer federal intervention, yet it had a higher percentage of newcomers than Pernambuco, where the establishment was ousted. Before-and-after comparisons show changes in education and occupation as well. Only 2 percent of the composite elite members who had entered politics before 1930 were

Table 3   Elite Generations Cross-tabulated by Selected Variables

| Generation | Political Experience | | | | Age |
	Republican Party Executive Committee	Oppos'n Party Executive Committee	Break w/State Establishment in National Crisis	Legislative Experience	Reached Elite Before Age 40
1	32.5%	5.8%	13.3%	71.7%	25.6%
2	29.2	17.7	25.5	60.0	29.3
3	8.5	33.3	48.6	52.6	69.0
χ²	0.000	0.000	0.000	0.001	0.000

| | Occupation | | Foreign Ties | Profession | | |
	Business	Export		Judge	Educator	Engineer
1	32.5	27.2	27.2	31.9	24.8	7.1
2	41.9	34.7	46.6	10.9	26.6	12.5
3	25.9	21.9	32.5	6.0	37.1	15.5
χ²	0.011	0.044	0.000	0.000	0.041	0.021

Note: "Foreign Ties," "Business," and "Export" are composite variables (see definitions above).

military officers, compared with 5 percent of those who entered after that year. Still, it is notable that this figure is not even higher, given Vargas's debt to his military supporters. The *bacharel* (law or medical graduate) group fell from 80 percent among pre-1930 elites to 68 among those who entered politics during Vargas's tenure. The proportion of businessmen likewise fell from 37 percent to 26 percent, which fact parallels their falling share in third generation elites, mentioned above.

Success within the Elite

Having sketched the general features of the composite elite and those of the three states, we are ready to ask, What characteristics distinguished the more successful from the less successful elite members? Borrowing a procedure from Peter Smith's study, we can stratify the positions attained to ask the question, Are there correlations between *success* (defined as the highest office held) and other attributes? We can group the coded political posts in the following ranking:

1. presidents, vice presidents, and ministers
2. governors and supreme court justices
3. federal, legislative, and executive posts other than minister
4. party executive committee members
5. state secretaries and presidents of the state courts
6. state legislative and executive posts other than secretary.

This ranking seems to be consonant with the power of the offices. Executive committee memberships were more important than all other state offices except that of governor, because they groomed candidates for so many other posts.[12] The governorship, however, was always a key position in the state political system and even in the federal constellation of power. Supreme court justices warrant inclusion in level 2 because of their prestige and relative independence of the executive during this period.

With such a ranking, we can correlate highest office held with the coded variables for members of the elite in order to find the attributes that seemed most helpful for getting ahead in politics.[13] We consider all correlations at the 0.05 level to be significant.[14] We also, somewhat arbitrarily, required a gamma value of plus or minus 0.3 for inclusion.

Among the political variables treated above, legislative experience had a fairly strong association with success, especially for the elite of São Paulo (+0.35). This fact supports our view of a more orderly progression of careers there than in Pernambuco. No statistically significant results distinguished abolitionists from nonabolitionists, or Historical Republicans from Monarchists.

In nonpolitical leadership, the role of prestigious lawyers and magistrates is especially striking in Pernambuco: in fact, there is a perfect correlation between success and leadership of the attorneys' organization (+1.0). Foreign economic ties were apparently important only in São Paulo (+0.32 for exporter and +0.31 for manager of a foreign company); interstate ties of various sorts appear most closely correlated with success in Pernambuco, e.g., +0.37 for out-of-state political office. Educational patterns reveal that *bacharéis* did best in Pernambuco (+0.33); that pharmacists fared badly in Minas (−0.45); that engineers did likewise in those two states, especially in Pernambuco (−0.61); and that, unexpectedly, a military education was the worst degree (a perfect negative correlation, −1.0) for climbing the success ladder in the Northeastern state.

Among occupations, it is notable that only two were positively correlated above the +0.3 level. Both, banking and real estate trading, were associated with ownership rather than professions, and both were exclusively correlated with success in São Paulo, at +0.33 and +0.51, respectively. (In that state, industrialists as well nearly reached the +0.3 level.) Family connections were associated with success in Minas Gerais (+0.36 for ties within the Minas elite).

"Success," however, need not be defined in terms of highest office attained, as in Smith's study, and we would offer an alternate definition here: the degree of success within the elite is indicated by the number of positions held. By this definition, Antônio Carlos Ribeiro de Andrada, the governor of Minas who in 1930 is supposed to have said, "Let's make the revolution before the people do," was the most successful: of the 753 members of the three state elites, only he held 11 posts. Almost two-thirds of the whole set held only one.[15]

Using this standard for success, we see a somewhat different constellation of "useful" variables. For "longevity" in the elite, it was decidedly harmful (−0.59) to have been a Historical Republican in Pernambuco, just as having supported Deodoro da Fonseca's abortive coup was quite harmful for the São Paulo set (−0.64). Legislative experience was clearly useful in the more orderly states of Minas and São Paulo (+0.47 and +0.62, respectively), and to have been a leader of the opposition was a strongly negative factor in Pernambuco (−0.54), but not elsewhere. In nonpolitical activities, leadership in an agricultural society was important in São Paulo, but doubly so was leadership in a lawyers' association in Pernambuco (+0.90).

For foreign ties, being an exporter was useful for staying in the elite in Pernambuco (+0.41), while having an interest in a foreign firm was important in São Paulo (+0.34). For interstate ties, it was predictably harmful for Mineiros to have been born out of state (−0.36) and even more so (−0.57), surprisingly, to have attended a *colégio* outside Minas; likewise, a career in the Federal District and especially in an interstate agency seemed to hurt Pernambucanos (−0.38 and −1.0). Since holding an office in another state helped the Northeasterners on the "highest office" scale, such fact may imply that they needed outside help to move up the ladder; but leaving their state base may have shortened their careers. (This view is also supported by the much lower correlation of success by the two definitions for Pernambuco than for the other two states, noted below.)

With respect to education, the in-state law degree was important in Pernambuco only (+0.37), and the bacharel background (in state or out of state) important for Pernambuco and Minas (+0.32 for both). Surprisingly, the lack of higher education was perfectly negatively correlated in São Paulo (−1.0) yet not statistically significant in the other two states.

For occupations, it was important for Mineiros to be lawyers to survive in the elite (+0.57), and they had much less chance of advancing politically if they were doctors (−0.48). To be a fazendeiro in Pernambuco was useful (+0.51). As anticipated, bankers did well in both the São Paulo and the Minas Gerais elites (+0.34 for both). Family ties in the same state elite were, as expected, positively correlated in São Paulo (+0.37) and even more so in Minas (+0.53), where any coded family tie (to contemporary state elites or to the imperial elite) was also strongly positive (+0.45). Contrary to expectations, ties in the same state elite were negatively correlated in Pernambuco (−0.45). Nonetheless, family links with the imperial elite were useful (+0.34) in the Northeastern state.

As for the degree of correspondence between attributes for success by the two definitions—highest office attained and number of offices held—there was considerable dispersion among the scores for the two rankings. The following regularities, however, were observable: for both Minas and São Paulo, legislative experience was important by both definitions of success, as was legal society leadership for Pernambuco. Association with a foreign firm was important in São Paulo for both types of success, and a bacharel background helped for both types in the other two states.

A test for strength of association between the two definitions of success yielded a relatively high score: +0.53.[16] It was higher still for the São Paulo and Minas subsets (+0.63 and +0.69), but much lower (+0.14) and not statistically significant for the Pernambuco group. Thus Pernambucanos who succeeded along the two tracks were much less likely to be the same people than those in São Paulo and Minas.

Cross-national Comparisons

In the concluding section of this chapter, we will explore the ways in which the regional elites of Brazil were similar to and different from other political elites. The exercise is tentative, because all the studies considered define elites differently. Most of the elites are national (though some include important state or provincial executives). Most are parliamentary elites, though a few are mixtures of executive, legislative, and other groups.[17] These comparisons will highlight what seem to be the distinguishing contours of the Brazilian political elite, as we will hereafter refer to the composite of the three state elites.

With regard to father's occupation, the Brazilian pattern, revealing upper-middle and upper-class fathers (over 95 percent), contrasts with political elites in three German regimes (Weimar, Nazi, and Federal Republic), where fathers of political elite members had lower-middle and lower-class occupations in the following shares: 47 percent (1925), 59 percent (1940), and 54 percent (1955).[18] Even in Porfirian Mexico (1900–11), 11 percent of the political elite had fathers with lower-class occupations of "worker" and "peasant." The share with lower-class fathers rose to 17 percent in revolutionary Mexico (1917–40) and to 24 percent in the post-revolutionary era (1946–71).[19]

On foreign birth, Brazil's elite may also be contrasted with Argentine senators and deputies in three transitional moments studied by Darío Cantón (1889, 1916, 1946). In Cantón's work, for three sets of senators and deputies, the foreign-born ranged from 10 to 53 percent, peaking in 1946. By contrast, only 0.6 percent of the Brazilian elite was foreign born, and fewer than 4 percent had at least one foreign parent. Both countries experienced mass immigration, but immigrants to Argentina enjoyed more political success, perhaps in part because the base population was smaller there.

Argentine legislators first took high offices at earlier ages than their Brazilian counterparts. In 1889, 85 percent of the former had entered the national parliament before reaching forty years of age, and another 4 percent had reached provincial office before thirty-five. Thus 89 percent of Cantón's Argentine elite in 1889 held state or federal offices by the age of forty, compared with only 35 percent of the Brazilian elite. In the Argentine congresses of 1916 and 1946, however, the share that entered politics before age forty dropped to 69 and 41 percent, respectively. Still, the latter rate was higher than that of the Brazilian elite.[20]

The studies of other Latin American elites cited in note 17 do not furnish data on kinship, but Brazil's elites were probably not unique in possessing extensive networks of relations. Robert Putnam notes that "43 percent of the cabinet ministers who ruled Holland between 1848 and 1958 were bound by kinship to other ministers; . . . approximately one-seventh of the deputies of the Third French Republic (1870–1940) were related to one another; and . . . about one-tenth of all U.S. congressmen from 1790 to 1960 had relatives who also served in Congress."[21] We suspect that kinship remains an undeservedly neglected variable in most political elite studies. If Latin American political leaders were also owners of factories and plantations or haciendas (as in the São Paulo case), would this fact not drastically alter our views of sectoral clashes?[22]

As for educational background, the several political elites for which we compared data showed that university graduates were overrepresented with respect to the general population by a factor ranging from eight-to-one for the United States to over 100-to-one for underdeveloped countries.[23] Brazil's elite clearly falls toward the far end of the range, since 93 percent had university degrees.

Comparisons of occupation are complicated by the facts that not all authors have used multiple coding and that definitions differ. In any case, professionals predominate everywhere. Brazil's elite stands out because of the large proportion of its members who were landowners or businessmen of some sort. The contrast is especially sharp with the elite in Mexico, where landowners did not constitute over 4 percent and businessmen reached only 6 percent, as compared with 25 and 34 percent in Brazil. (Smith in fact devotes an entire chapter of his book to the lack of integration between the economic and political elites.) The same pattern held true for the last parliament of France's July Monarchy (1846–48), in which only 13 percent of the deputies were businessmen. Of all bourgeois deputies, only a tenth were in business occupations. Patrick and Trevor Higonnet comment, "This last figure is surprisingly small for a regime that was . . . described by Marx and Tocqueville as a joint stock company ruling the many for the material advantage of a selected few. . . . the great majority had no direct connection with the business world."[24]

Two other parliamentary elites for which occupational data are available are the Spanish and Dutch chambers of deputies. In seven Spanish parliaments, 1879–1979, "businessmen" and "farmers," the only two property-holding groups identified in the study of this elite, together averaged 18 percent of the total membership. In the

Dutch chamber for the years 1848–1967, the average for four periods (defined by the extent of suffrage) was 11 percent.[25]

Most curious of all, perhaps, is the case of the United States political elite (1877–1934), consisting of presidents, vice presidents, and cabinet members, of which only 13 percent were businessmen and 2 percent landowners. Of the United States national leadership from the 1790s to 1940, Putnam remarks, "The proportion of businessmen (or sons of businessmen) entering the political elite has remained relatively small and essentially unchanged throughout the period during which America moved from an overwhelmingly agricultural society to an overwhelmingly industrial society."[26] These data are in apparent conflict with an earlier study of United States cabinet members, in which a majority were identified as businessmen during the period 1889–1949. In any case, the latter work shows that professionals rather than property owners dominated even in the executive elites (national cabinets) of Britain, France, and Germany.[27]

If we except the conflicting findings for the more narrowly defined United States elite (i.e., an exclusively executive elite), the low level of participation of proprietors is notable everywhere outside Brazil. The only elite that approximates that of Brazil with regard to property ownership is Argentina's. Proprietors made up 24 to 45 percent of the Argentine parliament in the three periods Cantón studied, and a weighted average is 31 percent. This figure is still a third below the Brazilian score of 47 percent. José Luis de Imaz's study of Argentina's elite includes entrepreneurs in his "governing teams," which also presumably include landowners. Entrepreneurs constituted 8 to 16 percent of the teams of 1936, 1941, and 1946, dropped in 1951, and then rose to 24 and 32 percent in the teams of 1956 and 1961.[28]

Thus the Brazilian political elite seems to have been more extensively penetrated by property owners than were other elites. Though property owners tend not to predominate in Western political elites, extensive research has nonetheless established the nonrepresentativeness of the latter groups. This literature shows that political elites tend either to be formed by professionals from relatively privileged backgrounds, linked with owners of property through social and economic ties, or to be formed (in lesser numbers) by the owners themselves.[29] And, as Ralph Miliband puts it, "The reason for attaching considerable importance to the social composition of the state elite in advanced capitalist countries lies in the strong presumption this creates in its general outlook, ideological dispositions, and political bias."[30] This observation seems a fortiori valid for the Brazilian elite, which manifestly felt no great injunction to represent the interests of the laboring classes of the city and countryside, not to mention other groups it all but excluded—nonwhites, women, and immigrants.

To be sure, our finding on the relatively high share of property owners in Brazil must be tentative. The multiple occupational coding for some elites (including Brazil's) leads to larger percentages than single coding. Robert D. Putnam's United States and Smith's Mexican data were coded for occupations at entry only, and occupational definitions are not identical. The Brazilian elite contains a larger proportion of Paulistas (residents of São Paulo) than it would in a full national study, yet Minas and even Pernambuco had relatively large shares of proprietors. The Paulistas and Mineiros did weigh more heavily in the political process than even their large numbers of ministers and presidents would indicate. Nonetheless, within these limitations, the fact that Brazil stands out in the degree to which proprietors held leading political positions tends to raise doubts—at least for the years studied—about the celebrated hypothesis of the "relative autonomy" of the Brazilian State from economic interests.[31]

Notes

1. The original studies are: John D. Wirth, *Minas Gerais in the Brazilian Federation, 1889–1937* (Stanford: Stanford University Press, 1977); Robert M. Levine, *Pernambuco in the Brazilian Federation, 1889–1937* (Stanford: Stanford University Press, 1978); and Joseph L. Love, *São Paulo in the Brazilian Federation, 1889–1937* (Stanford: Stanford University Press, 1980). For a discussion of the three methods of defining political elites, see Robert A. Dahl's classic article, "A Critique of the Ruling Elite Model," *American Political Science Review* 52 (June 1958): 463–69. We wish to thank Professors Levine and Wirth for supplying additional data on fathers' occupations.

2. Explicit definitions and a list of variables and values appear in Love, *São Paulo*, pp. 277–87.

3. Peter H. Smith's *Labyrinths of Power: Political Recruitment in Twentieth-Century Mexico* (Princeton: Princeton University Press, 1979), for example, included 6,000 persons in a study of the period 1900–71.

4. Occupational and educational data are from the 1940 census.

5. Eul-Soo Pang and Ron Seckinger, "The Mandarins of Imperial Brazil," *Comparative Studies in Society and History* 14, no. 2 (March 1972): 217–18.

6. Foreign ties included importing and exporting; economic interests in foreign firms or immigration schemes; representation of foreign firms or governments; foreign birth, or that of spouses or parents; residence or study abroad; and foreign decorations or titles.

7. Interstate ties included birth, secondary schooling, professional careers, or government posts in other states or the Federal District, excluding service in Congress or cabinet posts.

8. Kinship was defined to include blood and in-law relations through first cousin. The imperial elite was defined as senators or titleholders of baronial rank or above.

9. José Murilo de Carvalho, "Elites and State-building in Brazil," (Ph.D. diss., Stanford University, 1974), p. 177.

10. See Love, *São Paulo*, pp. 162–63, 165.

11. Ibid., pp. 117–18.

12. See Joseph L. Love, "Um segmento da elite política brasileira em perspectiva comparativa," in *A revolução de 30: Seminário internacional,* Coleção Temas Brasileiros, vol. 54 (Brasília: Editora Universidade de Brasília, 1982), pp. 63–64.

13. After Smith, we will use the gamma coefficient of correlation: see *Labyrinths,* pp. 107–8.

14. Graduation from college and practicing a liberal profession did not yield statistically significant results when correlated with highest office attained, because there was little variance: over nine-tenths of the whole elite were graduates and professionals, so these attributes were almost assumed for presence in the elite.

15. For an analysis of movement from one position to another, see Love, "Um segmento," pp. 59–64.

16. Gamma was used.

17. These studies are, Darío Cantón, *El parlamento argentino en épocas de cambio: 1890, 1916, y 1946* (Buenos Aires: Editorial del Instituto, 1966); Salustiano del Campo, José Félix Tezanos, and Walter Santín, "The Spanish Political Elite: Permanency and Change," in *Does Who Governs Matter? Elite Circulation in Contemporary Societies,* ed. Moshe M. Czudnowski (DeKalb, Ill.: Northern Illinois University Press, 1982), pp. 125–53; Hans Daalder and Joop Th. J. van den Berg, "Members of the Dutch Lower House: Pluralism and Democratization, 1848–1967," in the same volume, pp. 214–42; Harold D. Lasswell, Daniel Lerner and C. Easton Rothwell, *The Comparative Study of Elites: An Introduction and Bibliography* (Stanford: Stanford University Press, 1952); Frederick W. Frey, *The Turkish Political Elite* (Cambridge, Mass.: M.I.T. Press, 1965); Patrick L.-R. Higonnet and Trevor B. Higonnet,

"Class, Corruption and Politics in the French Chamber of Deputies, 1846–1848," in *Quantitative History*, ed. Don Karl Rowney and James Q. Graham, Jr. (Homewood, Ill.: Dorsey, 1969), pp. 129–47; José Luis de Imaz, *Los que mandan (Those Who Rule)*, trans. Carlos A. Astiz (Albany: State University of New York Press, 1970); Robert D. Putnam, *The Comparative Study of Political Elites* (Englewood Cliffs, N.J.: Prentice-Hall, 1976); Smith, *Labyrinths*; and Wolfgang Zapf, *Wandlungen der deutschen Elite: Ein Zirkulationsmodell deutscher Führungsgruppen, 1919–1961* (Munich: Piper, 1965).

18. Lower-class occupations alone were 14.5 and 16 percent respectively. Derived from Zapf, *Wandlungen der deutschen Elite*, p. 182.

19. Smith, *Labyrinths*, p. 77.

20. Cantón, *Parlamento argentino*, pp. 46, 77. We recomputed percentages to eliminate missing information and obtained a single rate for each cohort by weighting the deputies and senators by the number in each chamber for the year in question.

21. Putnam, *Political Elites*, p. 61.

22. See "Topical Review: The Theory of Sectoral Clashes," in *Latin American Research Review* 4, no. 3 (1969): 1–114.

23. Putnam, *Political Elites*, p. 27.

24. Higonnet and Higonnet, "Class, Corruption, and Politics," p. 132.

25. Derived from del Campo et al., "The Spanish Political Elite," p. 129, and Daalder and van den Berg, "Members of the Dutch Lower House," pp. 225, 227.

26. Putnam, *Political Elites*, p. 188.

27. Lasswell et al., *The Comparative Study of Elites*, p. 30.

28. Imaz, *Los que mandan*, p. 27.

29. John D. Nagle, *System and Succession: The Social Bases of Political Elite Recruitment* (Austin: University of Texas Press, 1977), pp. 233, 248–49; Ralph Miliband, *The State in Capitalist Society* (New York: Basic Books, 1969), p. 66.

30. Miliband, *Capitalist Society*, p. 68.

31. For the general proposition of relative autonomy in Brazil, see Raymundo Faoro, *Os donos do poder: formação do patronato político brasileiro*, 2d ed., 2 vols. (Porto Alegre: Globo, 1975). For the period under review, see Mauricio Font, "Coffee Planters, Politics, and Development in Brazil," *Latin American Research Review* 22, no. 3 (1987), pp. 69–90. For literature on "relative autonomy" in other periods of Brazilian history and the argument that state policies favored the economic interests represented in government, see Joseph L. Love and Bert J. Barickman, "Rulers and Owners: A Brazilian Case Study in Comparative Perspective," *Hispanic American Historical Review* 66, no. 4 (November 1986): 743–65, and the reply by Love to Font in *LARR*, forthcoming, 1989.

Michael L. Conniff

The National Elite

All organized societies select elites to conduct public business and to make decisions affecting their populations. Since the turn of this century, Brazilians have used several methods with varying results to choose their political elite. This chapter will focus on the characteristics and selection of public officials in the executive branches of government, from mayors to presidents.[1]

Before the Republican coup of 1889, political tradition in Brazil had reserved the highest offices for a small elite chosen by the hereditary monarch and his aides. Democratic procedures were utilized only for filling local, provincial, and some parliamentary offices. The long-term trend, however, was toward increased use of elections and gradual expansion of the electorate.[2] After the overthrow of the monarchy, the 1891 Constitution provided that elections be held for virtually all executive and legislative posts. But as we will see, that mandate was not immediately honored. In a broad sense, twentieth-century political history has been accompanied by attempts to perfect a democratic system for the selection of leaders. Generally speaking, this has been resisted by incumbent politicians, who have tried to extend their time in office or to choose their successors.

Democracy is not an absolute: people select their leaders with varying degrees of representation, secret balloting, freedom from coercion, and open competition for public posts. The Brazilian experience during this century has ranged from a virtual lack of democratic procedures at the beginning to their widespread prevalence during the 1950s. It might be clearer to use the term "selection" to refer to the choice of political leaders in Brazil, to avoid applying criteria by which elections in the United States and Western Europe are judged. Nor is the attainment of democracy permanent. During the 1960s and '70s Brazilians lost most of their political rights under a military-technocratic regime. Only in the mid-1980s were they restored.

A final generalization is in order. In the early part of this century, the political elite coincided closely with the social, economic, and intellectual elites. Increasingly, however, access to public office became available to individuals from the middle class, so that the political elite no longer overlaps as much with the others. Political careers have become avenues of upward mobility for talented persons with the right qualifications. This trend brought a degree of democratization to Brazilian society, because leadership was no longer restricted to a small number of persons.

Collective Biographies

Modern data processing has made it easier to compare large numbers of individuals, using a technique called prosopography or collective biography. The preceding chapter by Joseph Love and Bert J. Barickman portrays the elites of three major states during the period 1889–1937 using such a method. This section provides demographic and career descriptions of several generations of the national political elite.

Just how big is the universe of political leaders in Brazil? Several years ago Aspásia Camargo estimated that it was approximately fifteen thousand persons, from local to national levels, including influentials who did not necessarily hold public office. Of that total, only about a thousand could be termed major decision makers. Finally, she estimated that about three hundred could be said to belong to the "inner circle" of persons who formulate and carry out long-term political strategies.[3] The present study concentrates on the intermediate level, i.e. the major decision makers.

I have created a general profile of the political elite in executive branch offices, based on a 5 percent sample of entries from the *Dicionário histórico-biográfico brasileiro, 1930–1983.*[4] The *Dicionário* contains data on about five thousand persons, who may be considered the political elite for this period.[5]

The first striking fact about the national political elite is its members' sex and advanced age: most were middle-aged or elderly men.

On average, they entered public office in their early forties, so that politics was virtually a second career. Once initiated, they stayed on for years, moving from one position to another. Nearly half held four offices, and three held twelve! Most of them began their careers in federal positions (55 percent), instead of in state or local offices. Moreover, the longer they stayed in politics, the likelier their presence on the federal payroll: by the tenth office, 88 percent were in the national government. So this elite was mostly middle-aged or older aɪ.J concentrated in the federal establishment.

As the century progressed, however, aspirants to the political elite entered office at younger ages. The first generation's average age when they attained their first office was 55 years; the second's 37; and the third's 32. (The generations included: 93 born before 1900; 136 between 1901 and 1920; and 21 after 1921.)

A slight majority of the political elite came from the Southeastern states of São Paulo, Minas Gerais, Rio de Janeiro, and Espirito Santo. The Northeast contributed 25 percent and the South 19 percent. This changed significantly over time, however, for by the third generation the Southeast supplied only 30 percent and the Northeast 35. This new profile may have been due to better alternative careers in the Southeast and to the post-1964 military government's favored treatment of the rural Northeastern states.

Several characteristics did not vary much among the generations. Virtually all (93 percent) were born in urban places (as defined by the 1950 census), and the majority (56 percent) established themselves professionally in states other than where they were born. This geographical mobility parallels the experience of the general population, which seems to pull up stakes and move every generation.[6] In addition, members of the elite had some form of postsecondary degree. That virtually all (94 percent) came from intact families is important because kinship plays a major role in politics. Finally, most had parents who were Brazilian and bore Portuguese surnames. The entry of children of immigrants into the political elite could be noted, however, in the occurrence of foreign parents (5 percent) and non-Portuguese surnames (18 percent).

As for education, the most frequent postsecondary degrees held by members of the elite were in law (44 percent), a quarter of them earned in schools outside their state of birth. Surprisingly, the next most frequent training was military (32 percent). Engineering and medical degrees ranked third and fourth (12 and 5 percent). As for timing, the median and modal year of graduation was 1930, which seems a remarkable coincidence with the revolution of that year.

Training for the political elite shifted over time. The most dramatic change was a decline in military background from the first to third generations, from thirty-seven to ten percent. This partly reflects the fact that first-generation politicians with military skills had a better chance of surviving into the 1930s and hence were overrepresented. This was especially true of the 1920s *tenentes*, or radical army officers, who helped Getúlio Vargas come to power in 1930. They made up 6 percent of the entire sample and 11 percent of the first generation. The second generation also had a large share of persons with military degrees (34 percent), which is partly due to the rise to prominence of officers who supported Vargas in 1937 or fought in Italy in World War II, the so-called *FEBianos*. The latter played a major part in the post-1964 administrations. These officers were also more likely than their predecessors to take advanced military degrees. Still, the smaller incidence of military degrees among third-generation politicians suggests that civilian training is replacing military as a likely road to high political office.

A final preparation for joining the political elite seems to have been some exposure to foreign life. Most members had such contacts, either through extended residence or study abroad or through business dealings.

Most members of the political elite had entered the professions for which they trained, especially those with law, medical, military, and engineering degrees. In addition, most branched out into other lines of work, for the average politician had 2.4 professions, according to my multiple-coded data. The most common additional careers were teaching, journalism, banking, and manufacturing, in declining order of occurrence.

The most marked trend with regard to the professions of the political elite was the decline of traditional ones like law and soldiering and the rise of new ones, like teaching, engineering, business, and the like. The 1950s saw a sharp increase in engineers and industrialists, for example, many of whom would occupy high offices in the post-1964 military-technocratic regime. Perhaps the most remarkable finding was that over half of the third generation exercised professions *other than* those mentioned above.[7]

Membership in associations and professional societies seemed to be essential for the political elite. *All* belonged to a professional group. In addition, 95 percent belonged to social clubs and 86 percent to commercial associations (especially important after 1950). Most also served as officers. A surprisingly small share (16 percent) belonged to the bar association, however, suggesting that many lawyers had allowed their practices to lapse. Only 11 percent were members of an academy of letters, the traditional bastion of the cultural elite.

Finally, we can gain some insights into the political elite by examining how its members behaved in moments of national crisis. Fully 87 percent supported the 1930 revolution, as might be expected since our data set is drawn from those active after that date. Two years later, in the depths of the depression and with the country in turmoil, the leaders of São Paulo declared war against Vargas and his administration in Rio. Fully 26 percent of the sample supported the revolt, especially those of the first generation. They managed to continue in politics due to Vargas's conciliatory posture after the war.

From 1937 until 1950, Vargas seemed to polarize the political elite. Generally speaking, the older generation (to which Vargas belonged) now supported him more than younger politicians. For example, the elite split about evenly with respect to the 1937 Estado Novo coup, but first generation politicians supported it while the second was mostly opposed. The latter may have sensed that their opportunities for upward mobility were going to be curbed. Their time came in 1945, when the second generation backed the military coup against Vargas more than the first generation. In 1950, *all* first-generation politicians for whom data were available supported Vargas's election, whereas the second generation split evenly. Finally, by 1954 the gap seemed to close, as first- and second-generation politicians split evenly over Vargas's ouster.

The 1964 coup did not seriously divide the elite: 82 percent backed it, though second- and third-generation politicians were more supportive than those of the first. Expectedly, the latter suffered a higher incidence of retaliation (jail, exile, loss of political rights) at the hands of coup leaders than did the former (18 vs. 12 percent). Thus, 1964 marked a passing of generations just as 1930 had. Since most of the political elite backed the coup, it also filled the ranks of the official party, the Aliança Renovadora Nacional (ARENA), after 1966.

This general portrait of the political elite can be compared with Sérgio Miceli's detailed study of persons who served in the 1946 Constitutional Convention.[8] The moment was important because it revealed a rift in the political elite, caused in part by the deep changes instituted by Getúlio Vargas in the preceding fifteen years. That year also marked the beginning of truly modern politics in Brazil, because the first national parties were formed in 1945.

Miceli found some similarities between the two leading parties, the pro-Vargas Social Democratic Party (PSD) and the opposition National Democratic Union (UDN). For example, both drew a larger proportion of their votes from rural and backward states in the Northeast than from the urban and industrial Southeast. In addition, both had substantial representation from the rural landowning class, the traditional source of political recruitment.

Miceli encountered sharp differences, however, between delegates of the two rival parties. The PSD had a large contingent of industrialists, as well as many former state officials linked to regional political machines. The PSD also drew in seasoned politicians, especially former mayors of medium and large cities. The latter, though still linked to the rural clans, often by kinship, were accustomed to newer political styles more atuned to working-class voters. The PSD favored expanding the powers of the state, protecting industry, and regulating private enterprise.

The UDN, on the other hand, was closely tied to financial groups in Rio, Minas, and Bahia. Moreover, the UDN delegation contained more upper status intellectuals and lawyers, many of whom could be traced back to pre-1930 political elites. They were not reactionaries, however—most had supported Vargas's Liberal Alliance in 1930—but rather they were disappointed revolutionaries who did not get jobs and favors from Vargas's regime. Miceli found that financial and business interests openly used the UDN for lobbying purposes. Because of this, the UDN was correctly seen as probusiness, procapitalist, and antiregulatory.

The two profiles sketched above can be contrasted with the results of a survey of mayors conducted in 1973 by the Instituto Brasileiro de Administração Municipal.[9] Responding to questionnaires, some 2600 mayors from towns and cities of all sizes provided information on themselves, their jurisdictions, and their attitudes toward government.

Most Brazilian mayors were middle-aged, had held other elective offices, and had only a primary school education. They were usually raised or had lived a long time in the town they served. About half were landowners and merchants, and the rest were professionals, government employees, or industrialists. The overwhelming majority belonged to the government party, ARENA. Opposition party mayors tended to be somewhat younger and better educated, and they represented larger towns and cities. All mayors professed a strong interest in promoting education, road construction, and health and welfare.

The mayoral level of administration might be termed the seedbed of local and state politics. From the mayor's office an ambitious politician could move up to the state legislature, to a state executive position, or occasionally to national office. Juscelino Kubitschek and Jânio Quadros are examples: after serving as mayors of Belo Horizonte and São Paulo, respectively, they eventually attained the presidency. Still, very few small-town mayors could expect to become part of the national elite, because they lacked essential qualifications.

Getting Power before 1930

Cronyism and the threat of force characterized the selection of the political elite during the Old Republic.[10] President Campos Salles (1898–1902) crafted a system known as the "politics of the governors." Governors of the several large states instructed their congressional delegations (whose selection they controlled) to give the president absolute authority to make and carry out financial decisions. In return, the president agreed to let the powerful governors be dictators in their respective states. They could rig elections, raise military forces, handpick their congressmen and senators, quash opposition, and stage-manage the judiciary without fear of federal intervention. The governors could call on the president for federal military reinforcements if necessary. Finally, the handful of powerful governors decided among themselves who would be the "official" candidate for president. That person rarely had opposition, since the governors had enough votes at their disposition to dominate the elections. Most presidents rose from the rank of governor of one of the major states—usually São Paulo or Minas Gerais. Indeed, an informal system of alternation between these two states, known as cafe com leite, existed from 1900 to 1930.

A second system of elite recruitment operated at the state and regional level, the so-called politics of the colonels, or *coronelismo*. Regional bosses, holding military rank from honorary commissions in the national guard, established mutually supportive ties with state governors. The colonels kept the local peace, held fraudulent elections for the governors' candidates, and occasionally contributed armed gunmen (*jagunços*) to the state militias. In exchange for these services, the colonels received public works monies and almost complete local autonomy. According to Victor Nunes Leal, "*Coronel* politics lay precisely in this reciprocity: *carte blanche* in the municipality to the local boss, in return for his electoral support for candidates nursed by the state government."[11] The politics of the governors and coronelismo may be sketched thus, with arrows indicating transfer of power and scarce political goods:

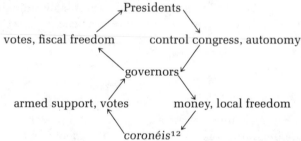

Rural elections had little democracy. The *coronéis* or their urban allies (called *doutores*) kept the voter lists. They valued voter loyalty above formal literacy and other requirements. On election day, the coronéis and their fellow landowners would herd their employees to the polling places. Votes were cast orally and in public, so that the coronéis could be sure their men did as they had been instructed. Afterward favors—such as liquor, food, a party, or money—would be distributed to the loyal voters. In close elections, the coronéis would resort to fraud, simply filling in fictitious votes in the roll. Such illicit votes were characterized as *do bico de pena,* or from the tip of the pen.[13]

The 1891 constitution gave states the right to establish and enforce election rules. State officials followed election procedures that benefited the group in power and ignored those that aided the opposition. They were usually not subtle in their methods. They conspired with congressional leaders to disqualify opposition politicians who managed to get elected, a procedure common enough to have its own term: *degola,* or throat-slitting. In the case of local elections, an opposition coronel might find that the state police had given his rival arms, ammunition, and license to use them to intimidate the opposition. The incumbent group, known as the *situação,* seemed to hold all the cards.

Because most votes originated in coronel-dominated rural areas and because rural population far outnumbered urban, city dwellers seldom bothered to vote. Their ballots counted little, even in local elections. Bosses and ward heelers (called *chefes* and *cabos*) in city neighborhoods managed to round up sufficient voters to win elections time after time. Their clients were usually poor folk in crowded city districts or in blighted suburban areas. In Rio in the late 1920s, when the city had about a million and a half inhabitants, it took only 17,000 votes to be elected senator, 1,000–3,000 to be elected congressman, and something over 600 to win a council seat. This pattern held in most major cities. Urban elections were usually more peaceful, but they were little more democratic than rural ones.[14]

Getting Power after 1930

The 1930 revolution changed and confused the means for getting power for about fifteen years.[15] For one thing, participation in the coup—so-called revolutionary credentials—became a primary qualification for access to the political elite. Second, the chief of the revolution, Getúlio Vargas, soon broke down the politics of the governors and crippled coronelismo. Thereafter, knowing Getúlio or his appointees in the statehouses and ministries became a vital prerequisite for executive appointments. Third, and perhaps most important in the long run, was the promulgation of a new election code in 1932, to be discussed in more detail below. Few elections were actually held during Getúlio's first administration (1930–45), yet expectations for democratic procedures grew because of the new legal system and the rhetoric of the government. Eventually such democratic aspirations led to the overthrow of Getúlio in 1945.

A more specific alteration of elite recruitment occurred because the recourse to civil war in 1930 brought large numbers of army officers directly into the political arena, reversing a tendency since 1894 to professionalize and remove them from politics. The tenentes were the most famous army officers to emerge powerful from the revolution, but many others were also bitten by the bug of ambition.

After relying on the tenentes for some time, Vargas came to rest his regime on the regular army, especially the minister of war. From that time on, a dozen or so top generals would normally be counted a part of the political elite of Brazil.[16]

The demise of the politics of the governors and the erosion of coronelismo occurred during Getúlio's first fifteen years as president. Employing everything from military superiority to personal manipulation, Getúlio managed to gain control over the governors of the major states—São Paulo in 1932, Minas in 1933, and Rio Grande in 1937. This meant that governorships in those states no longer led directly to the presidency; it also meant that access to the political elite became easier via the federal bureaucracy than via state party machines. The final demise of the politics of the governors was signaled in November 1937, when Getúlio promulgated the Estado Novo Constitution and publicly burned the state flags, symbolizing the preeminence of federal government over states' rights.

The collapse of gubernatorial politics in the 1930s left the coronéis in limbo, but Getúlio soon took them under his paternalistic wing. Many became clients of his subservient governors in the major states. The new arrangements no longer included recourse to violence, however, because Getúlio preferred concentrating firepower in the hands of the regular army. The armed federalism of the Old Republic disappeared as the federal army came to dominate the state elites. The new coronelismo featured patronage (federal as well as state) in exchange for loyalty to the political elite. After 1946 most of the coronéis joined Getúlio's Partido Social Democrático (PSD) and delivered their votes for him and his candidates. In this form, coronelismo lasted in some areas into the 1950s.[17]

In the long run, the electoral reform of 1932 proved very disruptive of elite recruitment, for it laid out rigorous democratic procedures for selecting officers at all levels of government. The main impetus for reform was the 1930 revolutionaries' belief that widespread fraud had prevented national development. They promised to render elections more honest. Joaquim Francisco de Assis Brasil, a backer of the revolution, had written a flaming denunciation of fraud during the Old Republic and suggested methods for correcting things.[18] His protégé, Maurício Cardoso, became minister of justice and promulgated an electoral code that overhauled the system from top to bottom. The vote was made secret and subject to federal supervision. New voter rolls were ordered, maintaining the literacy requirement but lowering the age to eighteen. Women were given the right to vote for the first time. Electoral tribunals at all levels were responsible for registering voters, overseeing elections, and tabulating and announcing election results. Between 1933 and 1935 a number of elections were held throughout the country, the first reasonably democratic ones Brazil had ever experienced. (The code contained flaws that would be addressed in 1935 and in the Agamemnon Law of 1945.) The impact of the electoral code was limited during the 1930s, however, because Getúlio eschewed elections as a method of recruiting the political elite. Still, the precedent and ideal had been established.[19]

After Getúlio's overthrow in 1945, political life in Brazil flourished, and elections became the foremost means of access to the political elite. Thomas E. Skidmore called the era from 1945 to 1964 an "experiment in democracy." Local, state, and federal elections were held frequently. Parties and coalitions proliferated during this era, and voter registration rose from 7.4 to 19.4 million. [See table 1.] The political elite stayed near the moderate middle of the ideological spectrum; except for the period 1945–48, they denied legal status to the communists, and no fascist party arose either. The political elite still protected the wealthy and propertied and did not tolerate threats to the established order. From the vantage of the 1980s, we can see that the liberal era from 1945 to 1964 marked the high point of democratic procedures for selecting public officials.

The liberal era also saw experiments designed to render elections more representative and honest. The 1932 code remained as a framework, but its various flaws were corrected and new techniques were designed to promote party formation. So-called ex officio voter registration was abolished after 1945. Instituted to facilitate registration following a purge of the old rolls, it had allowed government agencies and employers to submit lists of employees for blanket registration, without verification of qualifications. This led to much abuse and was discontinued in the late 1940s.

Chapas, privately printed ballots, were replaced by official ones in the late 1950s. From early in the century, politicians had handed out lists with candidates' names printed on them to be submitted as votes. This way the voter did not have to memorize the names of candidates and posts. The composition of slates led to extremely complicated preelection negotiations. In states where the elite was regimented into a disciplined party (such as the Republican parties

Table 1   Brazilian Election Turnouts, 1902–82

Year	Total Population	(millions) Electorate	Turnout	Turnout as %	Turnout Growth Rate
1902	18		0.6	3%	
1906	21		0.3	1	
1910	23		0.6	3	
1914	26		0.6	2	
1918	29		0.4	1	
1922	32		0.8	2	
1926	33		0.7	2	
1930	36		2	5	
1934*	38		2	6	
1945	46	7	6	13	
1950	52	11	8	16	6.4%/yr
1955	60	15	9	15	
1960	71	16	13	18	
1966*	83	22	17	21	
1970*	91	26	22	25	6.6%/yr
1974*	104	36	29	28	
1978*	116	46	38	33	
1982	125	59	48	40	
1984	132		55	42	
1986	140		69	49	

*Legislative and executive other than presidential.

Sources and notes: Intercensal population figures before 1934 and after 1978 were extrapolated; the rest are from Raimundo Pereira et al., Eleições no Brasil pos–64 (São Paulo: Global, 1984), p. 66, as are figures on the electorate. Turnouts are from Joseph L. Love, "Political Participation in Brazil, 1881–1969," Luso-Brazilian Review 7, no. 2 (1970): 9; Maria D'Alva Gil Kinzo, a'Novos partidos: O início do debate," in Voto de desconfiança: Eleições e mudança política no brasil, 1970–1979, organized by Bolívar Lamounier (Petrópolis: Vôzes, 1980), p. 223; and recent press reports. Percentages, calculated before rounding, may not replicate. Turnout in highest legislative race is used. Null and blank votes are included.

of Rio Grande do Sul and Minas Gerais), the executive committee simply composed an official slate based on cronyism, seniority, and loyalty to the machine. Local contests might turn competitive, but the official ballot usually prevailed.

In urban areas, fluid coalition building preceded elections. Politicians would agree to print one another's names on their ballots, exchanging roughly equal numbers of votes. A politician might print several runs with different candidates' names to represent various agreements. Last-minute deals and double-crosses occurred. As one of Rio's major dailies commented in 1926, "Politics in the Federal District are surely the most difficult in the country. Infinitely fragmented, without a leader who has sufficient support to be elected on his own merits, local politics live off of agreements, counterbalances, and unstable combinations which, like bubbles, appear and disappear with ease."[20]

By the 1950s, individual deals had become party deals, and the complexities became nearly impossible to follow. Party professionals were the agents of these dealings, trying to get their ballots into voters' hands moments before they went into the booths. Between 1955 and 1960, the electoral authorities replaced private ballots with official ones, ending much confusion but not fazing coalition politics.

By the early 1960s Brazil had a reasonably efficient and representative system for choosing the political elite. Its main shortcomings were continued manipulation of rural voters by landowners and the disfranchisement of millions of illiterates.

Keeping Power

Winning high office and hence joining the political elite did not end a politician's work. Staying there and winning reelection became important on-going tasks. The threats to continuity were threefold: an opposition candidate might defeat the incumbent at the polls; the incumbent's party might be defeated by a rival and bring widespread replacements; or a generalized movement or revolution might eliminate all officeholders in a single sweep. The defenses against these threats were necessarily different.

Individual defeat in an election was the most immediate concern of officeholders, so it required the greatest variety of protections. In those states where political organization was fairly advanced, group solidarity in the form of a party was probably the safest defense. As long as one played by the rules and obeyed the party chiefs, one would be assured a place on the official ballot and hence reelection. In addition, politicians kept latent campaign organizations ready for mobilization by appointing their aides and workers to public jobs. The bureaucracy, in large agencies and jurisdictions, could become a virtual party in itself if the politician screened appointees carefully over a long period of time. Government employees usually voted for the incumbents rather than risk wholesale dismissals by a new-comer. Politicians reinforced this tendency by granting special favors to their employees, such as social security benefits, vacations, accident disability insurance, and shorter hours. Thus, much could be done to lower the risk of losing office to a challenger.

Special networks of friends-in-high-places also provided safety and advantages for politicians. Anthony Leeds described a kind of old-boys' network called a *panelinha*.[21] This was usually a handful of men who had graduated from the same school or came from the same town and kept in touch throughout their careers. They regarded one another as *homens de confiança*, or trusted and discreet friends who could always be counted upon. The typical panelinha would have a politician, a financier, a real estate specialist, a journalist, and a businessman, all of whom could exchange favors for one another. They could enter into business partnerships or bail each other out of sour deals. The politician could call upon his friends to finance his campaign and to recruit outside support. The panelinha could in turn call upon the politician to help write laws or use his influence to win special contracts or other favors. The politician who represented a particular group was known as a *testa de ferro*, or stalking horse. Such networks, though hard to discern, were widespread among professionals and remained intact for decades. The panelinha was obviously one way the political elite and other elites interacted with one another.

Postsecondary training also created collegial groups that acted in politics. Since 1831 a secret society of São Paulo law school students and graduates, called the Bucha, formed a large network for politicians and professionals. Highly influential at critical moments, the Bucha also served as a model for groups in other states and in later times. Military academy graduates likewise identified with their turma, or class cohort, and used it for political and professional favors.[22]

Because of the preference for an insider's approach to political action, lobbying in Brazil did not resemble the pluralist model found in many Western democracies. Politics was not an open forum for the clash of competing interests, where leaders weighed sides and made decisions based on the merits of the case. Instead, personal contacts and friendships, commitments, and family ties determined a leader's stand. Competitive, autonomous interest groups acting aggressively in the decision-making process would not prosper in this environment. Indeed, political scientist Philippe Schmitter, who had expected to find such associations in 1960s Brazil, proved they did *not* flourish. His findings caused many students to rethink their notions of political culture in Brazil and to hypothesize a corporative, closed approach to decisionmaking.[23]

The typical politician, whether from the Old Republic or the liberal era, cultivated a smooth style and avoided controversy. He was, in Sérgio Buarque's words, the *homem cordial,* the affable one who got along with everyone and smoothed ruffled feathers. He could take a stand if forced to and could be eloquent in the defense of an idea, but his instinct was to avoid actions that might offend or alienate followers. The term *conciliação,* or conciliation, was often used to describe the goal of Brazil's working politician.[24] Using unorthodox means (the famous *jeitos*), he reconciled opposites and resolved contradictions. He posed as an individualist and a statesman, even though he was usually beholden to his friends and subject to his party's authority. The traditional politician of Brazil created personal relationships with his supporters by remembering names, citing kinship ties, providing free professional services (especially lawyers and doctors), and feigning genuine interest in his constituents' problems. Indeed, the illusion of personal relationships with huge numbers of voters is called *personalismo* in both Brazil and in Spanish America.

Two typical defenses against individual or party defeat in elections have always been fraud and manipulation of the rules. The varieties of fraud are practically endless and resemble those in other democracies. (Note, for example, the ingenious infiltration of a Rio vote-computing firm in 1982 by federal agents who wished to rig the election against Leonel Brizola.) Manipulation of election rules by incumbents is found elsewhere, too, but seems to have become a specialty of Brazilian politicos in this century. Such tactics probably inhibited the circulation of persons into and out of the political elite.

The final challenge to those in power is a national coup d'état that purges incumbent politicians. Two such coups have occurred in this century, the so-called Revolutions of 1930 and 1964 (led respectively by Getúlio Vargas and General Humberto Castello Branco). In each case, the victors removed a large number of officeholders and reconstituted the political elite. In 1930, most Paulistas and many Mineiros found themselves barred from federal and even state positions. Rio Grande do Sul gaúchos close to Vargas made up a new elite.[25] In 1964, the military weeded out high officials of the previous government, especially those with leftist tendencies. The ranking generals in the army became the core of the restructured political elite. Such blanket changeovers have not been revolutionary in the socioeconomic sense, yet they have brought deep changes in the recruitment, structure, philosophy, and interactions of the political and other elites.

Prevention is virtually the only defense against a coup d'état. Leaders of such movements are usually successful only if they exploit divisions within the political elite, as they did in 1930 and 1964. To avoid such divisions and thereby avert civil wars and coups, the Brazilian political culture has built-in accommodation procedures. José Honório Rodrigues's *Conciliação e reforma* argues that the elite will always try to coopt opponents or preempt hostile movements rather than face wholesale dismissal. Throughout its history the Brazilian elite has been viscerally conservative (that is, disinclined to serious change) yet willing to reform to avoid more radical disruptions. This has meant that the Brazilian elite usually undertakes innovations long after they have been adopted elsewhere. Rodrigues argues that this puts Brazil some fifty years behind the times but it also produces a highly stable political elite. Compared with other Latin American experience in this century, the two Brazilian "revolutions" have been mild indeed.[26]

Twice this century those at the top of the political system decided to suspend elections or to impose drastic restrictions in order to control access to the political elite. The first time was during the Estado Novo, between 1937 and 1945. Getúlio Vargas, who had sponsored an advanced electoral code and a democratic constitution, decided to replace both with a dictatorship. The second time was after the army high command seized power in 1964 and found itself unable to control elections. It then restricted access to political office. These two periods, amounting to almost three decades, were not merely temporary departures from democratic circulation. They are part of what theorists call Brazil's authoritarian tradition.[27]

According to some authors, the weight of the past favors a system of government in which a privileged elite controls public office and jealously protects its perquisites.[28] Advocates of this authoritarian approach deny the legitimacy of elections and warn of the dangers of political competition. Radical ideas, unbridled ambitions, demagoguery, and instability all accompany open politics. The proper method of governance, in this view, is for those in power to recruit their own colleagues and to provide an orderly, stable regime. If these leaders are wise and sensitive to public wishes, the regime will be more representative than any elected one. A compelling argument for this case is the fact that major institutions—the church, the army, the bureaucracy, and the professional associations—will lend their support to an autocratic regime in exchange for guarantees of institutional privileges. In all, the tradition of an authoritarian elite in Brazil is powerful and runs counter to the democratizing tendency begun in 1891. Those in office are tempted to invoke it, a ploy known as *continuismo*.

Oddly enough, the recently ended military regime eschewed individual continuismo—no general stayed in the presidency longer than his allotted period—but played institutional continuismo to the hilt. The army high command made absolutely certain that it kept control over appointments and elections. The generals went to extreme, even ridiculous, lengths to manipulate election rules. David V. Fleischer calls this "electoral engineering." *Legendas, sublegendas, voto distrital, biônicos, cassação,* and *chapa única* made their debut, often promulgated as decrees and termed *pacotes* (packages), or surprise decisions. (See the glossary for definitions of these and other terms.) The generals also rigged legislation on parties to keep control over the political elite. Government manipulation alternated between tawdry and farcical.

The electorate, having little control over the rules of the political game, resorted to a new tactic: the protest vote. Since the vote has been mandatory since 1932 and noncompliance carries some sanctions, abstinence was not a viable option. Instead, millions of voters inserted blank or defaced ballots in the boxes. These blank and null votes represented an indictment of the government's tactics and helped undermine its legitimacy. Partly in response, the military began allowing more serious choices on the ballots. From then on, the number of blank and null votes diminished and virtually disappeared by the mid-1980s.[29]

The reasons for these bizarre government procedures and the citizenry's reaction lie in the nature of the military-technocrat coalition that ruled the country for twenty-one years and in its relationship to the civilian political elite. The generals seized power in 1964 partly at the behest of the political elite itself. João Goulart had issued an unmistakable challenge to the political class: swear loyalty to him and his advisers or face expulsion from office. The political elite (*sans* Goulart and his people) preferred a military coup to threats from Goulart. The political elite expected (and Castello Branco intended) that the military would stay in power only a short time in order to remove the radical threat posed by Goulart and his supporters. Afterward they would return to business as usual. The political elite was sorely disappointed when in the course of 1965 and 1966 radical army officers subverted Castello's plans and provided their own brand of *continuismo*: the top generals would choose presidents from among themselves, and they would appoint civilians to the cabinet, statehouses, and federal agencies. Obviously the political elite had lost control over its own destiny.

During the military years, a political elite continued to exist, occupying many positions in government, but it changed composition and no longer managed access, interelite relations, or even the extent of power exercised. In a sense, the elite survived on the scraps that fell from the military table. Their goal during the first three army presidencies (Castello Branco, Artur de Costa e Silva, Emílio Garrastazú Médici) was to survive, if possible with a modicum of dignity.

Beginning with Gen. Ernesto Geisel in 1974, the army presidents followed a course known as *distensão* and later *abertura*, or political decompression and opening, that envisioned a gradual return of power to civilians. Then the political elite sought to broaden its control over its own ranks, including more recruitment through elections, executive appointments according to party patronage, broader limits on ideological discourse, freedom from the two-party straitjacket, and less interference in politics by the military officers and their technocrat allies. The years 1974–85 saw the civilian elite gradually recover these rights as the military removed itself from power.

Thus, looking back over the past nine decades, we can generalize that the political elite has been quite successful in keeping power. Throughout the Old Republic the chiefs in the major states and in Rio managed the system with infrequent challenges and resort to force. Vargas upset the system and rebuilt the political elite, drawing on some existing elements but bringing in many new actors as well. During the two decades of the democratic experiment, the political elite controlled public affairs almost without interruption. The 1964 coup shook up elite control almost as much as Vargas's revolution, but in the end a reconsolidated elite achieved hegemony again.

One last aspect of the political elite requires discussion before moving on. Beginning in the 1930s and continuing into the 1960s, some politicians developed so-called populist movements. Some of the best known were Adhemar de Barros, Carlos Lacerda, Getúlio himself in the 1950s, Jânio Quadros, Leonel Brizola, Miguel Arraes, and João Goulart. These leaders abandoned the traditional rules of the game and wrote their own. The populists enjoyed great success at the polls and hence did not need the endorsement of the usual bosses and brokers. Populism was a way to vault ahead in politics without following the usual paths. The elite maintained its internal regulations but suspended the rules to accommodate the populists.[30]

Populists did not usually constitute a threat to the established order; they merely gathered up new voters by vowing reform and broad representation. They promised democracy and a better life for all. Persons with authoritarian leanings, however, disliked the populists for several reasons. First, they destablized the system by bringing in many lower-class voters and by ignoring the rules of the game. Second, they often created foreign relations problems by stressing national welfare over profits for foreign investors or the satisfaction of international obligations. Finally, the populists could appear demagogic and irresponsible in their pursuit of new voters.

Authoritarian-minded politicians claimed that the populists threatened the nation by arousing the masses and disturbing the system. In 1964 they asserted that Goulart was undermining private property, respect for law and order, and traditional values. Certainly since the Estado Novo, authoritarians have always opposed populists, in what might be termed a populist-authoritarian counterpoint.[31] This is probably why the moderate Castello lost control over right-wing generals in 1965. The latter set their sights on extirpating populism itself from the political culture, rather than just eliminating a bad president. The political elite was the loser, because it too was marginalized in the process.

Losing Power

Until now we have discussed the characteristics of Brazil's twentieth-century political elite and how it got and kept power. We have
already spoken of some ways individuals are excluded from the
elite: through their defeat in an election, the fall of their party or
faction, or in a generalized coup by an outside group. Other ways to
lose power existed, however, and they will be discussed briefly.

Voluntary withdrawal constituted a fairly common way to lose
power. The most dramatic example was Jânio Quadros's resignation
as president in August 1961, after just seven months in office. His
motives, never fully clarified, seem to have been frustration with
congressional opposition and a vain hope that his resignation would
be refused and that he would be given broader executive powers.
Politicians also withdrew from the scene due to old age, although
this alternative occurred less frequently than we might imagine. The
average age of politicians in general and upon retirement seems
unusually advanced.[32] Power has a strong appeal to members of the
political elite, tempting them to stay on indefinitely.

Assassination was another way politicians were removed from
the scene, though since the 1930s it has become less frequent. During the Old Republic skirmishes and civil wars among the coronéis
left hundreds, perhaps thousands, dead. The assassination of vice
presidential candidate João Pessoa in 1930 helped trigger the revolution later that year. Another celebrated murder attempt, against
Carlos Lacerda in 1954, helped precipitate military agitation against
Vargas. For the most part, though, such extreme tactics disappeared
by the 1950s.

In the late 1960s, the military government began to employ torture
and eventually murder to curb guerrilla and terrorist activities. They
were not indiscriminate in such repressive measures, compared
with the governments of Argentina and Chile, for example, but they
nonetheless murdered several hundred people, many of them inno-
cent of crimes.[33] Brazil's political elite was barely affected by this,
because the victims were from political factions that had rarely won
elections or appointment to public office. Still, government terror-
ism cast a pall over most political activities and certainly had an
inhibiting effect on discourse.

Two final methods of losing political power have seldom been
seen in Brazil: impeachment and suicide. Impeachment is rarely

attempted because the executive branches are stronger than their legislative counterparts. Suicide occurred only once on the national scene that we know of: when Getúlio Vargas shot himself during a military crisis in 1954. Brazilian politicians apparently have such strong ego commitment to their careers that they cannot contemplate self-destruction. The same psychic defenses that ward off depression after lost elections, fall from power, and personal defeats probably also protect against suicidal impulses. Members of the political elite seem to have no doubts about the legitimacy of their leadership.

By Way of Summary

Beginning in the 1890s, the characteristics of the political elite of Brazil changed markedly, as did the methods of access to and tenure in high public office. The regionalized political elite of the early twentieth century became a national one. Democratic procedures have gradually supplanted ones based on cronyism and threats of violence. The political elite is now partly recruited from the middle socioeconomic strata (contrary to practice at the turn of this century), and it no longer represents only the interests of other elites. Business, intellectual, cultural, religious, and military elites must bargain with their political counterparts to protect their rights and jurisdictions. With the exception of the Estado Novo and the military era—times of frankly authoritarian rule reminiscent of colonial and nineteenth-century Brazil—steady progress has been made in expanding the electorate and perfecting methods of voting. Indeed, in 1985 the newly installed civilian government extended the vote to illiterates, the last major group excluded from the franchise. Fraud has diminished, along with manipulation of election rules, again with the exception of the military era.

In the late-1980s the political elite appears to be regaining its authority and self-confidence, recovering from two decades of military rule. It seems to be taking up the liberal promises of the 1890s and the democratic practices of the 1950s. Whether or not populist leadership will return is an open question at this point. The military certainly issued a stern condemnation of such politics. On the other hand, the elections of Leonel Brizola as governor of Rio de Janeiro and Jânio Quadros as mayor of São Paulo suggest that populism is still a viable approach. That in turn raises the possibility of an authoritarian reaction, such as those of 1937 and 1964. Would the political elite defend the populists as preferable to autocrats? Would the elite be able to contain internal debate and division over other major issues, such as the national debt, foreign investment, land reform, privatization of public enterprises, international alignments, or inflation? Given the problems Brazil faced in the 1980s (inherited, some point out bitterly, from military mismanagement), the political elite will be more challenged that at any other time in this century. Only time will tell if the old formulae will work or if new ones can be devised.

Notes

1. Congressmen have been more throughly analyzed than executive branch politicians: see the literature survey by David V. Fleischer, "Thirty Years of Legislative Recruitment in Brazil," Johns Hopkins University, Center of Brazilian Studies, Papers Series, no. 5 (Baltimore, 1976), pp. 8–11. There is a great deal of overlap between the sets, of course, since most politicians move back and forth between executive and legislative positions.

2. Joseph L. Love, "Political Participation in Brazil, 1881–1969," Luso-Brazilian Review 7, no. 2 (December 1970): 3–24.

3. Aspásia Camargo, "Os usos da história oral e da história de vida: trabalhando com elites políticas," DADOS 27, no. 1 (1984): 12.

4. Israel Beloch and Alzira Alves de Abreu, eds., Dicionário histórico-biográfico brasileiro, 1930–1983, 4 vols. (Rio de Janeiro: Editora Forense-Universitária/CPDOC/FINEP, 1984–86). Sonny Davis provided valuable research assistance for this portion of the study, and Joe Love generously allowed us to use part of the codebook for his study in chapter 2.

5. Note that local officials who did not rise to national level politics are underrepresented and that I excluded a few politicians who did not occupy executive positions at least once in their careers. Moreover, the data base is limited to those who were prominent after the 1930 revolution, so the information about those who also served before is necessarily incomplete. Only a minority of 1930 incumbents who opposed the revolution continued in politics. I will indicate any apparent biases in the text.

6. See Thomas W. Merrick and Douglas H. Graham, Population and Economic Development in Brazil: 1800 to the Present (Baltimore: Johns Hopkins University Press, 1979).

7. Cf. Fleischer, "Thirty Years," pp. 21–25.

8. Sérgio Miceli, "Carne e osso da elite política brasileira pós-1930," in História geral da civilização brasileira, vol. 10: O Brasil republicano, ed. Boris Fausto, 2d ed. (São Paulo: Difusão Editorial, 1983), pp. 557–96.

9. Cleuler de Barros Loyola and Ana Maria Brasileiro, eds., *O prefeito brasileiro: Características e percepções* (Rio de Janeiro: IBAM, 1975).

10. See the classic study of Old Republican politics by the late Victor Nunes Leal, *Coronelismo: The Municipality and Representative Government in Brazil*, trans. June Henfrey (Cambridge: Cambridge University Press, 1977), esp. pp. 132–35. Cf. Gláucio Ary Dillon Soares, *Sociedade e política no Brasil* (São Paulo: Difusão Européia do Livro, 1973), chs. 1, 5.

11. Leal, *Coronelismo*, p. 41.

12. After Joseph L. Love, *Rio Grande do Sul and Brazilian Regionalism, 1882–1930* (Stanford: Stanford University Press, 1971), p. 120.

13. Leal, *Coronelismo*, pp. 12, 124.

14. Michael L. Conniff, *Urban Politics in Brazil: The Rise of Populism, 1925–1945* (Pittsburgh: University of Pittsburgh Press, 1981), pp. 65–69.

15. Soares, *Sociedade e política*, ch. 2.

16. Eurico de Lima Figueiredo, ed., *Os militares e a revolução de 1930* (Rio de Janeiro: Paz e Terra, 1979).

17. Thomas E. Skidmore, *Politics in Brazil, 1930–1964: An Experiment in Democracy* (New York: Oxford University Press, 1967).

18. Joaquim Francisco de Assis Brazil, *Democracia representativa—do voto e do modo de votar* (Rio de Janeiro: G. Leuzinger and Filhos, 1893).

19. Soares, *Sociedade e política*, ch. 3.

20. Conniff, *Urban Politics*, p. 68.

21. Anthony Leeds, "Brazilian Careers and Social Structure: A Case History and Model," *Contemporary Cultures and Societies of Latin America*, ed. Dwight B. Heath and Richard N. Adams (New York: Random House, 1965): 379–404; Peter McDonough, *Power and Ideology in Brazil* (Princeton: Princeton University Press, 1981), pp. 22–23.

22. John W. F. Dulles, *The São Paulo Law School and the Anti Vargas Resistance (1938–1945)* (Austin: University of Texas Press, 1986), pp. 5–14, passim.

23. Philippe C. Schmitter, *Interest Conflict and Political Change in Brazil* (Stanford: Stanford University Press, 1971), pp. 366 and conclusion.

24. José Honório Rodrigues, *Conciliação e reforma no Brasil: Um desafio histórico-cultural* (Rio de Janeiro: Editora Civilização Brasileira, 1965). See Sergio Buarque de Holanda's explanation of the "cordial" Brazilian style in his *Raizes do Brasil* (Rio de Janeiro: Editora José Olympio, 1948), pp. 203–24.

25. Carlos E. Cortes, *Gaucho Politics in Brazil* (Albuquerque: University of New Mexico Press, 1974).

26. Rodrigues, *Conciliação e reforma*.

27. See, for example, Douglas A. Chalmers, "Political Groups and Authority in Brazil: Some Continuities in a Decade of Confusion and Change," in *Brazil in the Sixties*, ed. Riordan Roett (Nashville: Vanderbilt University Press, 1972), pp. 51–76.

28. Raymundo Faoro, *Os donos do poder: Formação do patronato político brasileiro*, 2d ed., 2 vols. (Porto Alegre: Globo, 1975).

29. Raimundo Pereira, Alvaro Caropreso, and José Carlos Ruy, *Eleições no Brasil pós-64* (São Paulo: Global, 1984); Gláucio A. D. Soares, "The Brazilian Political System: New Parties and Old Cleavages," *Luso-Brazilian Review* 19, no. 1 (1982): 39–66; Bolivar Lamounier, organizer, *Voto de desconfiança* (Petrópolis: Editôra Vozes, 1980).

30. Conniff, *Urban Politics*, "Introduction."

31. Conniff, *Urban Politics*, pp. 135–38; Aspásia Alcántara de Camargo, "Authoritarianism and Populism: Bipolarity in the Brazilian Political System," in *The Structure of Brazilian Development*, ed. Neuma Aguiar (New Brunswick: Transaction Books, 1979), pp. 99–125.

32. David V. Fleischer, "As bases socio-econômicas do recrutamento partidário, 1945–1965," paper for the symposium "Partidos Políticos no Brasil," Rio de Janeiro, March 28–30, 1979, p. 28.

33. Archdiocese of São Paulo, *Torture in Brazil*, comp. Jaime Wright, trans. Joan Dassin (New York: Random House, 1986).

Frank D. McCann

The Military

Both elites and masses are found in the military. The officer corps constitutes a functional elite regardless of socioeconomic origins, while the enlisted ranks are drawn from the lower end of the socioeconomic scale. The military is a bridge between the upper and lower limits of the society. Its function, to defend the country from external aggression and internal disorder, sets the military apart from other elites, though at times the other elites have co-opted the military to act as defender of their interests. A theme that ran through the history of the Brazilian army from the Paraguayan War to the 1930s, with gradual modification thereafter, was that the civilian elites did not understand national defense and consequently did not value the military. Not surprisingly, subthemes were alienation, frustration, and resentment, and a steady effort across the officer generations to correct the situation. The resulting drive to expand the influence and power of the military flowed from the psychology of resentment and alienation.

In this chapter the term military will be synonymous with army, because though Brazil has a navy and an air force, their roles in social, political, and economic history have not been as salient. The army is superior in physical and political power. Much of its history as an institution deals with the process of attaining that power, of eliminating competitors. Further, *military* is used here, as in much of the literature, to mean the officer corps.

The Brazilian army is a cadre force, composed of a permanent corps of professional officers (about 13,000), sublieutenants and career noncommissioned officers (about 20,000), and roughly 110,000 troops, mostly made up of one-year draftees, who after their training are placed on the reserve list. This has been so since the obligatory service law went into effect in 1916. As a result, the life of most units consists of continuous basic training. Because the draft system reflects the social system and historical patterns, the majority of soldiers are drawn from the lower classes; this forces the military elite to come face to face with the masses and many of their problems. In the process the army serves as a structural linkage between the masses and the elites.[1] Throughout the Republican period, the officer corps has used terms such as citizen soldiers, the people in uniform (o povo fardado), and the nation in arms (a nação armada) to describe the army. Generalíssimo Manoel Deodoro da Fonseca, chief of the provisional government after the deposition of the imperial dynasty (1889), declared that "the soldier . . . ought to be henceforth the citizen in arms, supporting and promoting Republican institutions."[2]

The military is the only elite whose existence is mandated by the constitution. It is a situational rather than a class elite. While the constitution also specifies a legislature, a judiciary, and an executive, the members of these are neither permanent nor recruited into a lifetime institutional commitment. In addition to its legal status, the military differs from other elites in that it has its own doctrines, as well as an intense sense of unity and tradition. It is also different in that its members are drawn from throughout the country, and in that its focus, interests, and distribution are national. It resembles to some extent the only other nationally dispersed elite, the Catholic clergy, but the military elite is more homogeneous. While the Catholic clergy share a common doctrinal allegiance, they are divided into many religious orders and diocesan priesthoods that have their own educational institutions, traditions, and control systems. Moreover the clergy have an extranational source of legitimacy and power as representatives of the worldwide Catholic Church. And, it should be noted that a high percentage of the clergy are foreign born.

From the angle of interaction between the elite and the masses, the army has functioned as a key vehicle for maintaining elite hegemony. Many of its repressive actions, such as Canudos (1897), the salvações (1910–12), and the Contestado (1912–15), had more to do with the agendas of other elites than with that of the officer corps. However, the so-called tenente revolts of the 1920s were symptomatic of a resentful suspicion that the political elite was deflecting the army from its true role and endangering the national well-being in favor of regional or personal interests. The disenchantment encouraged officers to support the Revolution of 1930, Getúlio Vargas's subsequent changes in the political system and in elite membership, and the various military interventions from 1945 onward that culminated in the Military Republic of 1964–85.

The Officer Corps

Who are the officers? Throughout the Republic they have been drawn largely from the urban middle class. While the middle and upper classes have long gone to lengths to avoid having their sons serve as enlisted soldiers, the opportunity for a free education attracted young men without better alternatives to the officer corps. Leading figures who fall into this category include Gens. José da Silva Pessoa, Pedro de Goís Monteiro, and Juarez Távora. Though a number of families were, and are, traditionally associated with the military, such as the Fonseca and Mena Barreto, because of its emphasis on education, merit, and performance the officer corps tended to be more open to advancement than was the case in the political-social-economic elites wherein family ties, friendships, connections, and money played a larger role.

There has been considerable discussion about the importance of officers' social-economic backgrounds in determining the military's political behavior in Latin America.[3] Alfred Stepan, in his study of the Brazilian army's involvement in politics, concluded that the "mere fact of middle-class composition of a military establishment cannot in itself explain political behavior or political intervention. . . . by *itself* it is almost never a determinant of the political behavior of elites."[4] Rather, he saw "life experience and career pattern variables" as having more value in determining attitudes.[5]

In the 1960s the military's conviction that the officers were not affiliated with a particular class became a justification for extending military control. Proponents of this view argued that the military was "the only institution without vested interests in the status quo . . . [which] freed it to act solely in the interests of the national good."[6]

A key factor in shaping officers' attitudes has been the military educational system. Unlike the American army, which accepts officers who have graduated from diverse colleges and universities, from Officers' Candidate Schools, and from West Point, all Brazilian regular army officers are graduates of the military school, and since the 1920s promotion has been tied to completion of various service schools. But taking the Republican period as a whole, the educational situation was much less uniform than this statement suggests. Coming out of the Empire, there were three military schools (Fortaleza, Porto Alegre, and Rio de Janeiro) that offered, respectively, a general high-school level program (three years), a Positivist-influenced science program (four years), and combat arms training (one year). Part of the last was taught at the so-called practical schools (escolas práticas at Realengo, Rio de Janeiro, and Rio Pardo, Rio Grande do Sul). In 1898, the Fortaleza and Porto Alegre schools were closed, Rio Pardo became a preparatory school, Realengo became the Escola de Tática, and the Rio de Janeiro school at Praia Vermelha was raised to the Escola Militar do Brasil. When the cadets at the last rebelled in 1904, it was closed and officer formation passed to two institutions in Rio Grande do Sul, the Escola de Guerra in Porto Alegre and the Escola de Aplicação de Infantaria e Cavalaria in Rio Pardo. This arrangement lasted only until 1911, when the two were merged into the Escola Militar do Realengo, in a suburb of Rio de Janeiro. Realengo prepared cadets until 1944, when the sole entry gate became that of the Academia Militar das Agulhas Negras in Resende in the state of Rio de Janeiro.[7]

These changes in location, number, and function were matched with changes in the military school curricula, teaching staffs, equipment, and living and training facilities. Such turbulence made it difficult to develop lasting traditions and a sense of commonality among the graduates. The changes necessarily deepened generational divisions. Through much of this century Brazilian officers have looked with envy on the continuity of tradition that West Point, Sandhurst, and St. Cyr provided the American, British, and French officer corps.

After graduation as *aspirantes*, the officers passed through a series of schools on their march to becoming generals. The sequence that follows has applied since the 1950s, but the educational prerequisite for advancement has existed since the 1920s. To reach major the eight-month advanced officers' course (Escola de Aperfeiçoamento de Oficiais) ESAO had to be completed; to ensure promotion to full colonel and to be considered for brigadier general an officer had to complete the three-year (two-year after 1982) general staff school (Escola de Comando e Estado-Maior do Exército, ECEME); finally, after 1949, upwardly mobile officers had to put in a year of study at the Escola Superior de Guerra (ESG).

An officer's class standing in these schools played a large part in his advancement. The importance of class rank as a key factor in promotion contrasts with the situation in the American army, where more frequent wars have allowed officers of mediocre academic achievement to display skills that resulted in promotions. Morris Janowitz's classic, *The Professional Soldier*, noted that in a sample of West Point graduates who reached high United States Army positions only 36.4 percent had been graduated in the top quarter of their classes.[8]

The friendships, alliances, and contacts that Brazilian officers made in these schools were of great importance. Given the small size of the officer corps and the even smaller classes, officers knew each other and experienced a greater degree of professional and personal intimacy than was the case in the larger, multi-entry American army.[9] Friendships and enmities could easily stretch across a lifetime of mutual studies, assignments, and experiences. The 1916 class of the Colégio Militar of Porto Alegre—the army's southern preparatory school—included future generals whose careers intertwined: Humberto de A. Castello Branco, Artur da Costa e Silva, and Amauri Kruel. Each had a distinguished student record, received training from both the French and the Americans, served with the World War II expeditionary force in Italy, and were top army leaders by the early 1960s. Kruel served as minister of war under Jânio Quadros, while the other two were the first and second presidents of the Military Republic.

Officers in a particular class formed a *turma* that was often a lifelong association. Lacking a Morris Janowitz–type sociological study of the Brazilian army, one can only speculate. The term *turma* is applied to the entire graduating class, but it can also be applied to a self-defined subgroup that functions like a *panelinha*. The latter term has a negative connotation and is frequently used to refer to a closed group of individuals who join together for mutual advantage. Turma, a Latin term for a group of thirty horsemen, has come to be applied to any group joined together for a common purpose. It is used the way Class of Such-and-Such is in the United States, but it is applied more broadly. The Brazilian army employs it to describe teams, squads, details, etc. Further, in Brazil it is used to denominate a group of friends.

The turmas that officers formed at certain stages of their careers were carefully maintained thereafter. The analytical problem is to determine which experiences led to enduring turma formation, especially turmas that embraced officers from a variety of arms and services. Early in the century the moves and closings of the various military schools may have had the effect of bonding together those who were graduates of a particular school. Certainly Castello Branco kept in contact with his Colégio Militar turma, to judge from the roles a number of them played when he rose to power. The Realengo turmas in the 1920s and 1930s seem to have formed close bonds, as did officers who served in certain Brazilian Expeditionary Force (FEB) units in World War II.

In the post–World War II period the General Staff has fostered the socialization process by deliberately reinforcing turma ties and by interlinking turmas. For some officers the process may have begun in one of the colégios militares at the age of twelve or thirteen. From the day they enter the Academia Militar das Agulhas Negras (AMAN) marching through the new cadets' gate until they leave through the aspirantes' gate, the educational and training experience forces them together in a world that emphasizes unity and performance. It is a world in which a cadet is rarely alone—in the first year he lives with eleven others in a barracks-like room divided down the center by face-to-face desks, and in subsequent years he shares similarly configured quarters with seven roommates; he marches everywhere in groups and dines at a round table that reinforces face-to-face contact with others of his turma.

Spread over forty-two weeks per year, the curriculum blends military training with postsecondary studies. First-year cadets receive eight hours per week of military instruction, while second- and third-year men receive twelve and sixteen hours respectively. The rest of their time is devoted to physical education, academic subjects, and study. Extracurricular activities and free time are scheduled between 1610 and 1700 hours. In January and February, fourth-year cadets are sent to units in the states of Rio de Janeiro, São Paulo, or Minas Gerais to assist in training recruits for four weeks, and then they return to the same units for two weeks in June and a week in October to gain experience with the same soldiers further along in the training cycle.

In academic subjects the emphasis is on textbooks, many of which are prepared by the officer faculty, for the cadets have no time for reading or research beyond the assignments. For the serious student the library offers no mental stimulation or solitude, as it is more of a splendid salon for formal receptions than a place of study or a source of books and periodicals. This is more a matter of deliberate policy than accident, for army leaders believe that the cadets are too young to research and reach independent conclusions. Such activity, they believe, is for mature minds. Consequently, courses tend to be sanitized of positions or interpretations that conflict with army ones. Of course it should be observed that few civilian universities have good libraries, and wide reading and research are not commonly part of an undergraduate education in Brazil. What is different between the two situations is that at AMAN this is a matter of policy rather than an imposition of fiscal constraints or weak student preparation.

In the first year at AMAN cadets are housed by turma, and thereafter they are quartered in multiturma groups by arms and services—infantry, artillery, cavalry, engineering, quartermaster, communications, and war materiel. This early branch selection mirrors Brazilian civilian university procedure, which also forces career or professional selection at the outset.

By contrast, in the United States branch selection for West Point and ROTC cadets comes in the fourth year, allowing the branches to make their choices based on grades and performance, and the cadets to make their bids based on greater information and experience.

Considering that the AMAN enrollment hovers around 1400 and that graduating turmas tend to be between 300 and 400, it ought to be relatively easy to know a large number of contemporary cadets. The cadet's roommates are from his turma, however, and since he marches into the dining hall with his company he is most likely seated with members of his own turma. Friendships and acquaintances are probably most common in the descending order of one's own turma/arm, the preceding and succeeding turma/arm, the remainder of one's turma, and finally random cadets from various turmas/arms. As the officer progresses from aspirante to colonel, the turma will become an increasingly important identification.

The army's educational system reinforces the turmas and seeks to knit them together across generations. Its personnel department makes an effort to form the new class at the Escola de Aperfeiçoamento de Oficiais from the same AMAN turma(s), and the same is true for those who pass the competitive examinations for ECEME. In the intervening years they have served together in units throughout

Brazil and have formed affective bonds with commanders and sub-
ordinates from other turmas.

They reach ECEME in early middle age, as majors and lieutenant
colonels from all branches, usually married and with children. Ex-
cepting the few with their own quarters, the student officers live in
apartments next to the school on Rio de Janeiro's Praia Vermelha for
the two-year course (reduced from three in 1982), forming tight
relationships that embrace whole families. Thereafter the ECEME
relationship takes precedence, for only command school graduates
move upward.

Within the turma, ties are maintained informally, by birthday and
promotion telegrams and by meeting for discussions when a number
are stationed near each other, as at Vila Militar in Rio de Janeiro or at
posts in the Federal District. As the turma members progress
through their careers they tend to expand the group's contacts, to
widen its network. Turmas may attach themselves to an upwardly
mobile officer, or such an officer may seek ties with a turma in which
he has *homens de confiança,* so that he has trusted lower-ranked
associates upon whom he can call when he has openings in his
command. Such groupings are known in army slang as *peixarias*
(schools of fish). Instructors at ECEME, who often are appointed for
their academic achievements and staff performance and who are
upwardly mobile by definition, establish such ties with the turmas
they teach, and often when they hold command positions they turn
to their former students to fill subordinate slots. There is a structural
link between ECEME and AMAN in that field-grade officers assigned
there are customarily ECEME graduates, and by regulation the history
and geography courses must be given by officers wearing the command school insignia. In this fashion the various officer generations
get knitted together, contributing to institutional unity. The ECEME
graduates are the shapers and executors of military doctrine. In a
broad sense they are an elite within an elite, but perhaps it is more
accurate to say that they are the military elite, since they fill the staff
positions in the national and regional commands and from their
ranks come all the general officers.[10]

The Troops

If the officers are the military elite, the troops are the military
masses. Obtaining and maintaining a sufficient number of soldiers

have been constant challenges in the history of the army. As the century opened, the army was trying to reconstruct itself after the disaster of the 1897 Canudos campaign, when it suffered 5,000 casualties and extensive demoralization. In the period from 1900 to 1910 the army's annual authorized strength was about 30,000 officers and soldiers, but contemporary testimony indicates that effective troop strength rarely reached 15,000, and in 1904 one officer commented that there were fewer than 10,000 troops. It appears that instead of supporting the legislated number of soldiers, the Ministry of War put its funds into maintenance of an inflated officer corps.[11] The turn-of-the-century economic crisis and the resulting tight money policies of the Campos Sales administration, however, undoubtedly stimulated the officer corps' instinct for self-preservation.

The soldiers of the era were the unfortunates of society. Though called volunteers, most entered the army from the ranks of the unemployed, some willingly, seeking food and shelter, but perhaps the majority under guard, having been seized by the police in sweeps called canoas—a term that goes back to the days of Indian slave hunting. In this way many Northerners were sent to the central and southern states. Illiteracy was general; many soldiers suffered from malaria, verminosis, and inadequate diet; and discipline was harsh, even brutal. In 1900, the minister of war observed that discipline in the ranks was not a problem because the soldiers were cowed, and little beyond guard duty and parades was expected of them. The Canudos campaign had shown the difficulties of taking such troops into combat, even against untrained but determined sertanejos. Indeed, that campaign made some officers imagine that the Brazilian army would be unbeatable if it recruited, trained, and properly armed the fierce sertanejos—one officer asserted that if that were done "national integrity, honor and unity" would never again be put at risk.[12]

Discipline in the ranks was based upon fear, as punishments were often capriciously applied. A retired general, who had served in the enlisted ranks at the start of the century, commented that the "dosage of disciplinary punishments" depended on a commander's mood. Officers, he said, confused the "duty to punish" with the "right to castigate."[13] Rough treatment was the only way officers could imagine welding together the poor soldierly material. They complained that they had to accept all who came their way or face gaps in the ranks. As one officer explained, "to reject them would be to leave the unit ineffective. The solution was, then, to take them and discipline them with a strong hand."[14]

The troops were poorly paid and their food left much to be desired. Until the great renovation and expansion of facilities in the 1920s, the barracks that housed them were frequently adapted rented quarters. Married soldiers and their families often lived in or around the barracks in circumstances that encouraged "a circle of dependency and obligations between officers and soldiers." Col. Francisco de Paula Cidade, a noted army historian, described the mental outlook as one of "dedication to the chiefs" in an atmosphere closed to the surrounding civilian community.[15] The army reflected the patriarchal nature of Brazilian society, with its patron-client relations.

Troop Recruitment

Thoughtful officers understood that an efficient army could not base its recruitment on forced levies of the hungry, unemployed, or jail-birds any more than it could tolerate its officers being philosophers who knew Auguste Comte's Positivism but not how to shoot, ride, or function in the field. Reformists pointed out bitterly that the 1874 obligatory service law did not function, and Article 86 of the 1891 constitution, which placed military duty on the shoulders of "every Brazilian," had not been made operative. This was partly due to the opposition of the great landholders, who did not want their labor force disturbed, and to the regional political elites, who did not want the federal government to have a strong army at its disposal. Even so, Congress passed a new obligatory service law in 1908, due to a surge of patriotism encouraged by the seizure of rubber-rich Acre territory from Bolivia (1903), the armed demonstration on Peru's Amazonian frontier (1903–04), the modernization of Rio de Janeiro, the hosting of the Third Pan American Conference (1906), Santos Dumont's successful flights in France (1906), and the Brazilian role in the second Hague Peace Conference (1907).

Brazil was awash in a rising tide of nationalism. Afonso Celso caught the mood of the era in his *Porque me ufano de meu pais* (Why I boast of my country) (1901) when he proclaimed, "the dawn of our greatness. We will arrive inevitably at the brilliance and full heat of its mid-day. . . . We will be the second or first power of the world." Celso also declared racial prejudice passé, urging Brazilians to be

proud of all the races and combinations that made up the people
(povo). Events such as Canudos, the acquisition of Acre, the string-
ing of the telegraph line to Porto Velho in the western Amazon, and
the establishment of the Indian Protective Service encouraged writers, and the urban coastal dwellers who read them, to look proudly
upon the face of the nation, which Euclides da Cunha asserted was
that of the "sturdy caboclo." In his Os Sertões (1902) he wrote that in
the people of the sertão, where "shadings tend to disappear," was
"the hardy nucleus" of Brazil's future, "the bedrock of our race."[16]

However much the 1908 law was the trend of the future, it did not
go into effect until 1916. The shifting nature of elite politics was
such that the very members of Congress who had supported its
passage refused the necessary enabling legislation. In addition, between 1909 and 1915, the reformist elements in the army officer
corps, who believed that officers should be apolitical, were pushed
aside by military politicians and interventionists. The 1909 presidential election cast Gen. Hermes da Fonseca, ex-minister of war
(1906–09), as the government candidate for president and Bahian
lawyer Ruy Barbosa as his opponent. The campaign centered on the
military's role in national life. Ruy apparently won the majority of
the small popular vote, but the "politics of the governors" system
declared Hermes the victor. In power, Hermes backed a series of
military interventions or attempted interventions, called the salvações, to remove entrenched oligarchies in several states and to
replace them with rival factions that often included army officers.
Some officers lost their sense of proportion. The January 1912 bom-
bardment of Salvador marked the movement's low point and cast a
shadow of disgrace on the army.

World War I and the work of military reformers contributed to a
different mood. The movement that resulted in the 1916 Obligatory
Service Law had the impetus of an energetic, one-man campaign
conducted in 1915 and 1916 by poet Olavo Bilac, the self-pro-
claimed "professor of enthusiasm" who headed the National Defense League. From 1916 to 1924, the league beat the nationalist
drums and gave valuable propaganda support for obligatory military
service.[17] Bilac believed that Brazil was going through "the gravest
of all the crises of its history." A vision of dismemberment terrified
him. Reflecting the prevalent middle-class notion that Brazil was
not a cohesive, unified nation, he saw the privileged classes wanting
only pleasure and prosperity; the lower classes living in "inertia,

apathy, and superstition;" and the foreign immigrants isolated from others by language and custom.

Bilac saw Obligatory Military Service as "a promise of salvation" for Brazil. The "militarization of all civilians" was the way to impart middle-class virtues to society and thereby give it the cohesion necessary to preserve itself. Military service was to be a means of massive social uplift; however, it was also important, in the middle-class view, that it act as a leveling force, bringing the upper classes down a bit. For Bilac, "generalized military service" would purify the dregs of society and make them "conscientious, worthy Brazilians." The military would provide the discipline and order to reconstruct Brazil by lifting up the downcast millions. He saw a middle-class-cum-military crusade correcting the damage that the rural elites had done to the people. He called upon the officers to improve themselves and then to perfect the people (povo), observing that "the people possess energies and virtues stronger and purer than ours." The nation—that is, the remade people under middle-class leadership—would be the army, and the army, reformed, re-structured, redirected, would be the nation, the Patria. The officer corps was the priesthood of the civil cult of the Patria and as such should be free from political involvements. The officer corps would be the regenerator and the disciplinarian; the middle class would govern and direct. All that the different elements of the people needed was to become aware of their unity, of their Brazilianness. When all Brazilians think of themselves as Brazilians, Bilac prophesied, "Brazil will be one of the greatest, one of the most formidable nations of the world."[18]

Bilac's speeches found echoes and amplification in the pages of A defesa nacional, the military review that reformist officers, recently trained in the Imperial German army, founded in 1913. It was a forum in which officers discussed the latest military innovations, current army affairs, and their dreams for Brazil's future. Its directors organized a nationwide network of representatives who looked after the collection of subscription payments and distribution of the publication, and sought out potential contributors and news items. Throughout its history, many of the regular contributors and members of its editorial board rose to the highest ranks in the army, and two board members, Eurico Dutra and Humberto de Castello Branco, became presidents. From 1913 to 1922, ten officers, or 0.3 percent of the officer corps of approximately twenty-seven hundred, served as editors. In any given year, about a dozen others (0.4 percent) served on its board, contributing financial support, articles, assistance with circulation, and anything else that was needed. These officers, in effect, formed a turma dedicated to army reform and improvement, as well as to their own career advancement.

In their first editorial, the reformers (soon called "Young Turks," after the military reformers of Turkey) proclaimed the army's defense mission as linked to "political-social transformation" of society. The army should educate and organize the citizenry; it should be the school of citizenship, demonstrating the superiority of the collective over individual good, and giving an example of total sacrifice for the Motherland.[19] The editors saw Brazil as "an improvised nation, without roots in the past, of indefinite ethnic formation, and, therefore, easy to break up." For that reason, while preparing against a possible external enemy, the officer corps had to be aware of the more likely internal enemy: "the lack of national cohesion."[20] The agitation of the editors, Bilac, and the National Defense League, as well as fear that an unprepared Brazil would be drawn into the European war, caused the Wenceslau Bras administration to put the 1908 law into effect in December 1916.

The results were not what the reformers had sought. The image they had of a citizen army simply did not accord with the Brazilian socioeconomic system. The reformers' ideal army was rather different from the real army. The army of 1915–16 was suppressing rebellions of sergeants seeking rank reclassification and of civilians in the Contestado seeking redress of economic and social wrongs. It was also sending troops here and there in Mato Grosso, Amazonas, Pará and Piauí to back up political and judicial decisions. Such an army did not easily attract sons of the middle class or the landed elites. Indeed, it had difficulty attracting any suitable citizens. Draft dodging became a chronic problem.

Obligatory military service was intended to be universal only in that all eighteen-year-old males were to register for a draft lottery. The number chosen through the lottery would depend on the military's needs at the time. To avoid wholesale illegal draft dodging, the system allowed legal exemptions to anyone holding a reservist card. Service in militarized shooting clubs, called tiros, participation in army maneuvers as a volunteer, or attendance at a school offering military training qualified a man as a reservist. Not surprisingly, tiro ranks swelled.[21] The lottery was intended primarily to create an army reserve, and regardless of the propaganda about producing cohesion and contributing to greater social equality, the "conscientious, worthy Brazilians" that the army incorporated were generally poor illiterates rather than middle- or upper-class youths. "The rich and the powerful," one military analyst observed in 1928, "almost always find an escape, a means to free themselves from obligatory service."[22] While the lottery had important institutional and political effects, it did not, before World War II, radically change the socioeconomic composition of the rank and file, which continued to bear a striking resemblance to that of the turn of the century. Brazilians would continue to display, in Gen. Eurico Dutra's phrase, a "visceral rebellion" against "the career of arms."[23]

The new recruitment system required changes in officer attitudes that were slow in coming despite the efforts of the *A defesa nacional* turma. The old punishments could not be used on draftees, the out-of-date regulations had to be revised, and new barracks had to be built throughout Brazil. The new system also changed the distribution of army units to give the army a physical presence in every state, thereby increasing the institution's ability to involve itself in state and national politics.

The recruitment system provided the mechanism and the justification for the army's physical expansion. To give the army a local image while avoiding the cost and administrative burden of transporting recruits to national training camps, the war ministry decided to train the new men in regional barracks. By mid-1918 every state had at least one garrison to accept and train the draftees and volunteers. The system also required expanding the number of effectives (18,000 to 25,000 in 1916–17) and increasing the army budget.

Studies from the 1920s and 1940s provide collective portraits of the Brazilian males called up for military duty. An army physician, Col. Dr. Arthur Lobo da Silva, using the 1922 and 1923 health examination records, compiled statistics on 38,675 men. His data included racial composition, level of education, occupation, health status, and height. Of the total, 547 were caboclo; 3,707 black; 11,711 mestizo (which included mulattoes); and 22,710 white. Interestingly, the last were the least healthy, with a 71 percent acceptance rate compared with 77 percent for mestizos, 80 percent for blacks, and 81 percent for caboclos. Whites, who were generally smaller than the others, also suffered higher levels of venereal disease, respiratory illness, and ear, nose, throat, and eye disorders. The whites' greater number of health-related rejections was due partly to the fact that most of the caboclos, mestizos, and blacks came from the North and Northeast, where examining boards were not as rigorous as in the central and southern states. Also, in the latter, the whites called up were from the lower classes; the better off found some means of escape.

Farm laborers made up the majority of those examined (37.5 percent), followed by workers (31.1 percent), and unskilled clerks— "individuals without breeding, without education, and without certain means of livelihood." Thirty percent of the total were illiterate, which was considerably better than the then national rate of seventy percent. Regarding illiteracy, the blacks were the worst off, followed in order by the caboclos, mestizos, and whites.

From the outset in 1916, the army sought to combat "the cancer of illiteracy" and to instill patriotism through regimental schools, but the early hopes of using the army to educate the populace proved illusory. The army simply could not take in enough recruits to have an impact on the problem. Out of a 1940 population of about 45,000,000, roughly 0.8 percent, or 360,000 youths, annually reached twenty years of age. Of these about 15 percent were not registered and had no legal existence, another 40 to 50 percent were physically excluded, leaving a group of about 180,000 from which to select. The tiros and school military training programs took about 35,000, who received certificates as second class reservists. Ideally the army wanted to take in 80,000 a year but lacked the facilities and training personnel. Those who legally escaped duty had to pay an indemnity, which went into the military budget.[24] In 1940, Minister of War Gen. Eurico Gaspar Dutra complained that almost 60 percent of those examined for duty were illiterate and nearly 50 percent were physically disqualified.[25] Obviously, if the recruits had included the sons of the middle and upper classes these percentages would have been lower.

Even after screening out infirm candidates, the army had a large percentage of soldiers with health problems. When the army assembled its World War II expeditionary force, its physicians examined 103,565 soldiers and 4,044 officers and found over 22 percent of the former and 3.7 per cent of the latter unfit either for combat duty (19.5 and 2.22 respectively) or for retention in the service (3.31 and 1.48).[26] Despite this weeding attempt, unhealthy men were sent to Italy. Two extreme examples were a soldier with epilepsy and an officer with chronic hepatitis who displayed periodic jaundice. And even the healthy were easily afflicted with sickness in the combat zone. In the winter of 1944–45, a battalion of six hundred had four hundred soldiers requiring hospitalization. Between July 1944 and May 1945, 8,480 of the FEB's 11,617 casualties were due to illness.[27] Health problems represented a serious reduction of combat efficiency, a constant threat to morale, and a drain on medical facilities. The army reflected the poor health and poor health care of Brazilian society.

The Army and Politics

World War I, which Brazil entered in October 1917, provided a compelling reason for immediate military expansion. Even though the government did not plan to send troops to Europe, army leaders argued that the cost of mobilization was low considering the protective insurance that military strength provided for Brazil's tremendous natural resource wealth. They also pointed out that military spending helped the national economy.[28]

This expansion provided the army with the physical structure that would allow it to play a greater political role in future decades. The number of authorized effectives rose to 30,000 in 1920, to 48,000 in 1930, to 93,000 in 1940, and to 163,00 in 1944.[29] Indeed, the army grew at a faster rate than the population itself. José Murilo de Carvalho noted that between 1890 and 1930, while the population increased 162 percent, the army expanded 220 percent.[30] Though Alfred Stepan observed that "political variables are frequently far more important for determining the role of the military in society than the absolute size of the armed forces," we are confronted with the parallel developments of the army's numerical growth and its increasing political involvement. While the former may not have caused the latter, it is difficult to imagine the turn-of-the-century army providing the muscle for the Estado Novo (1937–45) or the Military Republic (1964–85).[31]

The political atmosphere that permitted army expansion also encouraged changes in the military's political role. The collapse of the "politics of the governors" in the Revolution of 1930 and the subsequent "inability of the political elites of the states to reconstruct civilian hegemony at the national level . . . opened the way to a greater role for the central government and for the central state in general, of which the armed forces were now a major component."[32] In the 1930s, the civilian elites' fears of social upheaval, of Brazil following the example of Spain into civil war, led them to support for the first time in Brazilian history a strong unified military. For decades army leaders had struggled to eliminate or gain control over the bulwarks of regionalism, the National Guard and the states' Policia Militar organizations; the former was abolished in 1918, and the Estado Novo placed the Policia Militar under army jurisdiction. The loss of their states' independent military power was the price the civilian elites paid for federal government protection of their interests. Of course, it was not completely a willing surrender as the Paulista revolt of 1932 showed. Federal control of military power enhanced the position of the central government and helped re-establish the hegemony that it had lost during the Old Republic.

In the process, as the army became the principal control vehicle of the central government, the idea of the army as a politically neutral institution, as an instrument of social reform, as the "vanguard of the people" was replaced with the conception of "the army as an essential part of the state and an instrument of its policies." An "ideology of conservative interventionism" presented the army as "the vanguard of the state" rather than of the povo.[33] The 1930s witnessed repeated purges of the officer corps as the likes of Gen. Pedro de Góes Monteiro, the military leader of the 1930 revolution, strove to eliminate partisan politics within the army, while pursuing the politics of the army nationally.

The restructured officer corps maintained the army dream of an organized, self-aware, industrialized Brazilian nation. During the Estado Novo, officers replaced civilians as state government leaders, industrial managers, censors, and propagandists; served with civilians on economic study commissions; negotiated agreements with foreign officers; trained in the United States; prepared for war with Argentina; became increasingly involved in internal antisubversive activities; and managed a combat division in Italy. These experiences produced an officer corps more aware of political forces and technocratic methods, and determinedly committed to national development. They shared the middle-class and elite fear that politicization of the masses would be a basic threat to their security, which they identified with national security. By 1945 the civilian-military technocracy, which would characterize the military-dominated authoritarian regime after 1964, had taken shape.[34]

In the late 1930s, the high command aimed at protecting the officers from political factionalism by supporting Vargas's abolition of political parties and by restricting access to the Escola Militar (Realengo). The only acceptable candidates were those who came from the military high schools, preparatory courses, or the enlisted ranks. By 1942, in addition to restrictions based on race, family background, religious and political beliefs, there was a "Law of Social Conformism and Elimination of Nonconformists" that "formed the moral basis of the Army's disciplinary structure," in the words of the minister of war. And Article 177 of the Estado Novo constitution authorized expulsions of officers whose dismissal the high command deemed "in the interest of the public service or for convenience of the regime." In Gilberto Freyre's land of racial democracy, Negroes, mulattoes, Jews, sons of immigrants from Poland or Russia, members of working-class families, sons of separated parents, or non-Catholics were excluded from the military schools. But even here the *jeito* or *pistolão* functioned, because excluded candidates with connections, or perhaps with a father who was a colonel, would be admitted as an exception by order of War Minister Dutra.[35]

While such practices are now only bad memories, another dating from that era continued until 1984. That was the custom of filling the ranks of the capital's guard units with tall, blue-eyed blond German descendants called up from Santa Catarina and Paraná. The breaking of the tradition of local training was justified by some officers who said that service in Brasília helped to nationalize the "immigrants"— many of whom were by now fourth- or fifth-generation Brazilians! Jehovah Motta had another interpretation when discussing the practice of stationing such troops in Rio de Janeiro in the late 1930s and 1940s: "we were trying to create, for ourselves and for the world, the image of an Arian, blond-haired nation, implicitly confessing the hurt or embarrassment or shame that our *mestiçagem* [miscegenation] and our negritude cause us."[36] Perhaps a simpler explanation was that the "Catarinas," as they were called, were taller than the average Brazilian, as size is a normal consideration in guard and police units. However, it may have been a classic case of *para inglês ver* (to impress the foreigners).

Worse, as the officer corps closed itself off physically from the masses, it closed its minds to the free development of ideas. The review *A defesa nacional* was a pale imitation of the lively magazine of earlier years. The officially sponsored *Nação armada* (The Nation in Arms) mirrored the high command line. And to limit intellectual contamination, officers were forbidden to attend civilian institutions of higher learning.[37]

These repressive measures produced a coherence and unity that had been lacking in the 1920s. The recruitment methods discussed above had given the army a national presence, while the expansion of the 1930s and 1940s gave the army numerical superiority over the military police in each state. By the early 1940s the approximately 49,000 military police in the various states faced an army that was approaching 100,000.

The World War II experience of fighting in Italy proved useful in a number of ways. It allowed the officers to measure themselves against a global standard and showed them what their troops, if properly trained, could accomplish. The campaign, and the expansion leading up to it, convinced the professionally oriented officers that by putting aside their apolitical preferences and working closely with military interventionists, such as Dutra and Góes Monteiro, they could improve the army's combat capabilities. The result of all this was to make the postwar army more political and interventionist. In the new army, even more emphasis was placed on officers' experiencing staff duty and attending the army's educational institutions. There was unwillingness to continue to enlist illiterates because of the technical knowledge required for modern warfare. The principal Brazilian military historian of the war period, Manoel Thomaz Castello Branco, observed that the barracks could no longer be "veritable schools for literacy. . . . The intention was laudable and the service highly profitable for the nation, still it was undeniably prejudicial to instruction, which was their essential mission."[38] Though attempts were made to improve draft procedures, the population simply grew too fast to permit army service for the millions of draftable age. Curiously, as the army's technical and educational level rose, it had the side effect of turning away the men who could most benefit from basic education. In the 1960s the army's promotional literature claimed that illiterates were being accepted and being taught basic skills, and random testimony indicates that this occurred in some units. Yet Alfred Stepan's contrary evidence suggests that the practice was not universal.[39]

Officer Recruitment

Increased professionalism and higher standards adversely affected the army's role as a vehicle of upward social mobility. Because the only entry into the regular officer corps is the Academia Militar das Agulhas Negras (AMAN), its records provide an accurate picture of the officer corps. In the post–World War II period, cadets from middle class families increased, while those from upper-class and unskilled lower-class families declined.[40] More disturbing, from 1950 to 1965 the number of applicants declined to the point that there were fewer than two candidates for every space. As the economy developed and diversified, high school graduates had more attractive options than the military could offer.

Increasingly, AMAN cadets were graduates of the army-supported high schools, which sons of military personnel attended tuition free. (Of the 269 cadets who graduated from the Campinas Escola Pre-

Table 1   Educational Origins of 1555 Cadets Enrolled at AMAN in 1985

Schools	No.	%
Escola Preparatória de Cadetes do Exército	800	51.4
Colégios Militares (see breakdown below)	566	36.3
Escola Preparatória de Cadetes de Aeronáutica	13	0.8
Colégio Naval	2	0.1
Admissions Examination (civilian high schools)	174	11.2
	1555	100

Colégios Militares	No.	% of Colégio Graduates	% of AMAN Cadets
Rio de Janeiro	153	27.0	9.8
Brasília	75	13.2	4.8
Porto Alegre	63	11.1	4.0
Recife	59	10.4	3.7
Fortaleza	53	9.3	3.4
Curitiba	50	8.8	3.2
Belo Horizonte	46	8.1	2.9
Manaus	34	6.0	2.1
Salvador	33	5.8	2.1
	566	100	36.0

Source: Brazilian army records.

Table 2 Religion of 1530 Cadets Enrolled at AMAN in 1985

Religious Affiliation	No.	%
Catholic	1195	78.1
Spiritist	112	7.3
Baptist	50	3.2
Evangelical	27	1.7
Protestant	17	1.1
Methodist	2	.13
Brazilian Christian	5	.32
Lutheran	3	.2
Presbyterian	6	.4
Mormon	6	.4
Adventist	3	.2
Umbandist	9	.6
Agnostic	1	.1
Unspecified	44	3.0
No Religion	50	3.3
	1530	100

Source: Brazilian Army Records.

paratória in 1982, 87% entered AMAN.) Of course, many of these students were sons of noncommissioned officers, whose own origins were not middle class, so a form of intrainstitutional upward mobility existed. In 1962–66, sons of military men made up more than 40 percent of the entering cadets, while graduates of civilian high schools represented only 7.6 percent of the corps of cadets. By late 1965, as AMAN began to shift from a three- to a four-year program, the situation reached a crisis, when enrollments in the new class totaled only 50 percent of capacity. In alarm the army offered admission without examination to the top three male graduates of recognized high schools. As a result, almost 50 percent of the first-year classes in 1967, 1968, and 1969 were civilian high school graduates.[41] However, the trend toward civilian sources of recruits has abated. The mental, health, and physical aptitude tests excluded large numbers of civilian school graduates: in 1977 of 1,145 civilians attempting the tests, only 34 were admitted (3 percent).[42] In 1985 only 174 or 11% of the academy's 1555 cadets were graduates of civilian schools; the rest were from the army's Colegio Militar system, the

Table 3   Profession of Fathers of 1413 First-Year Cadets: 1982, 1983, 1984, 1985

Upper		Middle		Lower Middle		Skilled Lower	
Fazendeiro	12	Upper Military	200*	Lower Military	550*	Tailor	2
Doctor	11	Business Mgr.	18	Bookkeeper	18	Plumber	1
Lawyer	20	Merchant	132	Salesman	21	Storeclerk	19
Dentist	7	Civil Servant	74	Insurance Rep.	4	Nurse	6
Judge	4	Architect	1	Bank Clerk	48	Railroad worker	8
General	10	Accountant	4	Small Farmer	7	Industrial worker	17
		Engineer	11			Airline worker	3
		Factory Owner	20			Mechanic	14
		Teacher	23			Driver	33
		Public Relations	1			Mason	9
		Chemist	1			Shoemaker	1
		Radio Announcer	1				
						**Unclassified	210
Totals	64		486		648		215
Percents	4.5		34.4		45.9		15.2

*Upper Military are majors through colonels and would be academy graduates. Lower Military are captains, lieutenants, sublieutenants, sergeants, corporals, and soldiers. In the first three ranks the men would be former sergeants who attained their status outside the educational and promotion system described above.

**AMAN officials believe that those cadets who do not list father's profession act from embarrassment, and they regard these cadets as being from lower-class families.

Data are from Brazilian army records. I assigned the class designations.

Escola Preparatoria de Cadetes, or air force or navy secondary schools.

As a result of its sources of recruitment, AMAN's cadets are much more homogeneous in educational background than is the case at West Point, and it is common to find officers produced by this system who entered military life at age 12 to 14. Stepan noted that "probably up to 90 percent of the present postwar generation of army officers entered the system around the age of 12."[43] Gen. Idálio Sardenberg commented that not even Catholic priests have such a homogeneous background.[44]

In a country that is about 80% Catholic, it is not surprising to find that 78% of the cadets at AMAN in 1985 said that that was their religious affiliation.

This homogeneity has social and educational implications that

Table 4   Race of Students, Graduating Turma 1982, Escola Preparatória

Race	Number	%
White	234	87.3
Negro/Mulatto	28	10.4
Oriental	6	2.2
	268	100

Race of Military Academy Graduating Turmas, 1962, 1975, 1984

	1962		1975		1984	
	No.	%	No.	%	No.	%
White	419	96.9	300	93.7	285	93.4
Negro/Mulatto	12	2.3	16	5.0	18	5.9
Oriental	1	.2	4	1.2	2	.6
	432	100	320	100	305	100

Note: Assuming that the number of Negro/mulatto and Oriental cadets was about the same in each class for 1962, when AMAN offered a three-year course, one could assume there were thirty-six of the former and three of the latter in the corps. The academy went to a four-year program in 1966, so for 1975 and 1984 multiply by four for a rough estimate. In informal conversations officers estimated an enrollment of about 20 percent negro/mulatto for the corps as a whole from the mid-1970s onward.

Source: Yearbook photos from Escola Preparatória and AMAN for indicated years.

are disturbing to officers and cadets alike. The shift that Stepan noted in his 1971 study, away from upper-class enrollment, has continued, with decreasing numbers of upper-middle-class entrants and consequent increases from lower-middle- and lower-class backgrounds. Table 3 provides an update on Stepan's data for the 1940s and 1960s and shows that lower socioeconomic family backgrounds are more common among 1980s cadets. Fewer AMAN graduates are sending their sons to the academy. In the 1982–85 period of the 760 cadets whose fathers were in the military, fully 550 were former sergeants (promoted to sublieutenants, lieutenants, or captains outside the career pattern described above) or current sergeants and corporals.

The decline in interest for an army career among sons of AMAN graduates may partly explain the increase in black and mulatto cadets, who now make up about 20 percent of the corps and perhaps as much as 40 percent of the students at the cadet preparatory school in Campinas (see table 4).[45]

The trend toward lower-class recruitment is seen most clearly by comparing the data on fathers' education between 1955 and 1979 with that of 1985:

Table 5a   Fathers' Education

Level	1955–79		1985	
	No.	%	No.	%
Primary	2151	25.15	781	50.0
Secondary	5428	63.47	455	29.0
Superior	973	11.38	211	13.0
No Declaration	0	0	108	7.6
	8552	100	1555	100

AMAN officials interpret "no declaration" as illiterate, which would mean that a total of 57.6% of the fathers of cadets enrolled in 1985 had less than a secondary school background.

The educational levels of cadet mothers in 1985 offer further insight:

Table 5b   Mothers' Education

Level	No.	%
Primary	1010	65.0
Secondary	231	14.9
Superior	14	1.0
No Declaration	300	19.1
	1555	100

Source: Brazilian army records. No data available on mothers' education for 1955–79.

While these figures indicate that AMAN is serving as a vehicle of upward mobility, they also explain why instructors at the academy are complaining about the cadets' lack of general education (cultura geral).

Table 6a   Preparatory Students' States of Origin

Region	State	1901–1902 No.	1901–1902 %	1982 No.	1982 %
Southeast	Minas Gerais	69	7.2	9	3.3
	Espirito Santo	5	.5	2	.7
	Rio de Janeiro	97	10.2	107	40.0
	Federal District	175	18.3	0	0
	São Paulo	41	4.3	90	33.5
South	Paraná	17	1.8	3	1.1
	Santa Catarina	17	1.8	1	.4
	Rio Grande do Sul	49	5.1	13	5.0
Central West	Goiás	29	3.0	1	.4
	Mato Grosso	41	4.3	2	.7
	Mato Grosso do Sul	0	0	2	.7
	Brasília, DF	0	0	1	.4
North	Roraima	0	0	0	0
	Amazonas	16	1.7	2	.7
	Pará	30	3.1	1	.4
	Acre	0	0	0	0
	Rondonia	0	0	1	.4
Northeast	Maranhão	41	4.3	3	1.1
	Piauí	14	1.5	1	.4
	Ceará	66	6.9	13	5.0
	Rio Grande do Norte	22	2.3	1	.4
	Paraiba	36	3.8	3	1.1
	Pernambuco	55	5.8	7	2.6
	Sergipe	42	4.4	0	0
	Alagoas	34	3.6	1	.4
	Bahia	58	6.1	3	1.1
Foreign		—	—	2	.7
		954	100	269	100

Note: These figures compare the military students enrolled at the Escola Preparatória e de Táctica do Realengo, Rio de Janeiro, in 1901–1902 and the graduating turma of the Escola Preparatória de Cadetes do Exército, Campinas, São Paulo, in 1982. For sources see 6b.

Table 6b   Preparatory Students' Regional Origins

	Preparatory (Realengo) 1901–02		Preparatory (Campinas) 1982	
	No.	%	No.	%
Southeast	387	40.4	208	77.0
South	83	8.6	17	6.3
Central West	70	7.3	6	2.2
North	46	4.8	4	1.4
Northeast	368	38.4	34	13.0
	957	100	269	100

Sources (for tables 6a and 6b): Ministerio da Guerra, *Relatório . . . J.N. de Medeiros Mallet . . . 1901* (Rio de Janeiro: Imprensa Nacional, 1901), p. 55, and *Relatorio . . . Mallet . . . 1902* (Rio de Janeiro: Imprensa Nacional, 1902), p. 33. *Revista da Escola Preparatória de Cadetes do Exercito (Turma Marechal Mallet) 1982* (Campinas: ESPCEX, 1982), pp. 73–95.

In this century the officer corps has been composed predominately of men from the Southeast and South of Brazil, where both military units and greater educational opportunities are concentrated. In 1901–1902 the Northeast contributed 38 percent of students at the army's preparatory school in Realengo, while in 1982 it provided 13 percent to the preparatory school in Campinas. In the same years the Southeast supplied 40.4 percent and 77 percent, while the South gave 8.6 percent and 6.3 percent. Though São Paulo, according to Stepan and other observers, has not been noted for sending its sons into the officer corps, its contribution increased from 4.3 percent of students in 1901–1902 to 33.5 percent in 1982. Regional origins of cadets at AMAN have been fairly consistent in the 1964–85 period. By far the largest contingent has come consistently from the state and city of Rio de Janeiro.

While social theorists might be pleased with indications that the army is serving as a vehicle for social mobility, army leaders are worried. Officers also remark upon the trend toward lower-class recruitment in the reserve officer training units, known as CPOR, and the problems they are having with such officers. In an interview, Minister of the Army Gen. Leonidas Pires Gonçalves observed that he did not want officers who would give five or ten years to the army:

Table 6c   States of Origin of AMAN cadets 1964–66 and 1985

		1964–66		1985	
		No.	%	No.	%
Southeast	Minas Gerais	57	7.2	84	5.4
	Espirito Santo	3	.5	7	.5
	Rio de Janeiro	19	3.4	637	41.4
	Federal District	233	42.0	0	0
	São Paulo	46	8.3	284	18.4
South	Paraná	13	2.3	57	3.7
	Santa Catarina	9	1.6	14	.9
	Rio Grande do Sul	80	14.4	136	8.8
Central West	Goiás	0	0	2	.1
	Mato Grosso	10	1.8	3	.2
	Mato Grosso do Sul	0	0	23	1.5
	Brasília, DF	0	0	16	1.0
North	Roraíma	0	0	1	.07
	Amazonas	1	.18	19	1.2
	Pará	6	1.08	17	1.1
	Acre	1	.18	1	.07
	Rondonia	0	0	0	0
Northeast	Maranhão	7	1.26	2	.1
	Piauí	6	1.08	12	.7
	Ceará	20	3.6	77	5.0
	Rio Grande do Norte	4	.7	16	1.0
	Paraiba	2	.4	13	.8
	Pernambuco	3	.5	77	5.0
	Sergipe	9	1.6	3	.2
	Alagoas	6	1.08	8	.5
	Bahia	22	4.0	28	1.8
		557	100.5	1537	100

he wanted men with a military vocation who would stay for a full thirty-plus-year career. Many officers expressed concern that men seeking to use the army to improve their status were not sufficiently dedicated to the institution. Certainly the army will have to give greater attention to remedial education and to focus its socialization in such fashion as to help these young men move into the middle class.[46]

Table 6d   AMAN Cadets' Regional Origins

	1964–66		1985	
	No.	%	No.	%
Southeast	358	64.3	1012	65.8
South	102	18.3	207	13.5
Central West	10	1.8	44	2.9
North	8	1.4	38	2.5
Northeast	79	14.2	231	15.0
	557	100.	1537	99.7

Sources (for tables 6c and 6d): For 1964–66, Stepan, *Military in Politics*, p. 38. The figures for 1985 are from Brazilian army records.

Whither the Army?

It is ironic that the economic development fostered by the Military Republic has provided the army with nationally made armament while depriving it of its traditional sources of officer recruitment. At the very time that the increasingly sophisticated technology of warfare demands a more highly educated officer corps, the army is unable to attract well educated candidates. The officer corps is not well paid. In September 1986 officers and their wives publicly protested their inability to make do on army salaries. Self-sacrifice for the national well-being is not an effective recruitment device.[47]

The purpose or mission of the army has bedeviled officers, because the constitutions have traditionally renounced wars of conquest, leaving the armed forces with a defensive role that was split into external and internal elements. But if there are no external enemies, which elements of the society should the army defend? The military's concept of Brazil then becomes key in determining its conception of its mission. And since military thinkers early conceived of Brazil as a "Motherland so worthy of better sons," the army's purpose was to provide those sons, to provide a nation for the "immense and dazzling country." This was the "grandiose task" that the *A defesa nacional* turma set before the army in 1916. The army was to be the formulator of the nation.[48]

Conclusion

Officer recruitment patterns in this century portray an institution with uneasy links to society. If its mission was to protect society, it needed to be an integral part of it rather than an institution set apart. In the postwar period the army sought to reform society from the top down by using the Escola Superior de Guerra (ESG) to integrate and militarize the civilian elites by inviting selected persons to study at the school and by organizing special courses for local elites across the land. In this fashion the officer corps sought to reduce its sense of isolation and alienation from society, whose elites and masses project values and attitudes very different from those of the military.[49]

Indeed, the attempt to reconcile its identity and alienation provided the psychological climate that led the military to take over the government in 1964. In the 1950s, the ESG's military-civilian student body had studied inflation, banking reform, land tenure, voting systems, transportation, and education, as well as guerrilla and conventional warfare. "In many of these studies, some of the fundamental aspects of Brazilian social and economic organization were depicted as needing change if Brazil were to maintain its internal security."[50]

By the 1960s, ESG doctrines became the army's blueprint for extending its influence into all aspects of national security policy formation and implementation. Confronting the deepening crisis of the early 1960s, the officer corps perceived the country as entering an era of subversive warfare such as they had studied in their ECEME courses on internal security. They had come to believe that Brazil's security and economic development could occur only if various aspects of the economic and political structure were altered and that the civilian elites were unwilling or unable to make the necessary changes. Moreover, they believed that they had the doctrines, the trained personnel, and the institutional will and force to do so.

After overthrowing João Goulart in 1964, the military kept power, rather than hand it over to other civilian elites as they had in 1930, 1945, 1954, and 1955. The Military Republic endured until 1985 partly because of the cohesion imposed during the 1930s. It is perhaps symbolic that General João Figueiredo, who as first in the 1937 Realengo graduating class was complimented by Getúlio Vargas, presided over the transition back to civilian rule (1979–85).

Figueiredo's career forms a bridge between the repression of the Estado Novo and the openness of the post-1985 Nova Republica. The gradual relaxation of military control under Presidents Ernesto Geisel and João Figueiredo responded to the conviction of the military professionals that continued political involvement was harmful to the best interests of the service and of the nation. Brazil had gone from being an importer of arms and munitions in the first half of the century to the world's fifth-ranked arms exporter in 1985, yet units lacked sufficient ammunition for marksmanship training. The example of Argentina's defeat in the 1982 Falklands (Malvinas) War weighed heavily on the minds of officers concerned with effective civilian support of national defense. Despite the fears of hard-line officers that their use of torture, terror, and sabotage would bring retribution from an elected civilian government, the pressures inside and outside the army for an end to the Military Republic were too great to ignore.

The trend toward lower-class entry into the officer corps worries top officials because of the strain this places on the military educational system. The officers who will command the army in the next century will have their roots in the masses to an unprecedented degree. But the history reviewed here suggests that the institution will absorb and change them to fit the needs of the service.

Notes

1. José Murilo de Carvalho refers to this relationship as "back and forward linkages . . . the first indicates the inflow of people from society into the army, the second the outflow of people from the army into society" ("Armed Forces and Politics in Brazil, 1930–45," *Hispanic American Historical Review* 62, no. 2 [May 1982]: 201). Size statistics available in public sources, such as newspapers, are often inaccurate because they are based upon the official authorized strength figures rather than actual strength. For example, a 1986 news story listed 17,610 officers, 38,800 sublieutenants and noncommissioned officers, and 140,000 soldiers. The figures in this chapter came from a staff officer who noted that there were about two-thirds fewer noncoms than needed and that troop strength was down to 30,000.

2. In a decree reforming military education, April 14, 1890, text in Edgard Carone, *A primeira república (1889–1930), Texto e contexto* (São Paulo: Difusão Européia do Livro, 1969), pp. 249–50.

3. See José Nun, "The Middle-Class Military Coup," in *The Politics of*

Conformity in Latin America, ed. Claudio Véliz (New York: Oxford University Press, 1967), pp. 66–118; and John J. Johnson, *The Military and Society in Latin America* (Stanford: Stanford University Press, 1964). Both regard origins as a central factor.

4. Alfred Stepan, *The Military in Politics: Changing Patterns in Brazil* (Princeton: Princeton University Press, 1971), pp. 52–53.

5. Ibid., pp. 53–54.

6. Ibid., p. 43.

7. For the history of military education, see Umberto Peregrino, *História e projeção das instituições culturais do Exército* (Rio de Janeiro: J. Olympio, 1967), and Jehovah Motta, *Formação do oficial do Exército* (Rio de Janeiro: Companhia Brasileira de Artes Gráficas, 1976).

8. Morris Janowitz, *The Professional Soldier: A Social and Political Portrait* (Glencoe, Ill.: Free Press, 1960), pp. 134–35. Cf. Stepan, *Military in Politics*, p. 51.

9. The size of officer corps in various years was 2,917 (1900), 3,597 (1920), 4,469 (1940), and 13,373 (1968).

10. The foregoing is based on interviews with officers. It would be unusual for colonels or lieutenant colonels to be assigned to AMAN unless they were ECEME graduates. Officers at AMAN serve in one of four capacities: the commandant's staff, the academic faculty, the corps of cadets, or a support function.

The academic sections consist of History, Geography, Economics, Philosophy, Public and Private Law, Psychology, Editing and Writing, English, Mathematics, Statistics, Computer Science, Physics, Mechanical Engineering, Chemistry, Descriptive Geometry, and Topography.

The corps of cadets is responsible for the professional military training of the cadets. It is headed by a colonel whose officers oversee training in the arms and services: Infantry, Cavalry, Artillery, Engineering, Quartermaster, Communications, and War Material. There are also officers who supervise physical education, horsemanship, special operations (mountaineering, jungle warfare, anti-guerrilla warfare), and parachuting.

Each of the cadet units has an officer as its commander. The cadets do not have a separate command structure such as that at West Point.

11. Augusto Sá, *Exércitos regionães e o problema de uma organização para o nosso exército* (Porto Alegre: n.p., 1905), pp. 12–14; Armando Duval, *Reorganização do Exército* (Rio de Janeiro: Imprensa Nacional, 1901)), p. 53. In 1901 legally the army was to comprise 1,914 officers and 28,160 soldiers; in reality it had 2,917 officers and 15,000 soldiers.

12. Henrique Duque-Estrada de Macedo Soares, *A Guerra de Canudos*, 2d ed. (Rio de Janeiro: Biblioteca do Exército, 1959), p. 403.

13. Dermeval Peixoto, *Memórias de um velho soldado* (Rio de Janeiro: Biblioteca do Exército, 1960), p. 108.

14. Ademar de Brito, *O 52o Batalhão de caçadores e a 3a Companhia de metrahadores pesados* (Rio de Janeiro: Biblioteca do Exército, 1944), p. 47.

15. Quoted in Edgard Carone, *A República Velha: Instituições e classes sociais*, vol. 1 (São Paulo: Difusão Européia do Livro, 1972), p. 355.

16. Euclides da Cunha, *Rebellion in the Backlands (Os Sertões)*, trans. Samuel Putnam (Chicago: University of Chicago Press), 1944, p. 481.

17. For the League's work, see Thomas E. Skidmore, *Black into White: Race and Nationality in Brazilian Thought* (New York: Oxford University Press, 1974), pp. 157–62.

18. The quotes are from *A defesa nacional (Discursos)* (Rio de Janeiro: Biblioteca do Exército, 1965). Skidmore discusses him in *Black into White*, pp. 153–55. For an analysis of Bilac's "burguesia militarizada," see Carone, *A república velha*, 1:164–68. For an extended discussion, see Frank D. McCann, "The Nation in Arms: Obligatory Service during the Old Republic," in *Essays Concerning the Socioeconomic History of Brazil and Portuguese India*, ed. Dauril Alden and Warren Dean (Gainesville: University Presses of Florida, 1977), pp. 211–43.

19. *A defesa nacional*, October 10, 1913, pp. 1–2.

20. "A organização nacional," *A Defesa Nacional*, March 10, 1916, pp. 177–79. For more on ADN, see Frank D. McCann, "The Formative Period of Twentieth-Century Brazilian Army Thought, 1900–1922," *Hispanic American Historical Review* 64, no. 4 (November 1984): 737–65.

21. Though women were not admitted to army ranks, a group of elite women formed a *tiro* unit named in honor of Hermes da Fonseca's first wife, Orsina da Fonseca. On the government side this was probably less an effort to recognize female equality than to attract support of elite women to the campaign for a modern army. The women's motivation was likely linked to their efforts to secure the right to vote; one of the leaders of the suffrage movement, Leolinda de Figueiredo Daltro, was one of the unit's organizers. Perhaps they hoped that a display of patriotism in an activity dear to President Hermes's heart would give them his support. Nevertheless, female suffrage had to wait for the 1930s. See June E. Hahner, "Feminism, Women's Rights, and the Suffrage Movement in Brazil, 1850–1932," *Latin American Research Review* 15, no. 1 (1980): 94–95.

22. Arthur Lobo da Silva, *A anthropologia do exército brasileiro*, Archives do Museu Nacional, 30 (1928): 36.

23. Ministério da Guerra, *Relatório . . . Gen. Eurico Gaspar Dutra . . . 1940)* (Rio de Janeiro: Imprensa Militar, 1941), p. 22. The usual length of service was one year if the recruit did satisfactorily; if not, he could be held for another six months. If the draftee was not fluent in Portuguese he stayed two years. This was designed to nationalize foreigners (Military Attaché, Rio de Janeiro, April 23, 1940, 6000, G-2 Regional, RG 165, Suitland Records Center, National Archives).

24. Ministério da Guerra, *Relatório . . . secreto . . . 1940* (Rio de Janeiro: Imprensa Militar, 1941), pp. 43–44.

25. Ministério da Guerra, *Relatório . . . Dutra*, p. 132.

26. Carlos Paiva Gonçalves (lieutenant colonel, Medical Corps), *Seleção médica do pessoal do a F.E.B.: Histórico, funcionamento, e dados estatísticos*, Biblioteca do Exército, vol. 162 (Rio de Janeiro: Aurora, 1951), p. 117.

27. Frank D. McCann, Jr., *The Brazilian-American Alliance, 1937–1945* (Princeton: Princeton University Press, 1973), pp. 369–71.

28. Ministério da Guerra, *Relatório . . . José Caetano de Faria . . . 1917* (Rio de Janeiro: Imprensa Militar, 1917), pp. 7–10, 15–17, 79–101.

29. Sources often disagree regarding size of army. In 1940 the U.S. military attaché reported that the army consisted of 4,469 officers and 73,175 soldiers (report cited in note 22). The 93,000 figure comes from Gen. Eurico Gaspar Dutra, *Exército em dez anos de governo do Presidente Vargas* (Rio de Janeiro: Imprensa Militar, 1941), p. 27.

30. José Murilo de Carvalho, "As forças armadas na primeira república: O poder desestabilizador," *Cadernos do Departamento de Ciência Política* 1 (Universidade Federal de Minas Gerais, March 1974): 141.

31. McCann, "The Nation in Arms," pp. 239–40; Stepan, *Military in Politics*, p. 26.

32. Carvalho, "Armed Forces," pp. 217–18.

33. Ibid., p. 219.

34. McCann, *Brazilian-American Alliance*, pp. 444–45; Carvalho, "Armed Forces," p. 221.

35. Ministério da Guerra, *Relatório . . . Dutra*, p. 22. The report noted that Article 177 had been used to force a few retirements. For the Estado Novo constitution, see Getúlio Vargas, *A nova política do Brasil* (Rio de Janeiro: José Olympio, 1938), p. 96. Cf. Nelson Werneck Sodré, *Memórias de um soldado* (Rio de Janeiro: Civilização Brasileira, 1967), pp. 188–90, and Carvalho, "Armed Forces," pp. 205–6.

36. Motta, *Formaçao do oficial*, p. 354.

37. Decree-law 432, May 19, 1938.

38. Manoel Thomaz Castello Branco, *O Brasil na II Grande Guerra* (Rio de Janeiro: Biblioteca do Exército, 1960), p. 577.

39. Stepan, *Military in Politics*, pp. 15–16.

40. Ibid., pp. 32–33.

41. Ronald M. Schneider, *The Political System of Brazil: Emergence of a "Modernizing" Authoritarian Regime, 1964–1970* (New York: Columbia University Press, 1971), p. 252.

42. *Veja*, November 30, 1977, p. 102; October 16, 1985, pp. 77–78.

43. Stepan, *Military in Politics*, p. 41.

44. *Veja*, November 30, 1977, p. 102.

45. *Revista Agulhas Negras*, 1979. Based on senior photographs in the AMAN yearbook.

46. Conversations with various officers in July and August 1986 and an interview with Gen. Leonidas Pires Gonçalves, Brasília, July 23, 1986.

47. Capt. Jair Messia Bolsonaro, "O salário está baixo," *Veja*, September 3, 1986, p. 154. He confirmed rumors that dozens of AMAN cadets had resigned and asserted that the reason in 90 percent of the cases was the financial crisis that the army's officers and sergeants were suffering and the resultant depressing perspective for the cadets' careers. He noted that a captain with eight or nine years of service received a total income of 10,453 cruzados a month, while a third sergeant got 4,134. At that moment, the official U.S. dollar exchange rate was fourteen to one, while the black market was 24. He further noted that officers spent about half their monthly salaries on rent. The article resulted in his being disciplined and in various demonstrations of solidarity by officers and army wives. See "Disciplina salarial," *Veja*, September 10, 1986, pp. 46–47.

48. Mário Travassos, "Para a frente, custe o que custe!" *A defesa nacional*, October 10, 1916, pp. 15–17; McCann, "Brazilian Army Thought," pp. 737–65.

49. On alienation in the 1945–64 period see Edmundo Campos Coelho, *Em busca de identidade: O exército e a política na sociedade brasileira* (Rio de Janeiro: Forense-Universitária, 1976), pp. 127–48.

50. Alfred C. Stepan, ed, *Authoritarian Brazil: Origins, Policies, and Future* (New Haven: Yale University Press, 1973), p. 56.

Part II: Economic Elites

Steven Topik

The Old Republic

A small group of men dominated the economy of Old Republican Brazil (1889–1930). The oligarchic state usually served their interests, so the wealthy class also was the ruling class. This chapter examines the nature of the economically dominant class and the means by which it shaped state policy.[1] To do that, first the propertied class is described. Then their expectations for state policy, their political organization, and the means by which they influenced the state are considered.

Brazil's Economic Elite during the Old Republic

The wealthy class was quite small. Although accurate data on property and income are scarce, several independent estimates agree that those who controlled most of Brazil's land, capital, and machinery constituted only one or two percent of the work force. (And only about one-third of the national population entered the remunerated work force.) This translated to roughly 70,000 men in 1890 and 135,000 in 1930 (virtually no women held important economic positions).[2]

The composition of the native economic elite mirrored the vastness, diversity, and relative backwardness of the Brazilian subcontinent. It is true that as a settlement colony, Brazil did not experience the sort of national, tribal, or religious schisms that fragmented African, Asian and even European countries.[3] The European families that immigrated and rose to prominence soon merged into the national society. Nonetheless, the wealthy class was unusually heterogeneous; it was splintered into many regional and local factions. The *classe conservadora*, as it was known, constituted a unified self-conscious class only in the sense that it mounted a common opposition to the demands of other classes and shared the desire for hegemony.[4] Otherwise, its members faced dramatically different economic prospects and operated in diverse sociopolitical settings.

The wealthy class's heterogeneity developed because of the country's geographical variety, contrasting settlement patterns, and lack of an integrated national economy. In the colonial period, each region fashioned its economy around a different export crop. This promoted differing growth rates and cycles. The European orientation of these economies, and their coastal locations, impeded internal integration. A poor transportation system further sustained regional compartmentalization and fragmented the ruling class.

The nineteenth century magnified regional diversity. The Northeast, formerly the most successful exporter, slumped as sugar lost its foreign markets. The Amazon enjoyed a short-lived boom (1890–1912) fueled by rubber. The South enjoyed steady but unremarkable growth based on products sold mostly within Brazil.[5] But the thriving economy of the Center, driven by coffee exports, underwent spectacular development. It came to overshadow the rest of the country.

As a result, just three of Brazil's twenty states, plus the Federal District, produced most of the export economy's riches. The state of São Paulo alone generated 40 percent of all exports. Together with Minas Gerais, Rio Grande do Sul, and the Federal District, it produced 60 percent of the agricultural crops, accounted for 75 percent of the industrial output and meat production, and held 80 percent of the nation's bank assets. The per capita income of these provinces and the federal capital was over double that of the poorer provinces, underlining the divergence between regions.

Within regions there were also sharp contrasts. Geography was partly at fault. The parched poor soil of the *sertão*, which stretched from the interior of the Northeast to Minas Gerais, supported only rudimentary agriculture and stock raising. The fertile well-watered land of the coastal zona da matta in the Northeast, the Paraíba valley, and western São Paulo, on the other hand, yielded abundant crops.

Human settlement patterns also contributed to the diversity. Some previously rich lands, such as the coffee plantations of the Paraíba valley, fell into decline because of soil exhaustion and erosion. At the same time newly opened frontier areas such as western São Paulo, offered cheap, bountiful plots while the vast and largely untapped interior lacked sufficient labor and transportation to support more than subsistence agriculture.

The changing demands of the world economy and the development of the domestic markets also caused regional differentiation and flux. Newly rich coffee planters in western São Paulo, cotton growers in the interior of Paraíba, rubber merchants in the Amazon, cacao planters in southern Bahia, and maté farmers in Paraná rose to challenge the traditional landed oligarchy of their respective areas. Industrialists, financiers, and other domestically oriented businessmen gained importance as exports fell from about a quarter of GNP in 1890 to around 15 percent in 1930.[6]

Regional and local differences in the pace and depth of development were reflected in the extent to which fully capitalist practices were implemented. In the more affluent Center and South, the end of slavery in 1888 brought the emergence of a labor system based predominantly on wages. Specialization and a money-based market economy prevailed. The economically dominant class, composed mostly of planters, was bourgeois. They viewed wealth as capital to be invested to create more wealth, and they invested principally in commodities and services. In the Northern rubber economy, merchants reigned. They invested in commerce more than production, since rubber gatherers (seringueiros) worked as semi-independent producers who exchanged their crop for needed supplies. The economy was fueled more by credit than by money. Markets were small and monopolized by merchants. The Northeast and more marginal areas of other regions were dominated by landlords who often were rentiers rather than entrepreneurs interested in increasing productivity. They attempted to monopolize the local factors of production—land, water, and capital—in order to rent them at a high price to small farmers. Money was not extensively used because farmers usually paid rent with a share of their crop.[7]

The diversity of regional and local economic settings meant that one could not speak of a unified national economic elite. It is more accurate to divide the ruling class into three tiers: the high bourgeoisie, the provincial barons, and the local notables. The boundaries among the tiers were neither precise nor impermeable.

On top were Brazil's high bourgeoisie, the dozens of magnates who sat at the commanding heights of the economy. They came overwhelmingly from the Center of the country. Though their fortunes were often founded in the countryside, where they maintained summer homes, they tended to live in the major cities. Rio de Janeiro, the nation's financial and governmental center, housed the greatest share of the country's wealthy aristocrats. São Paulo came increasingly to rival the federal capital but did not overtake it during the Old Republic. This small group of men had a hand in the largest, most profitable enterprises in the country, sometimes in regions outside the Center.

The provincial barons constituted the second tier. They were chiefly the prominent planters and ranchers from areas other than the Center. Less tied into the international economy and less capitalist in their undertakings, they usually invested in their own, less lucrative regions. When they participated in the larger enterprises of the Center, they usually served as junior partners or minority stockholders. They lived mostly in or near provincial capitals.

The third level was composed of the local notables. They based their fortunes on land, though some were merchants. Their investments were generally restricted to small, marginal, nonexporting geographic areas; their activities involved less capital, were less diversified, and more likely relied on precapitalist practices than those of the other two tiers.[8]

Since the high bourgeoisie was economically and politically most important, it will receive the most attention in this essay. The top echelon of the economic elite was notable for its diversified portfolios. Often, the same man owned plantations, banks, commercial establishments, and factories. The Prado family of São Paulo provides a good example.[9] Though their wealth was originally grounded in coffee production, they soon branched out. Patriarch Antônio Prado was simultaneously one of Brazil's largest coffee producers, president of the São Paulo Railroad, president of the Banco de Comércio e Indústria, partner in one of the largest export houses (Prado Chaves), founder of Brazil's first meat-packing factory, and partner in a glass factory. Import-export merchants similarly diversified. Francisco Matarazzo began importing and distributing lard but soon moved to general imports and exports and eventually built Brazil's largest industrial empire. He also founded a bank and became a large-scale landowner. Francisco de Paula Mayrink illustrates another path. He started working for the Banco Comercial do Rio de Janeiro and went on to found and preside over five other banks. He also established an immigrant colonization company in São Paulo, was president of the Sorocabana Railroad, founded five smaller railroads, headed the Lloyd shipping company, and helped organize the company that operated the Santos docks. Finally, he was president of the largest streetcar companies in Rio, São Paulo, and Belo Horizonte and owned sugar and flour mills and coffee plantations in addition to extensive urban real estate.

Such diversified directorships and portfolios were common until the depression of the 1930s. Thereafter greater sectoral specialization developed; it became more difficult for a single individual to accumulate the capital, technology, and knowledge for such diverse undertakings. In addition, ownership became more diffused as publicly held corporations became more important than private firms. But before the end of the Old Republic large concerns, controlled by just a few members of the classe conservadora, held sway.

In agriculture latifundia predominated. Only 4 percent of landholdings in 1920 accounted for 60 percent of privately held land. In the most prosperous export-oriented regions, concentration was even more extreme. In São Paulo, 2.5 percent of the holdings encompassed 45 percent of the land. In 1935 the situation remained much the same: 14 percent of the coffee plantations contained 57 percent of the trees. Ownership of land in sugar-rich Pernambuco showed a similar pattern: 2 percent of the agricultural holdings accounted for 43 percent of the land. Vast land empires arose in the frontier areas of Goiás and Mato Grosso. The Brazil Railroad alone was said to own 140,000 square kilometers. In comparison, land in the American South after the Civil War was much less concentrated: only 11 percent of the land was held by estates larger than 500 acres.[10]

In the export trade a few mercantile houses dominated. Eight coffee firms shipped two-thirds of Brazil's harvest. Eight rubber jobbers exported over half the annual crop. A few large commercial houses oversaw imports as well.

Transportation was mostly in the hands of a few firms. Just before World War I, two companies controlled two-thirds of Brazil's railroad mileage. These conglomerates broke up in the 1920s, but as late as 1930 seven companies still held over half the tracks. The same concentration was evident in the maritime shipping sector: six firms carried half the coffee exports. One firm (Lloyd Brasileiro) handled 61 percent of all passengers and, together with two others, accounted for 84 percent of all coastwise cargo.

Finance was equally concentrated: one bank held almost a fifth of all bank assets, and a dozen banks accounted for two-thirds of all banking activity. These banks conducted mostly the business of the wealthy, for large mortgages dominated their loan portfolios.[11]

Even manufacturing in the Old Republic was dominated by a few firms. The conventional wisdom has been that artisans and small workshops prevailed in Brazil's underdeveloped economy. In a sense that was true. In the first fairly accurate national industrial census, conducted in 1920, almost three-quarters of all manufacturing companies employed nine or fewer workers. On the other hand, those employing over one hundred people represented only 4 percent of the firms, but they accounted for 55 percent of production (by value), employed over 60 percent of the laborers and horsepower, and possessed two-thirds of the capital invested. Thus the wealthy class fashioned oligopolies in the key sectors of the economy.

Foreigners as Investors

Foreigners occupied an important place in Brazil's economy. Although the native bourgeoisie, which controlled the production of the country's exports, was among Latin America's strongest, foreigners dominated many complementary fields. In many analyses capitalists from abroad are not considered part of the national ruling class; as citizens of other countries they had no vote in Brazil, nor could they stand for office. Indeed the owners of the largest European and North American enterprises usually did not even reside in Brazil. They also lacked familial and cultural ties to Brazil. Foreign capitalists exercised enormous influence over the economic policy of the Brazilian state, but they did not have monolithic interests. Foreign economic involvement and interests were almost as diverse as those of Brazilians.

They were divided first, of course, by nationality. The British held over half of all foreign investment throughout the period. The French were second; they flooded Brazil's capital markets in the decade before the First World War but pulled back after the war. North Americans began at that point to invest heavily. Germans and Belgians were the other two sizable investing nationalities. Together, Europeans and North Americans increased their capital in Brazil over sixfold during the Old Republic, from around U.S.$400 million in 1889 to approximately U.S. $2.6 billion in 1930. In all Latin America only Argentina received more foreign investment in this period than did Brazil.

The relationship of foreign capitalists to the Brazilian economy and state varied according to the nature of their investments. Non-immigrant foreign capitalists, having expertise in particular areas, such as railroads, public utilities or banking, generally became involved in less diverse activities than did the Brazilian high bourgeoisie. When they enlarged their stake in Brazil, they generally integrated horizontally into like activities; sometimes they integrated vertically into related fields. Their greater sectoral specialization occasionally brought them down on different sides of issues of economic policy. Portfolio investors, who loaned money to the state or private firms, had somewhat different concerns from direct investors who held equity shares in Brazilian companies. Over 40 percent of all foreign investment was in the form of loans. In fact, Brazil was the largest debtor in Latin America. Until 1906 all federal loans were placed by the London Rothschilds banking house. Thereafter a few other banks became involved. These lenders were particularly well placed to influence Brazilian public policy.

Foreign merchants' interests sometimes conflicted with those of international bankers. The former were preoccupied with Brazil's international flow of goods rather than its ability to repay loans. Centered in Brazil's import and export trade, they had a grip on the economy's key pressure points. British, German, French, and North American merchants handled 90 percent of coffee exports in 1900 and two-thirds in 1930. Together with Portuguese exporters, they controlled a similar proportion of rubber shipments. They played a large role in imports and domestic distribution as well.

Direct investors in Brazilian enterprises constituted the third category of foreign capitalists. They had a more direct link to the Brazilian economy than the international lenders because they actually owned part of the economy and were at the mercy of its ebb and flow. They had more capital invested than merchants. The most important foreign-owned companies had been created in London, New York, or Paris to undertake specific activities in Brazil. Their strategies were based primarily on business conditions within Brazil. Some large foreign firms were established by immigrants who laid down deep business and familial roots in Brazil. Within a generation these companies usually became Brazilian. Only in the 1920s did multinational corporations begin to enter and subject companies to the more global logic of internationally integrated conglomerates.[12]

Foreign direct investors owned vital parts of the export economy. They played a large part in railroading. Although the pioneer lines of the 1880s had been paid for by Brazilians, British and French investors soon bought them out. Just before World War I foreign railroad firms owned or leased some 80 percent of Brazil's track. This proportion declined to a quarter by 1930.

Europeans were in control of banking as well. In the nineteenth century they dominated the exchange market and held an important share of the note discount and short-term loan business. They continued to issue half of all loans and discounts until World War I, but their position declined to one-quarter of the loan market by 1930.

Foreigners had been reluctant to invest in consumer goods manufacturing during the nineteenth century because of the limited size of the domestic market. They preferred those endeavors that supplied foreign trade, such as gold mining and sugar refining. By the early twentieth century, however, many foreigners began building factories. The incomplete 1907 industrial census revealed that the country's largest factory was British owned and that three of the next nine largest were foreign owned. After World War I the pace of foreign investment in manufacturing, particularly by North Americans, accelerated. This new group poured some U.S.$200 million into Brazilian factories by 1929. Foreigners were especially evident in (1) technologically advanced lines like electrical supplies, automobiles, and pharmaceuticals; (2) heavy industries, such as petroleum, electrical energy, cement, and steel; and (3) export sectors, like meat packing and mining. Foreigners also predominated in consumer goods industries, though most owners in this sector were immigrants who remained in Brazil and whose children became citizens. The largest companies producing beer, cigarettes, matches, shoes, and textiles were foreign owned. Government data were not clear about the extent of foreign ownership of industry, but from scattered evidence one can estimate that foreigners controlled roughly one-half of all industry in 1930.

Brazil's small wealthy class, then, composed of nationals and foreigners, dominated the oligopolized export economy. Despite frequently overlapping interests, the owners of Brazil's means of production were split by substantive differences. The various tiers and sectors of the ruling class were divided by nationality, economic prospects, the extent of their ties to the international economy, their integration into the national economy, and their adoption of capital-

ist methods. Consequently their demands on the state differed, as
did the means they employed to win favorable results.

The Proper Role of the State

The type of state aid that the ruling class sought was determined by
the structure of the export economy. It made fairly modest demands
because the export economy of the Old Republic required relatively
little state assistance compared with the planning and entrepreneurial role the state would assert in the drive to industrialize after
1930. The low level of skill and technology necessary to run plantations and light industries obviated both a sophisticated educational
system and institutes dedicated to research and development. The
relatively small, compartmentalized domestic market required little
state coordination or planning. The absence of substantive rural
labor movements or urban worker organizations before World War I
allowed the state to ignore the regulation of labor and the provision
of social services.

Influential members of the Republican classe conservadora, particularly from São Paulo, sought to decentralize the government for
political reasons. They believed that the imperial system had favored the declining elite of the Northeast and the Paraíba valley to
the detriment of the new rich. They also maintained that the imperial government had been guilty of excessive regulation, a large
public debt, and exaggerated administrative costs. These hindered
capital formation and thwarted entrepreneurship. The Republican
leadership hoped that by ending what they perceived as government
meddling in the private sphere they could unleash the country's
productive energies and take advantage of its vast resources.

The Republic in fact failed to lessen the state's economic role, but
the new regime did decentralize authority.[13] The provinces won the
right to tax exports (and they illegally taxed imports) as well as
contract foreign loans, which in some cases greatly increased revenues. They also received lands that had formerly belonged to the
central government. Furthermore, legislation on water and mineral
rights fell into their jurisdiction. Provincial governments could also
award railroad concessions within their territory and public utilities
in the provincial capitals.

Although in principle all provincial governments shared the same
economic powers, in reality only the richest gained much autonomy

from republican decentralization. The poorer provinces found themselves strapped for funds and unable to borrow sufficiently abroad. Consequently they were unable to offer railroads or public utility companies enough incentives to make their concessions attractive. Often they controlled only the less fertile areas, since their unassigned lands had all but disappeared. They had to appeal to the federal government for help. Municipalities, like the poorer provinces, did not gain many new powers from the Republic. The largest, most affluent cities were either provincial capitals, and thus subject to provincial authority, or the federally supervised capital in Rio de Janeiro. The remaining municipalities had authority over zoning, public utilities, local justice, public works, and some government offices but controlled few funds to undertake any economic initiatives.[14]

Despite the Republic's decentralization, the federal government remained very important. Although it lost many powers to the provinces, the central government continued to oversee the key areas of international economic relations and to serve as the supreme arbiter in relations among the provinces. Thus monetary policy, taxes on foreign trade, trade treaties, railroads that spanned more than one province, and international ports and shipping remained under its purview. Since the federal government still took in 50 percent more revenue than all of the provinces and municipalities combined, it also had the greatest capacity to finance new projects, aid entrepreneurs, and redistribute the tax burden.

The level of government to which members of the ruling class made appeals depended on the favor they sought and where they had political influence. The high bourgeoisie and foreign capitalists were very much concerned about the rates of interest, exchange, and inflation as well as customs duties and trade treaties. Only the federal congress could influence these. The prosperity of the federal treasury attracted capitalists who sought special concessions and loans. Being nationally prominent and generally from the most influential provinces, the upper tier of the ruling class could win federal support. These magnates also appealed to the governments of the Center-South provinces, which had considerable resources at their disposal.

Provincial barons usually did not enjoy sufficient weight to influence federal policy or to gain favors from Rio. Also concerned about such things as the exchange rate and inflation, they knew that they

were powerless to affect them. Instead, the provincial wealthy mostly restricted their requests to concessions, exemptions, and loans
from the provincial governments.

Local notables, finally, had to content themselves primarily with
control of local government and justice. Unlike the other two sectors
of the ruling class, which, being better integrated into the capitalist
economy, sought purely economic favors from the state, local notables more directly employed the state as an extra-economic tool to
grab land, assert access to water, coerce labor, and punish competitors.[15]

Brazil's economically dominant class thus desired limited state
economic activity, but still sought special favors. The division of
state power among the federal, provincial and municipal governments and the heterogeneity of the ruling class meant that numerous
paths existed for garnering state aid.

Means of Influencing State Policy

The nature of the ruling class and the political system, as well as the
limited demands that the wealthy placed on the state, dictated that
they would usually employ personal influence rather than political
parties or trade organizations to mold public policy. Widespread
personalist politics, fragmented political parties, and the lack of
sectoral specialization all contributed to an emphasis on individual
appeals rather than organized efforts. The sorts of favors that the
classe conservadora commonly sought, such as tax exemptions,
concessions, or loans, benefited only an individual or a specific
company. Only when the issue affected many people, such as monetary policy or the valorization of coffee, were organizations likely to
be the principal vehicles.

Personal influence was exerted in many ways. The most direct
method was for the capitalist to hold office himself. (This path was
closed to foreigners.) Occasionally the rich held high government
posts. Francisco de Paula Mayrink and Antonio Prado, mentioned
above, held public office. Minister of Finance Joaquim Murtinho,
famous for his financial reforms of 1899–1920, was also director of
the largest agricultural company, a major bank, and the only railroad
in his native Mato Grosso.[16] These men used their positions to
enhance their own fortunes. But such a direct link between the high
bourgeoisie and federal office was not the rule. On the provincial

level, the correlation was stronger between those who controlled the means of production and those who held office. Nonetheless, even in São Paulo, where an unusually high percentage of office holders were coffee planters, the richest planters were usually not politicians.[17] On the local level, however, the notables were usually the *coronéis* who ran the government though they did not always occupy an official position.

More commonly the propertied class influenced the government by placing relatives in high positions. This had been the practice under the Empire.[18] Because of the extended nature of the Brazilian family and the strong ties of loyalty that it involved, economically dominant families continued under the Republic to have politically well placed members.[19] In addition to blood relations, the wealthy could count on ritual kin such as *compadres*. A related variant was the mentor-protégé relationship, whereby a wealthy person (often a landowner) sponsored a younger man's career.

In the cities the wealthy were not limited to family and clan contacts for gaining public favors. Companies frequently hired high-level politicians and bureaucrats as legal counsel to further their aims. The contractors whom government engineers were supposed to supervise sometimes hired them as consultants.[20] Another tactic was for large companies to appoint government officials as board members. For example, Alfredo Maia (minister of transportation), Jorge Tiberiçá (governor of São Paulo), and José Paes de Carvalho (governor of Pará) served as directors of companies while in office.

When such acceptable means could not be employed, wealthy businessmen resorted to outright bribery. Official corruption was not an invention of the Republic. On December 14, 1889, the *South American Journal* noted that "for more years than can be well counted the administrative branch was rotten to the core." The first years of the Republic, especially during the boom-and-bust *encilhamento*, were notorious for bribery and corruption. The purchase of government favors continued afterward. The North American entrepreneur Percival Farquhar specialized in this sort of dealing. His biographer wrote, "So small is the oligarchy in Brazil, that Farquhar knew or once employed or his aides once bribed a substantial percentage of its members."[21]

Government concessions and favors could not, however, be granted solely on the basis of influence and bribery. Petitioners had to couch their bids in terms defensible to the general public. These appeals can be sorted into four groups. First, the favor seeker could stress that his company would actually increase government revenues by expanding the tax base, increasing national production, or improving the balance of payments. Second, he could promise to Europeanize or modernize Brazil with the latest technology. Third, he could propose to help other sectors of the economy with infrastructure or orders for raw materials. Finally, he could suggest that his concession would contribute to the general welfare by creating jobs, lowering the cost of living, improving sanitation, or providing homes for the poor. The particular mix and emphasis given to each of these approaches depended upon both the petitioner and the favor being sought.

Foreigners could use several additional methods not available to Brazilians for gaining government favors. They could, for example, play to the common Brazilian perception that foreign investment was a confirmation of economic health and of international optimism regarding Brazil's future. The *Gazeta do Comércio e Finanças* of February 13, 1897, reflected such a bias when commenting on the founding of a French bank in Rio de Janeiro: "This expansion of French capitalists says much in our favor and demonstrates that the credit of Brazil, despite the machinations of implacable enemies, cannot be easily demoralized in the productive markets of that country." Thus Brazilian officials were often honored by European requests for concessions and happily granted them.

When Brazilians were less cooperative, foreign investors had additional weapons. They could either promise to bring foreign capital into Brazil if awarded a concession, as Farquhar did when he leased the Sorocaba Railroad from the state of São Paulo, or threaten to tarnish Brazil's foreign credit. The great banking houses such as Rothschild's were in a particularly good position to use such threats to keep loan payments punctual. Smaller foreign companies had to appeal to other investors or to their governments. The British Corporation of Foreign Bond Holders, composed of private capitalists, determined the credit rating of borrowers. The French government employed the Paris capital market as an arm of foreign policy. It refused to allow the state of São Paulo to float a bond issue in Paris in 1906, for example, because it opposed the coffee valorization scheme the bond was supposed to fund. The German government acted in a similar fashion.

In addition to menacing with the loss of credit, foreign companies occasionally threatened to call for an invasion by their home country's armed forces. Since no such invasion ever occurred, we may surmise that such extreme threats were seldom employed or that no company had sufficient power to bring it about. For the most part, foreign investors' general perception of Brazil's creditworthiness was more important in influencing the government than was direct intervention by foreign powers. In both cases, Europeans and North Americans were in a position superior to that of their Brazilian counterparts.

Trade Associations

Trade associations tended to play a secondary role in influencing government policy, though their importance grew over time. The Republic inherited very few trade associations from the Empire. No national agricultural group existed until the formation of the National Agricultural Society in 1897. The regional agricultural societies that had existed before 1889 had done little more than disseminate technical information. Likewise, industrialists had not been represented politically: the Sociedade Auxiliadora de Indústria Nacional, which Pedro I founded in 1828, concerned itself only with farming techniques. Merchant associations in the major cities wielded a good deal of influence, but they too lacked national coordination and were partially neutralized by the fact that so many of their members were foreigners.[22]

The weaknesses of trade associations even after the turn of the century may be traced to several causes. First, personal and family loyalties, and reliance on them for lobbying, undermined efforts to institutionalize the various economic sectors. Second, the oligarchic political system, with neither national parties nor honest elections, made it less likely that organized lobbying would be effective. Third, the country's regional diversity and lack of a unified marketing system retarded the formation of producer groups. Problems that capitalists faced in one part of the country were distinct from those in other areas. Moreover, since little economic integration had taken place before World War I, there seemed to be little need for producer coordination at the national level.

Finally, the very composition of the economic elite, made up of persons with highly diversified business interests, impeded any real

structural coordination. Trade associations reflected this situation.
The São Paulo Commercial Association, composed largely of merchants, also represented industrialists. In both Rio de Janeiro and
São Paulo, integrated commercial and industrial centers existed.
Minas Gerais sponsored a convention that was even more expan-
sive, the Conference on Agriculture, Industry, and Commerce. Such
amorphous constituencies blunted the ability of organizations to
speak to specific issues. They often spoke as representatives of the
classe conservadora, rather than as agents of particular sectors.

After the turn of the century, more functionally discrete organizations appeared, reflecting the growing complexity of the economy.
The Brazilian Industrial Center was formed in 1902 and the Federation of Commercial Associations in 1912. At state and local levels,
more and more specific trade associations appeared as well.

The foreign component of the economic elite still undermined the
efficacy of associations, in commerce as well as industry. Of the eight
employer organizations that responded to a questionnaire in the
1920 census, six had foreign membership in excess of 80 percent.
These foreigners, no matter how wealthy, could not hold public
office. Worse, they (and by extension their associations) were not
seen by the general public as interested in the welfare of the nation.[23]

Finally, the lack of organized opposition from other classes, particularly before World War I, removed an incentive for the economic
elite to organize. When unions and middle-class reform groups
became more assertive in the 1910s and 1920s, employers' associations became more active in response.

Despite these weaknesses, the trade associations did influence
government policy. Sometimes they did so because of their leaders'
connections and official experience. Examples of such links are
Inocêncio Serzedelo Correia, a political leader as well as founder of
the Industrial Center; Gabriel Osório e Almeida, a high administra-
tor also associated with the Industrial Center; Miguel Calmon, minister of state and president of the National Agricultural Society; and
Leopoldo Bulhões of the Commercial Association of Rio de Janeiro.
Not all trade association leaders, however, had political experience.[24]

The vitality of the trade associations derived in part from the fact
that they arose spontaneously from the economic elite in order to

further their interests. Hence they were not beholden to the government or to any other entity.[25] Indeed, some of them performed functions usually under the purview of the government such as data collection, foreign trade promotion, stock market supervision, and so forth. Their principal impact on government policy, however, was in the realms of tariffs, monetary policy, and taxes.

Most business associations lobbied intensely for tariffs that would benefit their members. Businessmen who joined special government commissions formed to study tariffs carried much weight because of their specialized knowledge of trade.

Commercial associations in the coffee-producing provinces also played important roles in the coffee price support schemes known as "valorization." During the first valorization (1906), these associations promoted sales of surplus stocks in Europe. In the second (1917), they advised the government on the amount and timing of purchases. Their participation became institutionalized in the 1925 valorization program, as the commercial associations had members appointed to the provincial boards that oversaw the program in São Paulo and Minas Gerais. Merchant groups also attempted to establish corners on sugar, rubber, and rice to drive up their prices. Only in the case of rice in Rio Grande do Sul was there government participation, and only there did the monopolists experience some success.[26]

Agricultural associations also fulfilled semi-governmental roles. Groups such as the Sociedade Nacional de Agricultura collected economic data, popularized new production techniques, and promoted the selection of better seed and breeding stock. They lobbied for the creation of the Ministry of Agriculture, which they then helped staff. Agricultural associations also had a say in the coffee valorization programs.

Industrial associations performed similar functions. In 1907 the Industrial Center carried out Brazil's first industrial census to provide the government with more accurate information about the sector and to demonstrate their own importance. Industrialists made their influence most felt on government tariff commissions, where they often successfully lobbied for protective duties on imports.

Despite these semi-public functions that trade associations undertook after the turn of the century, business organizations remained distinct from the state. In fact, early state efforts to organize the private sector into cooperatives and syndicates failed. The first truly corporatist body came only in 1923; the government created the National Council of Commerce and Industry to bring together ministry officials and representatives of commercial, financial, and industrial associations. This council received little authority or funding, however, and hence had little impact on national life. At the same time, the federal government created the National Labor Council to reconcile the interests of capital and labor. It also enjoyed little success.

Conclusion

Members of Brazil's small, economically dominant class were extremely powerful. They controlled most of Brazil's land, capital and machinery; consequently they held the fate of most other Brazilians in their hands. Despite its small numbers, the classe conservadora was divided markedly by the extent of ties to the international economy, integration into the national economy, and adoption of capitalist methods. It was also kept apart by Brazil's small, compartmentalized domestic market. This fragmentation was further exacerbated by the personalistic, family-based nature of the political system and the absence of any serious well-organized threat from contending classes.

Because of the rural, underdeveloped nature of the export economy, the wealthy exercised their power mostly in the private sphere while limiting the state's reach. Because of their heterogeneity, when the rich did seek political favors, they tended to exert influence through individual rather than group action. Trade associations were slow to develop. Still, as the economy became more complex in the early decades of this century, and as the middle and working classes became more assertive, the government began to intervene more in social and economic relations. Trade associations became more vigorous in response. Since most members of the economically dominant class believed a weak state to be in their own best interest, however, they remained reluctant to infuse the business organizations with much authority and continued to seek individual rather than class solutions to problems. When the Great Depression, industrialization, urbanization, growing militancy among industrial workers, and an activist president all worked to expand the state's sphere of influence in the Vargas years, planters, bankers, merchants, and industrialists found themselves insufficiently organized to resist.

Notes

1. I use the term "state" to refer to the complex of federal, provincial and local governmental agencies and the institutions they control. Although Brazil was divided into 20 "states" during the Old Republic, I refer to those subunits as "provinces" to avoid confusion.

2. This small group probably owned over half of all national wealth. The highest echelon of this group probably increased its share of national resources over the course of the Old Republic because of the rise of large-scale capitalist enterprises.

3. Brazil's indigenous population was exterminated or pushed to the frontier rather than coopted into the national elite. See John Hemming, Red Gold, The Conquest of Brazilian Indians, 1500–1760 (Cambridge, Mass.: Harvard University Press, 1978).

4. The term translates "the conservative class"; it was used at the time to describe the economic elite.

5. Paraná's economy was based substantially on maté tea exports but its share of the regional economy was overshadowed by Rio Grande do Sul's domestically oriented agricultural and ranching pursuits.

6. See Steven Topik, "The State's Contribution to the Development of Brazil's Internal Economy, 1850–1930", Hispanic American Historical Review 65, no. 2 (1985): 203–28.

7. The Northeast had a rural bourgeoisie as well who invested in modern sugar usinas or cotton gins, but in most provinces they were not dominant.

8. Clearly a man could be a member of all three tiers. If he were part of the high bourgeoisie, he also was a member of the local notables in the municipio in which his investments were based and numbered among the provincial barons in those states. However, for the purposes of this analysis, he would be considered only as a member of the highest tier to which he belongs. As part of the high bourgeoisie he would have access to many resources and have concerns quite different from those of the segment of the ruling class with only local investments and influence.

9. Darrell E. Levi, The Prados of São Paulo, Brazil: An Elite Family and Social Change, 1840–1930 (Athens: University of Georgia Press, 1987).

10. Edgard Carone, A República Velha, vol. 1 (São Paulo: Difusão Européia do Livro, 1970), p. 15; Thomas H. Holloway, Immigrants on the Land: Coffee and Society in São Paulo, 1886–1934 (Chapel Hill: University of North Carolina Press, 1980), p. 160; Robert M. Levine, Pernambuco in the Brazilian

Federation, 1889–1937 (Stanford: Stanford University Press, 1978), p. 26; Monitor Mercantil (Rio de Janeiro), December 23, 1915.

11. In 1909 two percent of the country's transactions received half the bank loans. The average loan was U.S.$30,000 at a time when per capita GNP was around U.S.$60.

12. Ana Célia Castro, As empresas estrangeiras no Brasil, 1860–1913 (Rio de Janeiro: Zahar, 1979); Richard Graham, Britain and the Onset of Modernization in Brazil, 1850–1914 (Cambridge: At the University Press, 1968); Dudley Maynard Phelps, Migration of Industry to South America (New York: McGraw-Hill, 1936); J. Fred Rippy, British Investments in Latin America (Minneapolis: University of Minnesota Press, 1959); Mira Wilkins, The Maturing of Multinational Enterprise: American Business Abroad from 1914 to 1970 (Cambridge, Mass.: Harvard Univesity Press, 1974).

13. See Steven Topik, The Political Economy of the Brazilian State, 1889–1930 (Austin: University of Texas Press, 1987).

14. See Victor Nunes Leal, Coronelismo, enxada e voto (São Paulo: Editora Alpha Omega, 1975).

15. See Linda Lewin, Politics and Parentela in Paraíba (Princeton: Princeton University Press, 1987), and Barbara Weinstein, "Brazilian Regionalism" Latin American Research Review 17, no. 2 (1982): 262–76.

16. Virgilio Corrêa Filho, Joaquim Murtinho (Rio de Janeiro: Departamento de Imprensa Nacional, 1951).

17. J. W. F. Rowe, Studies in the Artificial Control of Raw Material Supplies: Brazilian Coffee (London: London and Cambridge Economic Service, 1932), p. 28.

18. Frank Roger Colson, "Economy and Society in a Revolution Polity, Brazil 1750–1894" (Ph.D. diss., Princeton University, 1979).

19. Jorge Amado illustrated the typical pattern with his fictional character Mundinho in the novel Gabriela, Clove and Cinnamon, trans. James L. Taylor and William L. Grossman (New York: Knopf, 1962). Mundinho called on his brother, a senator from São Paulo, to secure federal monies for improving the port works at Ilheus. For case studies see Lewin, Politics and Parentela, and Eul-Soo Pang, Bahia in the First Brazilian Republic (Gainesville: University Presses of Florida, 1979).

20. For example, see Charles Anderson Gauld, The Last Titan: Percival Farquhar, American Entrepreneur in Latin America (Stanford: Institute of Hispanic American and Luso-Brazilian Studies, 1964), p. 167.

21. Ibid., p. 297.

22. Eugene W. Ridings, "Class Sector Unity in an Export Economy: The Case of Nineteenth-Century Brazil," Hispanic American Historical Review 58, no. 3 (August 1978): 432–44, passim; and "Business, Nationality and Dependency in Late Nineteenth Century Brazil," Journal of Latin American Studies 14, no. 1 (1982): 55–96.

23. Michael L. Conniff, *Urban Politics in Brazil: The Rise of Populism, 1925–1945* (Pittsburgh: University of Pittsburgh Press, 1981), pp. 37–41.

24. Joseph Love, "Um segmento da elite política brasileira em perspectiva comparada," in *A revolução de 30* (Brasília: Universidade de Brasília, 1982), pp. 84–85; Edgard Carone, *O centro industrial do Rio de Janeiro* (Rio de Janeiro: Editora Cátedra, 1978), pp. 171–72; Barros, *Associação comercial no Império e na Republica* (Rio de Janeiro: Gráfica Olímpica, 1975), pp. 177–78.

25. Some, however, were started with government support and received small subsidies well into this century.

26. See Joan Lamayso Bak, "Cartels, Cooperatives, and Corporatism: Getúlio Vargas in Rio Grande do Sul on the Eve of Brazil's 1930 Revolution," *Hispanic American Historical Review* 63, no. 2 (1983): 255–75. The state generally supported efforts to drive up the price of agricultural exports but ignored the industrial cartels of products, such as matches and cigarettes, destined for the home market.

Eli Diniz

The Post-1930 Industrial Elite

Writings on the relationship between state and society in Brazil, and on the political roles of various elites, have differed greatly in their conclusions. Authors at one extreme stress the weakness of the state. They argue that the state is controlled by internal or external pressures exerted by economic interests and that these sectors are relatively autonomous.[1] At the other extreme, we find those who, for different theoretical reasons, stress the independence of the state in its relations with civil society. In this view, the state operates according to some internal logic of its own and maintains a certain autonomy vis-à-vis external pressures.[2] Over the past several decades, this latter view has become more widely accepted, so that a near-consensus now favors the hypothesis of a strong state and a weak civil society.

Interpretations of Brazilian economic elites have also varied along similar lines. A generation or so ago, rural elites were thought to be extremely powerful. Writers characterized them as ensconced in their domains while dictating policy to the government. Their power and arrogance allowed them to put their own interests ahead of the nation's. This view also underwent revisions, however, as alternative hypotheses emerged. Newer studies found the elite in general to be inherently weak because of its fragmentation. An amorphous entity without internal organization, the elite was in fact many distinct factions unable to organize themselves functionally or regionally. This disorganization prevented the elite from assuming leadership roles in politics or economic development. This new view applied to modern urban sectors as well as to the traditional rural elite. The reasons for this situation dated back to the early twentieth century.

From colonial times until the end of the Old Republic in 1930, agrarian and merchant elites exercised effective economic power. While they managed to control politics at the local and regional level and thereby to monopolize wealth, power, and status, they never became a national elite. Therefore, they did not achieve the strength and unity that would have allowed them to exert their influence in national issues crucial for the future of the country. Instead, a patrimonialist, bureaucratized, and centralizing state emerged beyond the control of the economic elites. In this way, Brazil did not see the emergence of a politically mature agro-mercantile bourgeoisie such as arose in the leading capitalist countries of Europe, especially in England.

This same theoretical divergence appears in studies of industrial elites. Some authors attribute to them a decisive role in creating an industrial order, while others stress their weakness and political irrelevance. The first interpretation (strong industrial class) arose in the 1940s and remained dominant until the early 1960s. Key features of this theory were the notions that Brazil had to industrialize and that factory owners would play a decisive historical role in leading the "bourgeois national project." Some of the major proponents of this theory taught and researched at the Advanced Institute for Brazilian Studies (ISEB) and at the United Nation's Economic Commission for Latin America (ECLA). These writers saw industrialists as proponents of urban-industrial development in peripheral societies.[3] According to this group, industrial elites would lead the creation of a new socioeconomic order, overcoming the existing backwardness. In order to achieve this, they would create and lead a progressive coalition that included workers and other reform-minded groups.

After the 1964 military coup this line of interpretation came under increasing attack by intellectuals. The 1964 overthrow of the so-called Populist Republic revealed certain aspects of elite behavior that were diametrically opposed to what had been hypothesized by proponents of the national bourgeois theory. Important sectors of the bourgeoisie allied themselves with the conservatives who, led by the military, came to power in 1964. They helped topple a constitutional government and implant a dictatorship. In the years immediately preceding the coup, the economic elites had never supported popular measures (like land reform) that might have harmed their own financial interests. Therefore, historical reality began to undermine the prevailing theory of a progressive bourgeoisie.

Soon after the coup, some authors began to attack the inconsistencies of the earlier theory, arguing that the model of a traditional sector and a modern sector both oversimplified and distorted Brazilian reality.[4] Others pointed out the error of attributing a revolutionary role to industrial elites. Since Brazil was a peripheral nation, it was trapped in a dependency relationship with international capitalism, and its elites would not have the power postulated by the progressive theorists.[5] Finally, yet another attack came from those who held that the Brazilian state was traditionally so strong that it prevented the economic elite from exercising much power. The state had always been capable of coopting and controlling potential rivals by bureaucratic means.[6] Eventually, this new approach began to treat Brazil's economic elites as basically irrelevant to the developmental process, at least since 1930.

I will argue that both of the above positions are extreme and lead to erroneous conclusions. First, the inability of economic elites to monopolize political power did not necessarily mean that these elites were passive in the political realm. Second, influencing political decision making was not the only way elites exercised power.[7] Elites, as political actors, have other ways of operating, such as excluding issues from consideration, setting governmental agendas, and creating a climate of opinion at high levels. Finally, an elite may organize very effective ideological campaigns, such as that mounted between 1974 and 1978 against state ownership of the economy (*estatizaçao*). Historically, such influences best characterized the relations between economic elites and the state in Brazil.

Linkages between the public and private sectors took various forms, among them the use of corporative and extra-corporative interest representation, as well as less conventional methods, such as tapping into bureaucratic rings, using clientelistic networks, or making informal contacts.[8] From the 1930s on, industrial elites actively defended their interests and helped chart the way toward a new industrial order.

The Rise of Industrial Interests in the 1930s

The Revolution of 1930, which marked the beginning of Brazil's contemporary history, has generated much debate. Some writers suggest that little substantial change occurred, apart from a replacement of the political elite: in other words, old wine in a new bottle.

Others, however, stress the changes wrought by the new elite, changes that brought on a new urban industrial order. On the political level, they point to the rise to power of persons committed to the project of industrializing the country. This latter view seems confirmed by comparisons of the various economic sectors in the years following the revolution. Internal as well as external events favored industrialization during the 1930s. The Great Depression was a major external factor. The sharp decline in capacity to import and the coffee support program designed to prevent bankruptcy created new opportunities for manufacturers. Among the internal factors we should note the replacement of the old agro-export elite by a new coalition less committed to protecting traditional economic groups.

Spurred by such stimuli, manufacturing activity experienced rapid growth in the 1930s. Fully 70 percent of the 50,000 industrial firms tabulated in the 1940 census had been formed in the preceding decade. Manufacturing as a share of the GDP rose from 21 percent in 1919 to 43 percent in 1939. Its average annual growth rate during the 1930s was 8.4 percent, compared with 2.2 percent for agriculture. During the years 1933–39, industrial production grew at the very high rate of 11.2 percent.[9] Agriculture nonetheless continued to be the largest sector of the economy. Shares of the economically active population in manufacturing and agriculture remained fairly stable between the 1920 and 1940 censuses. The primary sector dropped slightly, from 70 to 67 percent, while the secondary rose from 14 to 15 percent and the tertiary from 16 to 18 percent.[10] Still, the trend was toward greater industrialization. By 1934 manufacturing output surpassed that of agriculture. Traditional finished goods (textiles, clothing, footwear, processed food, beverages, building materials, tobacco products, and furniture) predominated, but their share of total output fell from 72 to 60 percent between 1919 and 1939. On the rise were new lines, such as metallurgical, mechanical, electrical, chemical, and transport goods.[11] Finally, comparing the industrial expansion of the 1930s with earlier periods of expansion, Anibal Villela and Werner Baer note that industrialization as a continuing process (not a temporary reaction to market conditions) only began in the 1930s.[12]

Looking back over the economic experience of the 1930s, then, we see the period as crucial in determining the future directions of growth. Economically, the principal shift was the rising share of industrial production in the GNP. Politically, this shift meant a decline in the power of those sectors dedicated to export agriculture and a rise in that of producers for the domestic market. The first Getúlio Vargas administration presided over this transition.

Throughout Vargas's first fifteen years in the presidency, the state gradually increased its influence over regional oligarchies. This centralization process had major implications for the various elites and their relationship to the state. First, it left the governors, even those of the major states, subordinate to the president. Second, it led to the encroachment of federal decision-making authority into new realms, such as economic and social planning. Finally, new and more effective tools for state regulation of the economy and society evolved. An outstanding example of this new style of government was the federalization of coffee policy under the National Coffee Council, later made into the National Department of Coffee. Other analogous agencies arose in the federal bureaucracy to oversee and control economic activity. Some of these agencies sapped the strength of regional economic elites, such as that of the São Paulo coffee oligarchy. On the other hand, these new regulatory agencies— corporatist in nature—allowed more freedom for industrial groups to lobby and pursue their interests. In sum, the new corporatist political-institutional structure signaled a redistribution of power available to different elites, the closing of some access channels, and the creation of new arenas in which pressure groups could court state assistance.

With regard to social change, greater differentiation occurred between the various economic elites. Unlike many authors, I believe that this differentiation led to greater socioeconomic complexity and political competition among the elites and that it was a major feature of the transition to an industrial society. The principal bone of contention in those days was to what extent the government should protect the traditional agricultural exporters. Proponents of change argued that the government should foster a shift toward urban and industrial priorities. Leaders of industry played an important part in forcing this shift.

During the first decades of this century, industrialists had progressed from relative indifference to a clearly formulated ideology in support of their sector. In so doing, they called into question the accepted wisdom of an international division of labor, according to which Brazil should always concentrate on agriculture. The 1930s saw further consolidation of this pro-industrialization rationale, as well as its growing sophistication. Industrial leaders proposed new means of stimulating production, instead of the traditional protectionism. They called for integrating the domestic market, more credit for manufacturers, and industrialization as a means of strengthening the economy and making it self-sufficient.

In light of this, we can conclude that increased differentiation among elites and their greater articulation with the state was an important long-term process begun in the 1930s. In particular, the industrial elite gained greater cohesion and an ideology that urged government support for their sector. They sought new means of communication and methods for negotiating favorable government policies. It was especially significant that in the 1920s industrialists formed their own interest groups, relying less and less on the traditional commercial associations.[13] After 1930, the corporatist consolidation of managerial groups into official *sindicatos* led to state-level federations and finally to the National Industrial Confederation.

The growing political force of factory owners, with a more complex and broader pro-industrial ideology, strengthened their influence in government policy making. Industrialists sat on many regulatory boards, side by side with technocrats, military officers, and representatives of other sectors, and they helped formulate drafts and proposals that ended higher up in the administration. This kind of activity assured them of channels for voicing their concerns and desires in the very heart of the government. Any number of important economic guidelines in the 1930s were influenced by leading industrialists.[14] The institution of council-style government led to regular negotiation between the industrial elite and public officials and made the executive branch the chief arbitrator among factory owners, technocrats, and bureaucrats. This trend was accentuated by the Estado Novo coup of 1937, which eliminated Congress and the parties as mediators. For the next eight years all negotiation was centralized in the executive branch.

Expansion of Industrialists' Influence, 1945–64

In the two decades following World War II, the accelerating growth of manufacturing reinforced its role as the most dynamic sector of the economy. Between 1946 and 1955 industrial production grew 122 percent, or at annual rates of 8.9 percent (1946–50) and 8.1

percent (1951–55). Under President Juscelino Kubitschek it reached a climax of 11 percent a year.[15] This deepening industrialization was reflected in the growing differentiation among subgroups of the factory owners themselves. Leadership now came from newer sectors, such as the consumer durable and automotive industries. By this time the most dynamic members of the industrial elite fought actively to secure more favorable governmental policies. A major issue was the degree to which foreign and state-owned enterprises should be allowed to expand at the expense of private Brazilian ones.

The major industrial associations, especially the São Paulo Industrial Federation (FIESP), became leading advocates of their interests vis-à-vis other sectors and in the halls of government. Moreover, because the government exercised considerable control over officially recognized associations, entrepreneurs gradually created their own unofficial groups with which to promote their interests. These so-called parallel associations, formed along sectoral lines and at the national level, were free of the government restrictions imposed on their official counterparts. Notable among the parallel groups were the Brazilian Association for the Development of Basic Industry (ABDIB), the Brazilian Association for Electrical Materials and Electronics Industries (ABIMEE), the Brazilian Association for Food Industries (ABIA), and the National Association of Automobile Manufacturers (ANFAVEA). This dual form of representation allowed greater flexibility and autonomy than was strictly permitted by the law, and it was designed to adapt to the bureaucratic complexities of the modern state. In sum, industrial groups sought to maintain their working relationships with key governmental decision makers.

The emergence of a dual network of industrial associations in the 1950s occurred simultaneously with the growing fragmentation of the sector. The forums for private-public sector consultation were within the agencies themselves. Among the most important in the 1950s were the National Bank for Economic Development (BNDE) and the Executive Groups (GEIAS) created by Kubitschek, such as that for the automotive industry. The latter brought together representatives of the various government agencies and private sector associations.

I would emphasize that during this time of accelerated industrialization and democratic institutions, government technocrats, in league with private sector representatives, usually managed to keep key decisions out of the public and partisan arenas. Party leaders had neither access to nor influence over the specialized agencies that, deep in the bowels of the government, took charge of modernizing the country's industrial park. Technocrats staffing these agencies created an antipolitical ideology that justified their immunity from partisan pressures. According to this view, legislators and politicians in general were neither competent nor serious enough to be entrusted with major economic decisions. Only those at the upper echelons of government possessed such qualifications. This technocratic mentality, strong in the 1930s, persisted in milder form through the 1950s and became dominant in the years following the 1964 coup.

In this way, the political socialization of the industrial elite, which had begun under an autocratic regime (Vargas in the 1930s), denigrated partisan activity as inefficient and geared only to satisfying special interests, not those of the nation as a whole. Such a bias persisted even during the years of participatory democracy. Lobbying, therefore, did not enjoy much favor among industrialists, because Congress was not considered an important arena for creating economic policy and because open advocacy of specific economic interests was held to be illegitimate.

Given their antipolitical and antilobbying ethics, industrialists naturally preferred to seek support for their projects within the executive branch and its specialized agencies. Not that they were always successful. The insider's approach was necessarily limited in scope to the narrow interests of the public and private sector participants. Broad issues of development policy could rarely be addressed effectively in the halls of government. Moreover, industrialists came together only in broader political campaigns when their sense of danger overcame their natural divisiveness; this happened infrequently. Two such instances were the coups of 1945 and 1964, when industrialists and major employer groups helped overthrow governments they believed threatened their interests. In the latter case, the industrialists formed a pact with the bureaucratic and military elites and joined them in creating a new phase of authoritarianism.

The foregoing analysis of the consolidation of the managerial elite since the 1930s demonstrates that important segments of the group were active and effective in defending their specific interests. Further, it shows that, when they felt they were in jeopardy, leaders of the industrial elite became politically unified and sought alliances with other groups to bring about a general economic, social, and political reorganization of the country.

Industrial Elites and the Authoritarian State 1964–74

The military-technocratic coalition that took control of the country in April 1964 attempted to promote the welfare of private sector investors and to raise the level of capitalistic development. They sought to preserve public order while simultaneously promoting economic growth, according to the so-called National Security Doctrine.[16]

The first decade of military rule can be broken into two subperiods. At first, under President Humberto Castello Branco and his finance ministers, Roberto Campos and Octávio Gouveia de Bulhões, most attention was given to dismantling the old order, that is, the perceived chaos of the João Goulart administration. This meant eliminating popular participation in government, curbing the power of unions, and silencing the most outspoken members of the old regime. On the economic side, the new government sought to clean house and legitimize its authority by following rational and technically sound policies. They attacked inflation by eliminating distortions in price structures and allocations of resources. The result was a classic stabilization program of reducing government expenditures, increasing tax revenues, curbing credit, and holding down salary increases. Predictably, these policies prolonged the economic stagnation until 1967—in sharp contrast to the heady growth of the 1950s. The structural changes introduced in 1964 and 1965 would bear fruit only in later years.

The second subperiod of the military years, from 1968 to 1973, saw high levels of growth in the Brazilian economy. Priority was shifted from anti-inflationary measures to rapid growth. The success of this approach, sometimes called the "economic miracle," allowed the government to claim legitimacy on the basis of its economic policies. Decision makers, led by Minister of Finance Antônio Delfim Netto, followed a capitalist development model that allowed strong government intervention, oligopoly in certain sectors, and internationalization of the economy. This strategy especially benefited large private, public, and multinational firms, forming what has been called the triple alliance. Average annual growth in GDP rose from 3.7 percent in the 1962–67 period to 10.1 percent between 1968 and 1974. Industry clearly led this growth, with average rates of 12.2 percent. The fastest expanding sectors of industry were transport equipment (especially automobiles), electrical appliances, and machine tools. More traditional areas—textiles, clothing, and processed food—grew more slowly. Other growth sectors included building and highway construction. Exports soared and experienced greater diversification in this period. For example, manufactures went from 7.2 percent of exports in 1965 to 27.7 percent in 1974.[17]

The new development strategy favored the producers of consumer durables, as a source of domestic growth and export expansion. Its success depended upon rising domestic demand for these goods—maintained by concentrating income in the upper-middle and upper classes and by easier credit—as well as on increased foreign demand, which was helped by liberalized export rules, special subsidies, and foreign capital. The achievement of high growth rates across a broad spectrum of the economy, the strengthening of key sectors like automobiles and electronics, and the expansion and modernization of public enterprises all helped give the government a positive image.

The military government's economic success during this period validated its strategies. A new ideology emerged, one that saw Brazil becoming a great power and gaining international recognition through its economic achievements. This euphoric vision of a new era, especially salient among members of the middle and upper classes, blinded them to failures in the political system. The economic miracle coincided with the greatest political repression—during the administration of Emílio Garrastazu Médici. This period saw widespread censorship, curtailment of civil rights, and control of labor and political organizations. Rapid economic growth masked the rigorous authoritarianism, and the strategy of the National Security Doctrine appeared strong enough to withstand political opposition.

During the first ten years of the military regime, the industrial elite remained supportive but altered its stance occasionally. In the years 1964–67, industrialists were ambiguous toward the government's policies, backing the political demobilization yet opposing the more severe elements of economic stabilization, such as contraction of credit and investment for the private sector. After Presidents Artur

Costa e Silva and Médici managed to trigger economic growth, however, most industrial groups pledged unquestioning support for the regime.

The prosperity of the miracle years produced general optimism regarding the development model followed by those in power. For a time, the economic, technocratic, and military elites found common cause. They agreed on such goals as strengthening the state, ameliorating social tensions, and suppressing political dissent, while still guaranteeing rapid economic growth. At the same time, a kind of military-industrial complex emerged, fostering expansion of the war materiel industry, modernization of the armed forces and communications networks, and development of strategic areas such as nuclear power. A large number of firms—private, public, and multinational—sprang up and helped knit closer links between business and military elites. Still, the legitimacy of this system depended entirely on continued growth and ever-greater profits.

Brazil's business elite accepted the centralization and autocratic decision making of the military years precisely because their interests were protected. It is important to note that during these years, business and industrial elites modernized their associations by creating parallel or extraofficial organizations. Indeed, nearly 65 percent of the parallel associations sprang up *after* 1964.[18] Access to decision makers varied during the military years. The emasculation of Congress tended to concentrate even more power in the executive branch. Yet, unlike Vargas, who formalized private sector participation in the various deliberative councils, the post-1964 leaders did not create normal channels of access to decision makers. The military governments gradually eliminated corporatist representation, beginning with labor unions. At first labor enjoyed membership on the National Planning Council (CONSPLAN), but it was not included in successor councils like the National Monetary Council (CMN) or the Economic Development Council (CDE). Business groups also found themselves left off such boards, but in their case informal and other arrangements guaranteed some level of participation.

The extreme complexity and differentiation of the bureaucracy during this period was paralleled by similar developments among the business associations. We found frequent contacts between the public Foreign Trade Council and major industrial groups, like ABDIB, the São Paulo Machine and Equipment Industry Association (SIMESP), and ABIMEE; between the public Interdepartmental Price

Council and the ABIA; between the public National Steel Council and its private counterpart, the Brazilian Steel Institute. Finally, some representatives of the capital goods industries found counterparts in such public agencies as the BNDE, the Industrial Development Council, the Treasury Department, and the Ministry of Industry and Commerce.

The authoritarian governments following the 1964 coup did not, then, exclude economic elites from power; rather, they redefined the channels of communication between private and public elites. Such a redefinition made the bureaucracy relatively permeable to private influence and hence raised the likelihood of the elites' interests being served.

By the same token, the erosion of formal representation and the centralization of power meant that decision makers at the cabinet level and those heading major agencies were relatively isolated from outside pressures. First, clientelistic and bureaucratic politics are effective only for achieving narrow, short-term goals, not for processing broad demands from a whole sector, such as the industrial elite. Second, centralization of power and isolation of the top level of government meant that industrialists could not influence longer-range decisions about the country's future.

From the Crisis to the Recession: Schisms in the Authoritarian Pact

Major social changes had accompanied the economic development of the late 1960s and early 1970s. Brazil now possessed the eighth largest GNP in the world. Manufactured goods rose from 20 percent of exports in 1968 to 57 percent in 1980, while the share of primary goods fell from 79 to 42 percent. Likewise, the secondary sector contribution to GDP rose from 19 to 34 percent between 1940 and 1980, while that of the primary sector fell from 26 to 13 percent. Changes in distribution of the economically active population by sector closely paralleled these shifts. Finally, the proportion of the population living in cities rose from 45 to 68 percent.[19] These data demonstrate that Brazil in the 1980s was no longer a rural country; moreover, it had a large and highly diversified industry.

Major socioeconomic changes such as these gave the urban-industrial sector greater weight in politics. For one thing, because voters in the cities came to outnumber those in nonurban areas, the predominantly rural bases of support for the military regime were undercut. In 1974 and after, the government party began losing more and more voters to the opposition party, whose main support was in the big cities of Brazil's Center-South.

The government increasingly found itself unable to translate fiscal achievements into political support. Indeed, the period following the economic miracle brought a gradual erosion of the regime's legitimacy. Discontent broadened with an economic slowdown in the mid-1970s, triggered by the rise in petroleum prices. These economic difficulties revealed the weaknesses of the development strategy adopted during the mid-1960s and early 1970s. The high priority given to raising savings rates grossly concentrated income and prevented large strata of the population from enjoying the benefits of economic growth. Thus, what was gained in capital accumulation was lost in social equity, an outcome that cost the government dearly in votes. So, beginning in 1974, the government attempted to create new bases of legitimacy by instituting a gradual process of decompression. Throughout Ernesto Geisel's administration (1974–79), this process—renamed *distensão* (relaxation) and then *abertura* (opening)—gained preeminence in the political dialogue.

The industrial elite's first protests against the regime occurred in the context of the *abertura*, and they reached a peak during the campaign against *estatização*, or state ownership and regulation of the economy. Their immediate goal was to reduce government regulation and even ownership in the economy. Industrialists began to regard the growth of the public sector during the miracle years as a threat. They saw their sector shrink in relation to the government's, and they began to fear that Brazil was headed toward a regime of state capitalism. Business elites began to unite in opposition to growing state intervention.

Although the campaign usually addressed economic issues, at heart it was a political movement, a protest against centralization of authority and the growing isolation of decision makers. From the businessmen's point of view, concentration of power in the upper layers of the bureaucracy excluded private interests like theirs from major decisions. Businessmen began to realize that while in the beginning a certain amount of state intervention had been appropriate, now the economy was completely controlled by a bureaucratic-military elite that threatened their position. They argued for a liberalization of the political system that would allow businessmen to exercise some control over decisions that affected their long-term interests. The state should restrict its economic activities to areas not competitive with private enterprise. With more political power, business groups could confine the expansion of the state and control its activities.

The business elites' proposal of liberalization was not far-reaching, however, for it sought only their own inclusion in the inner circle of decision making regarding political economy. Missing were other items usual in a liberal agenda, such as extension of the franchise to the working and popular sectors. When the campaign against state hypertrophy lost steam, the businessmen's protest did not end. Instead, they began demanding broader participation in a more open political arena. Spokesmen for the more dynamic industrial groups joined with others in supporting the abertura process, especially around the time of the 1978 elections.

Business and industry leaders also began to criticize the degree to which their official organizations were subordinated in a clientelistic relationship to the state corporate structure. This process culminated in the 1980 ouster of the traditional progovernment directors of FIESP by industrialists in the vanguard of new developments, led by Luís Eulálio de Bueno Vidigal. This new group revitalized interest group representation among industrial elites by taking an independent stance vis-à-vis the state. They hoped to collaborate with the government as equals in order to find a way out of the late 1970s stagnation. They did not attack the authority of the regime but rather offered to help it find new sources of legitimacy. Therefore, they sought to liberalize the authoritarian pact, not destroy it.

The economy plunged into recession in 1981, however, and business elites became even more critical of the government, opening up schisms in the pact. They began to call for continued abertura, which they now called redemocratization.

Final Considerations

A major feature of the last two decades has been the rise of the urban-industrial sectors of society, so that by the mid-1980s they became dominant. Simultaneously, several leading industrial groups gained strength. Apart from the economic importance of these trends, they also led to greater political influence on the part of industrial elites.

The growing participation of industrial elites in setting guidelines for political economy paralleled their advocacy of liberalization of the military regime, especially since the late 1970s. They became leading critics of the authoritarian experience and played an important role in redemocratization. Many commentators attributed the decline of the military government's legitimacy to the withdrawal of businessmen from the so-called authoritarian pact. According to this line of reasoning, businessmen belatedly coalesced into a bourgeoisie intent upon creating a political regime more in keeping with their interests, now that the economic miracle had played itself out. Some analysts even spoke of a veritable bourgeois revolution, in which the elite developed a sophisticated consciousness of its role in governing the country. In this view, the industrial elites were destined to assume leadership of the redemocratization process itself.

I am not inclined to accept this view of the rise to hegemony of an industrial bourgeoisie in the 1980s. The protests raised by industrialists in the 1970s did not signal their withdrawal from the authoritarian pact but merely their inconformity with current policies. They wished to build a more responsive system for creating consensus between the public and private sectors. Later their demands would become shriller but still moderated by the lack of a platform that could unify the industrial elites. In truth, the industrial elites never formulated a plan for a transition to a new political order. Their agreement on rejecting the authoritarian past did not lead to consensus with regard to the political future.

I do not see this weakness as temporary or circumstantial. Throughout the history of Brazilian industrial expansion, businessmen have been able to reach some degree of ideological coherence and self-identity as a sector yet have not come up with a plan for exercising political hegemony. The various subgroups of industrialists became specialized and differentiated according to their specific demands on government, without creating an overall program that would unify the entire class. Historically, only in critical moments did businessmen act in harmony; they fragmented again when the immediate threat was past. This instability derived in large part from a lack of consensus regarding the proper organization of bourgeois society. Liberalism coexisted with the authoritarian-corporatist tradition imbedded in Brazil's legislation. Attacks on state hypertrophy were accompanied by acceptance of state intervention as a means of reducing conflict, especially when labor disputes threatened to violate the corporatist rules of the game.

The current transition to an open political system implies the institutionalization of conflict, which also implies a challenge to businessmen's preference for orderly resolution of disputes. The business community still maintains a corporatist outlook inherited from the transition from agrarian export activities to industrial capitalism. Recent events do not suggest that businessmen have come to embrace pluralist relations between state and civil society. Instead, they believe that each sector should present its case to a neutral state according to its particular competence and interest.

This residue of corporatist ideology is best seen in industrialists' reactions to recent labor actions. They agree that the corporatist union structure inherited from the Estado Novo needed to be altered, but they still wish to apply strict limits to labor activity. The right to strike must be institutionalized and invoked only when mediation fails. In other words, the conflict must be contained between the interested parties themselves.

The industrial elite's narrow outlook is also seen in debates over the proper degree of state ownership and regulation of the economy. Business leaders proposed that the state sell only some enterprises back to the private sector; in other sectors the government should merely freeze public ownership at current levels when privatization was impractical. In addition, when it came to guaranteeing more public participation in shaping economic policies, businessmen preferred a narrower approach. They stopped short of advocating a stronger legislature, strengthened parties, greater press access to decision making, and so forth.

In conclusion, Brazil's industrial elite has not made a radical break with the authoritarian heritage of the past. One cannot be certain at this point which social group or elite will emerge as the leader in defining a liberal political ideology for the current democratization of the country, but it is clear that the business elite is not in a position to assume control over the process. Its mentality is still closely focused on self-interest and cannot easily expand to include issues of overall national policy. Thus, the business elite cannot advocate greater participatory democracy or accept the labor unions as partners in a new social pact. The business elite is not weak and disorganized; rather, it is incapable of leading the redemocratization process because of disagreements over key questions regarding the return to open, competitive politics. I do not expect the business elite to overcome these divisions soon or to create the sort of consensus that that would allow it to lead a latter-day bourgeois revolution.

Notes

1. We should include the Marxist and neo-Marxist analysts in this camp, because they emphasize the decisive role certain elites play in setting state policy. The latter place the peripheral or developing nations in an international system dominated by the capitalist powers.

2. In this group see especially Philippe C. Schmitter, *Interest Conflict and Political Change in Brazil* (Stanford: Stanford University Press, 1971).

3. In this school, the works of Hélio Jaguaribe and Alberto Guerreiro Ramos stand out. See, for example, the former's *Economic and Political Development* (Cambridge, Mass.: Harvard University Press, 1968), and the latter's *O problema nacional do Brasil* (Rio de Janeiro: Editôra Saga, 1960).

4. See, for example, Fernando Henrique Cardoso, *Empresário industrial e desenvolvimento econômico* (São Paulo: Difusão Européia do Livro, 1964), and "Hegemonia burguesa e independência econômica: raizes estruturais da crise política brasileira," in *Brasil: Tempos modernos*, Celso Furtado et al. (Rio de Janeiro: Paz e Terra, 1977), pp. 77–109.

5. A classic statement of this position is André Gunder Frank's *Capitalism and Underdevelopment in Latin America* (New York: Monthly Review Press, 1969).

6. Nathaniel H. Leff's *Economic Policy-Making and Development in Brazil* (New York: John Wiley & Sons, 1968), emphasized the autonomy of the state in making economic policy and the relative passivity of the elites.

7. For a discussion of this issue, see Peter Bachrach and Morton S. Baratz, "Two Faces of Power," in *The Bias of Pluralism*, ed. William E. Connolly (New York: Atherton Press, 1969), pp. 51–64.

8. According to Schmitter's classic study, state corporativism is a system of interest articulation that is not competitive. Instead, it is based on a limited number of hierarchically organized and functionally distinct groups in which membership is obligatory. These groups are recognized and legitimized by the state. See his article, "Still the Century of Corporatism?" in *Trends toward Corporatist Intermediation*, ed. Philippe C. Schmitter and Gerhard Lehmbruch (Beverly Hills: Sage Publications, 1979), pp. 7–52. "Bureaucratic rings" are ties between technocratic and business elites within the bureaucracy itself, usually formed through their cooptation by a high governmental official. See Fernando Henrique Cardoso, "On the Characterization of Authoritarian Regimes in Latin America," in *The New Authoritarianism in Latin America*, ed. David Collier (Princeton: Princeton University Press, 1979), pp. 43–44.

9. Anibal Villela and Wilson Suzigan, *Política do governo e crescimento*

da economia brasileira, 1889–1945 (Rio de Janeiro: IPEA/INPES, 1973), pp. 210–12.

10. Werner Baer, A industrialização e o desenvolvimento econômico do Brasil (Rio de Janeiro: Fundação Getúlio Vargas, 1977), p. 15.

11. Ibid., p. 217.

12. Werner Baer and Anibal Villela, "Crescimento industrial e industrialização: revisões nos estágios do desenvolvimento econômico do Brasil," DADOS 9 (1972): 123.

13. See Eli Diniz, Empresário, estado, e capitalismo no Brasil, 1930–1945 (Rio de Janeiro: Paz e Terra, 1978), ch. 7, and Philippe C. Schmitter, Interest Conflict and Political Change in Brazil (Stanford: Stanford University Press, 1971), part 2.

14. Diniz, Empresário, estado, e capitalismo, chs. 4–6, discusses these agencies, especially the Federal Council on Foreign Trade (1934–), the Technical Economic Council of the Treasury Department (1937), the National Council for Industrial and Commercial Policy (1943), and the Economic Planning Commission (1944).

15. Luiz Carlos Bresser Pereira, Desenvolvimento e crise no Brasil entre 1930 e 1983 (São Paulo: Editora Brasiliense, 1983), p. 39.

16. Alfred Stepan, The Military in Politics (Princeton: Princeton University Press, 1971).

17. Werner Baer, The Brazilian Economy: Growth and Development, 2d ed. (New York: Praeger, 1983). On multinationals in this period, see Peter Evans, Dependent Development (Princeton: Princeton University Press, 1979), and Richard S. Newfarmer and Willard F. Mueller, Multinational Corporations in Brazil and Mexico (Washington, D.C.: Government Printing Office, 1975).

18. Eli Diniz and Renato Raul Boschi, "Autonomia e dependência na representação de interesses Industriais," DADOS 22 (1979): 25–48. Cf. Renato Raul Boschi, "National Industrial Elites and the State in Post-1964 Brazil: Institutional Mediations and Political Change," (Ph.D. diss., Dept. of Political Science, University of Michigan, 1978).

19. Wanderley Guilherme dos Santos, "A 'pós-revolução' brasileira," in Brasil, sociedade democrática (Rio de Janeiro: José Olympio, 1985), pp. 223–336.

Part III: The Masses

Eul-Soo Pang

Agrarian Change in the Northeast

From the late nineteenth to the midtwentieth century, the rural masses of Northeast Brazil became a recognizable subsociety, yet at the same time they were gradually integrated into the larger social, economic, and political systems of the nation. Socially, they were transformed from invisible herds of backlanders into a restive problem people. The citizens in the Center-South considered the Northeastern *sertanejos* to be an embarrassment and, worse, an impediment to the nation's progress. Economically, the masses shifted from subsistence farming and stock raising to laboring in capitalist commercial agriculture, typically in cane fields and sugar refineries. But at the same time their numbers grew too large for the regional economy to support, and a mass exodus to the coastal cities and to the prosperous Center-South began. Politically, the masses remained irrelevant in national and even state affairs. Perhaps most of all, the rural masses of the Northeast became an painful reminder of the backwardness that other Brazilians were trying hard to escape.

This chapter concentrates on two major subjects: the penetration of capitalism into the formerly isolated backlands (*sertões*), and the resultant advent of social banditry and messianic or millenarian movements among the rural poor. Post-1870s capitalism was the single most important contributor to the other changes that swept the region. This chapter also seeks to dispel some of the myths surrounding banditry and messianism in the Northeast by linking these phenomena to capitalist modernization. This hypothesis should serve as theoretical underpinning for the otherwise descriptive narrative.[1]

Background

Beginning in the 1870s, Brazil's socioeconomically precapitalist Northeast began to modernize, lagging, however, behind the more progressive Center-South. The stimulus for development in both regions had been the growing interaction with the commercial and industrial nations of the North Atlantic, principally England. To the extent that such trade relations expanded, they dictated a shift from slaves and coerced workers to free wage laborers. As the Center-South became more intimately linked with international capitalism, a greater shift to free labor occurred. In addition, international linkages brought capital, technology, and modern business methods to the region.

Change brought on by the penetration of capitalism, first through trade and later through direct investments of capital and technology, caused wrenching adjustments in practically every aspect of life. The slow, seignorial pace of colonial existence, rooted in the plantation system, suddenly had to accommodate the steam engine, electricity, railroads, international trade and banking, and myriad other elements of nineteenth-century progress. Many Brazilian peasants could not make the adjustments and reacted in dysfunctional ways. For them, modernization presented a veritable crisis. In the cities of the Center-South, the reaction was trade union organization and strife, as well as urban protest of various sorts.

In Brazil's Northeast, the reaction against late-nineteenth-century modernization can be called the agrarian crisis. It was characterized by a state of persistent upheavals (organized and unorganized) and instability precipitated by structural changes, which were induced by a shift to modern modes of production, usually capitalistic. Some aspects of the crisis still persist, as evidenced by the continuing exodus of people from the Northeast to the Center-South, but its most pronounced symptoms disappeared by the 1940s.

Several major elements of the agrarian crisis require some discussion. The most radical change in the labor system was the abolition of slavery in 1888, which required new inducements to keep workers on the job. Changes in capital and technology also occurred, the most pronounced of which was the introduction of steam-powered sugar mills, called engenhos centrais, in the 1870s and 1880s; these were in turn replaced by even more powerful mills, called usinas, veritable factories in the fields. The third major change was the emergence of a central state after the 1930 Revolution. During the next several decades, President Getúlio Vargas and his successors curtailed the powers of regional and local officials and at the same time imposed peace on the unruly backlands.

Land ownership and income distribution inevitably suffered alterations during this period. Many members of the old landowning class were displaced by the new entrepreneurial usina owners. The latter needed to control vast areas in order to fill their voracious refinery capacity, so they bought up inefficient plantations and displaced smallholders and peasants as well. Because the usina owners sought to modernize the ailing sugar industry for a greater return on capital invested, they often called upon the government for low-cost interest and guaranteed loans, transportation infrastructure, and suppression of labor strife. In view of the intense competition from the usinas, many undercapitalized cane growers and refiners abandoned their lands and moved to cities. Others sold off parcels of land to retire debts or converted the land to subsistence farming. By 1910 a kind of *república das usinas* had replaced or refashioned the traditional sugarocracy.[2] Social banditry and messianism emerged as forms of popular resistance to the newly consolidated capitalist sugar elite and backlands ranchers.

Social Banditry

In his celebrated book, *Primitive Rebels*, Eric Hobsbawm argues that the cause of social banditry was an unconscious desire to protest social injustice. Alternatively, Maria Isaura Pereira de Queiroz argues that it was caused by a "structural crisis" in primitive society.[3] Yet other hypotheses have been advanced by North American scholars. Billy Jaynes Chandler's biography of Brazil's most famous bandit, Lampião, summarizes the causes of banditry as economic backwardness, periodic droughts, extreme dispersion of authority under the Constitution of 1891, and "the fragility of the institutions of law, order, and justice."[4] Ralph Della Cava, biographer of Brazil's most revered messianic leader, Padre Cícero Romão Batista, attributes the rise of his movement to the socioecological limits of the Northeast.[5] Chandler and Della Cava agree that the rural movements they studied were engendered by the closed agrarian system and by the stress implicit in economic stagnation and modernization.

Frederico Pernambucano de Mello focuses on social and psychological factors that drove the wretched and leaderless peasants into lives of banditry. He distinguishes three different types of bandit— the professional, the avenger, and the fugitive—and believes that up to 1930 the first type predominated in Brazil's Northeast. Most were motivated by the instinct of survival, not by political or ideological beliefs.[6]

Despite these different interpretations of banditry, most authors agree on the changes sweeping the region that helped engender it. In the 1890s the new elites of the Northeast, owners of the usinas and their clientele, collaborated with their Center-South counterparts, who created a new system of government, a highly decentralized republicanism. In the process, they denied the rural masses real participation in politics, although some hired hands were coopted into the base of the system as gunmen and others were allowed to vote if they took orders from the local chieftain. Faced with this situation, which was compounded by chronic ecological disasters, and exploited by a highly impersonal capitalist mode of labor, many rural poor sought to build new societies of their own in the isolated backlands, effectively withdrawing from the established political order. Thus arose the bandit gangs and messianic communities.[7]

In all nonindustrial societies, a peculiar triangular relationship prevailed between landowners, bandits, and peasants, one that helped define roles and perceptions. An alliance of any two could lead to persecution of the third. Often the bandits appeared to ally themselves with the peasants against the overlord class, so that the former became folk heroes to the alienated masses, who received both moral and material support.

Still, though some have romanticized the bandits as Robin Hoods, recent findings suggest that bandits were hardly revered by rural folk.[8] Linda Lewin's work on Northeastern bandits concludes that they were more feared than loved by peasants. Moreover, she believes that writers who romantized banditry in popular literature did so because they represented the agrarian elite that hired bandits as gunmen and enforcers. Lewin, then, finds that bandits were simply adjuncts of the oligarchical system of rule in the Northeast. As such, their actions were defined by the elite, not by inchoate feelings of dissatisfaction.[9]

Fear was used to legitimize a bandit's authority, according to studies from Sicily and England. In turn, this practice defined a particularly hierarchical relationship between the outlaws and the masses. In the retaliatory or "reactive" phase of banditry, brigands seldom emerged as social heroes. Only later would their advocacy of popular social and economic issues transform them into folk heroes and champions of the oppressed masses against the established order. In this framework, Robin Hood was a product of the era of England's economic transformation from feudalism into capitalism. So was Emiliano Zapata, a victim of the unbridled agrarian capitalism that swept ruthlessly through Morelos in the 1880s and 1890s. Pancho Villa, too, was a product of the capitalism in the mining and ranching industries that spilled over the border from the United States in the same decades. This list of comparisons could be expanded almost endlessly.

Citing parallel cases from Mexican history raises a theoretical issue of some importance: When does banditry become transformed into revolutionary activity? The answer seems to hinge on the degree of suffering experienced by the general population (urban as well as rural), as well as on the bandit's ability to articulate and parlay localized grievances into national issues. No less important is good timing: if an archaic society was undergoing a sudden economic transformation, a bandit could emerge as a revolutionary leader. But without an ideology with broad appeal, social banditry would have remained localized unrest.[10]

None of the Brazilian social bandits gained the status of a national revolutionary folk hero like Zapata and Villa. Instead, the agrarian crisis in Brazil, while sharpening the differences between city and countryside, remained a localized phenomenon. What occurred in the backlands was resisted by the urban sector throughout the country. For their part, those who ruled the hinterlands, the famous *coronéis*, viewed urban development with great suspicion. Thus Brazilian banditry lacked a broad ideology and remained local and reactive.[11]

The backlanders' contacts with the Prestes Column illustrate the foregoing. In 1924 a group of army rebels and urban unemployed (including some recent European immigrants) captured the city of São Paulo to protest a variety of ills in the country. Forced to abandon the city after a month, the rebels set out on a march that lasted over two years. The group was named after army Captain Luís Carlos Prestes, who became effective leader later in the march. Their odyssey took them thousands of miles through the backlands, and at one point they numbered 1500 men, including soldiers, policemen, unemployed workers, middle-class intellectuals, and restive immigrants. They hoped to call attention to the economic backwardness of the region and the misery of its inhabitants. They also expected to spark protest movements and perhaps even revolution among the rural poor. Logically, the bandits of Brazil's Northeast should have made common cause with the Prestes Column. Instead, they rejected the rebels' entreaties and collaborated with efforts by the authorities to capture them. Lampião himself fought briefly against the Prestes Column. Thus, the distrust of urban groups by the rural poor kept the bandit leaders from devising a broader ideology that could serve as a basis for a truly national movement.[12]

By the same token, the landowners succeeded in preventing the masses from identifying with and joining the column or the bandits. In various places, landlords organized "patriotic battalions" to fight the Prestes Column. Traditionally, landowners held great power over their hired hands and tenant farmers, since they provided status and a means of subsistence. Hence the column and the bandits alike could only prey on and recruit peasants on the fringes of the great rural domains.

Brazilian social banditry can best be seen as political resistance against local authorities, rather than against the central state. In keeping with the the country's Latin-Catholic tradition, the rural poor usually believed in the goodness of the faraway king or president and despised local officials who abused their delegated authority. Bandits shared this outlook and often blamed all local and regional authorities for their people's suffering. This antielite stance generated some peasant sympathy for the outlaw gangs.

An early bandit to enjoy much notoriety in the Northeast was Manuel Batista de Morais, better known as Antônio Silvino. His career began after a brush with the law involving the death of his father in a backlands clan war. His father had been a foreman on a sugar plantation, and he was related to the Feitosas of Ceará, a legendary warring clan whose roots went back to the seventeenth century. Antônio Silvino served as a soldier in private clan wars between oligarchic families. Eventually he became a bandit leading his own band of gunmen.[13]

The king of the Brazilian bandits was unquestionably Virgulino Ferreira da Silva, better known by his nom de guerre, Lampião. Born in the backlands of Pernambuco in 1897 or 1900, Virgulino was one of nine children in a peasant family. Local politics had long centered on a bloody feud between two rival clans, the Pereiras and the Carvalhos. Virgulino's family was allied with the Pereiras, so the father and male children were recruited into the Pereiras' private army to fight the Carvalhos. When the latter managed to gain access to the ruling elite in state politics, Virgulino and his family became outlaws. Although forced to leave their native state, Virgulino's family continued the struggle, only to become embroiled in another clan war in another state. Their father was eventually killed by the Alagoas state police, and Virgulino and his brothers became full-time bandits and recruited others into their band. Somewhere in his early career, Virgulino lost his personal/clan commitment to armed struggle and became a mere cog in a vicious wheel of rural violence.[14]

Most of the bandits' followers shared the bonds of loyalty to family and clan that motivated Silvino and Lampião, but they were also members of the dispossessed peasantry victimized by the agrarian crisis. When they joined the bandit group, they transferred to the leader the loyalty they had felt to family. The bandit leaders themselves continued to respect traditional social structures and often served as mentors or patrons for their men.

Bandit groups were microcosms of the larger rural society of the Northeast, and as such they exhibited many of the existing values. For example, they respected marriage and baptism rites, ritual punishment for female violators of marital fidelity, and the mutually protective relationships with agrarian overlords. Once a movement was organized, the members adopted the hierarchical structure of command usual in the backlands. The authority of the bandit leader was recognized and seldom challenged by his followers. Marriage too lent legitimacy to the bandit chiefs: Lampião had his Maria Bonita, Corisco had Dadá, Zé Baiano had Lídia, Círculo had Moça, and José Julião had Enêdina. Priests officiated at the marriages of at least some of these couples, and their children were regarded as legitimate, even though they might be orphaned later.[15]

Besides marital alliances and family, bandit society also respected the tradition of machismo. Lampião was said to have killed one of his men for disobeying orders, and Zé Baiano, his fierce black deputy, was known for his penchant for punishing unfaithful women with his infamous branding iron. Extramarital exploits by the men themselves, however, played an important role in reinforcing the image of chief and leader. Lampião and Corisco, for example, were notoriously promiscuous. One police officer who trailed them testified that the former had deflowered at least two hundred women. Still, some thirty years after Corisco's death, Dadá told a Rio newspaper reporter that neither her husband nor Lampião was a womanizer.[16] Regardless of the facts, it is clear that a macho image played a role in leadership.

Scholars of social banditry have turned up conflicting evidence with regard to the relative isolation or integration of their subjects. Hobsbawm and Queiroz suggest that all bandits break their ties with the larger society, while Anton Blok found that his bandits remained closely tied into Sicilian society.[17] The former view seems to hold for the Brazilian case, probably due to the low degree of economic development. Few sugar plantations, refineries, or cattle ranches were owned by coffee planters of the Center-South, so absentee ownership did not exist. The ties between the Northeastern sertão and Rio were minimal and fluid. The uneven spread of capitalism was probably most responsible for the isolation of Brazil's bandits. In Sicily, by way of comparison, land was bought by northern bankers and industrialists of Milan, who hired local foremen, often from the ranks of the Mafia.

The coronel played a pivotal role in the drama of Northeastern banditry. Sporting a real or assumed commission in the National Guard, he enjoyed quasi-legal authority to rule the backlands without interference. At the regional level, he served as a power broker, mediating between the peasant masses and the national government in Rio. The coronel used local gunmen to control elections, distributed patronage, dispensed justice of a personalistic sort, and acted as communal spokesman to the outside world. Most of the rural population existed peaceably under the coronel's rule, but persons left at the margins and denied minimal subsistence were available to the bandit leaders.

Shut out from direct participation in politics by the coronéis, Brazilian bandits worked as entrepreneurs of violence and as hired guns for rival power contenders. They were usually able to cultivate temporary alliances with landlords and even petty officials, especially when electoral competition became more intense in the 1910s and 1920s. As a highly mobile group, bandits became sources of political intelligence for competing coronéis. Bandits hired out as election enforcers, killed personal as well as public enemies of their employers, and received protection from legal prosecution. This mutually protective system, known as *coiteirismo*, kept the bandits available to but not totally under the control of coronéis. The *coitei-ro* was a local politician, probably also a merchant, landowner, or professional. He secretly kept in touch with and protected the bandits in exchange for their occasional services. Not infrequently coiteiros were relatives or family friends of the bandits.[18]

Between 1926 and 1931, Lampião and his band moved into a new phase by establishing a semipermanent community and preparing for reentry into normal life. According to the rules of coiteirismo, this should have been possible: the coiteiro often helped former bandits start anew in the western lands of Goiás, Mato Grosso, and Minas Gerais. Indeed, Lampião managed to settle down as a ranch foreman in Santa Brígida in northeastern Bahia. There he met Maria Bonita, who became his wife and comrade-in-arms. In 1931, however, state police forces identified Lampião and set out to eradicate him and his band. Lampião summoned his men and set out on a new life of crime, accompanied now by Maria Bonita.

At about the time that state police flushed out Lampião, the federal government launched a campaign to end banditry once and for all. Lawlessness seemed on the rise at the time, due to the breakdown of authority following the 1930 revolution. Federal agents combed the sertões in 1931 and disarmed the private troops of leading coronéis for fear that they might initiate counterrevolutionary activities. This was especially true in the Cariri Valley (Ceará), the middle São Francisco River Valley, and Lavras Diamantinas (both Bahia), where coronéis provided the bulk of the pre-1930 peace-keeping services. Once coronéis were disarmed, bandits began operating openly again. The first years of revolutionary government were chaotic because of the depression, droughts, political instability, and military revolts. As the government sought to impose a new order from the top down, the bandits took advantage to expand their activities.

A businessman in Salvador spoke for many when he called drought and banditry the "two ills of Bahia" in 1931. Local commerce lay exposed to thieves without the coronéis' protection. The Commercial Association of Bahia called for a joint federal and state campaign to eradicate banditry. By that time, a guerrilla war had broken out along the Bahia-Sergipe border between state police and Lampião's men. War refugees flooded the coastal cities. In addition,

Lampião's erstwhile deputy, Corisco, took Queimadas and threatened Bomfim, in an effort to create a free territory. For the next two years, banditry thrived in the backlands of the Northeast, unchecked by local authorities and by the weak government in Rio.

The central government survived São Paulo's revolt in 1932 and proceeded to consolidate its power over the entire country in 1933 and 1934. Meanwhile, federal officials saw that interstate and export trade, jeopardized by bandit attacks, was critical for rebuilding the nation from the ravages of the depression. The Federal Foreign Trade Council, for example, put much emphasis on reviving Bahia's cacao exports to the United States and Europe. The Rio government began to put pressure on state authorities to clean up banditry. By 1934 a consensus had emerged to take forceful action.

A special mobile task force of some sixteen thousand men was assembled in 1934 to eliminate bandits from the backlands. The peasantry, caught between the legal authorities and the bandits, began to withhold support from the latter. The bandits' mystique was undermined by financial considerations: the revival of commercial agriculture required federal aid, which would not be forthcoming for zones still under bandit control. Lampião suffered personal setbacks as well, when his brother was killed and he himself lost an eye. Maria Bonita and Dadá pressured the men to sue for peace. The end was not far.

The central government managed to consolidate its power over the countryside by the mid-1930s by either neutralizing or absorbing the coronéis into the new political hierarchy. State police and judicial institutions gradually spread their jurisdictions throughout the territory, and the masses no longer followed the coronéis blindly. Banditry, too, became an anachronism, losing its popular support or at least the tolerance for it. Coiteiros no longer dared protect bandits. By 1940 Brazil had become fairly well integrated economically, and federal authority in Rio was recognized throughout the land.

Banditry virtually ended in the late 1930s. Lampião and Maria Bonita were killed in a shootout, and Dadá lost a leg in an ambush that killed Corisco. The other bandits were hunted down and either imprisoned or killed.

The early 1940s also marked the shift of Brazil's economy from a predominantly rural to an urban industrial basis, and such institutions as Volta Redonda (Latin America's first modern steel mill) and the Vale do Rio Doce Company (a state-owned mining corporation) shifted ever-larger shares of the capital base to public ownership. Thus the agrarian crisis of the Northeast was not solved but rather passed into history as the country modernized.

Messianic Movements

While social banditry did not go beyond the stage of a primitive reaction to the agrarian crisis in the Brazilian Northeast, messianic religious movements were far more successful in penetrating the local and regional power structures. At the outset, all the messianic movements exhibited "heretical and revolutionary" qualities, so they remained underground and poorly organized in their early forms. Their constituency was much the same as that of the social bandits: the agrarian proletariat and peasantry.

Rui Facó, the late journalist-historian, was the first to formulate the fascinating hypothesis that banditry and messianism come from the same origin, i.e., structural problems brought on by concentrated landownership and the ecological difficulties of life in the Northeast.[19] The timing of such movements and the backgrounds of their leaders support this notion. Such collective action typically took place during the emergence of a modern economic system in a formerly primitive region, accompanied by the penetration of a full-fledged capitalist state.[20] Successful modernization measures further strengthened agrarian capitalism and its new elite, while they uprooted peasant communities. Peasants were forced to either become a rural proletariat or migrate to the cities to become wage laborers. In this crisis setting (from the peasant point of view), a religious leader could easily become a savior by helping the dispossessed adapt to or withdraw from their troubled existence.

No less important in the formation of messianic groups was the redefinition of church-state relations that occurred in the 1890s. The leaders of the republican coup of 1889 disestablished the church and wrote the separation of church and state into the 1891 constitution. Simultaneously, the traditional landowning class, which had been a principal supporter of the church, fell on hard times and was not able to sustain the church or its charitable activities. Thus, the peasantry was forced to search for new religious guidance outside the institutional church, and they increasingly joined messianic movements. The rural masses withdrew from the capitalist order to pursue a utopia on earth, led by religious fanatics. As in the case of medieval Europe, the promise of a better future was the key to mobilizing the dispossessed in northeastern Brazil.[21]

The two best-known messianic communes in the Northeast, Canudos (Bahia) and Joaseiro (Ceará), were founded at the height of the agrarian crisis. Not only did they become political centers of some importance, but they also functioned as enclaves with their own internal organization, which often put them in conflict with the surrounding society. For example, the demographic weight and economic success of Joaseiro drew the attention of local coronéis and national politicians alike. In both Canudos and Joaseiro, no attempt was made to proselytize the outside world; rather, their leaders sought to create self-contained communities that could live in harmony with the rest of society. They did not reject capitalism, but neither did they wish to become integrated into the world economy.

Since messianic communities offered no immediate threat to the traditional elite, political accommodation was possible, especially when the communities were prosperous and had many voters. For example, Canudos and Joaseiro actually contributed to the economic growth of the surrounding regions. In the process, they acquired political power that politicians were eager to preempt. Furthermore, because the sparse foreign immigration to the region compounded the labor shortage on plantations, landowners began to view the communities as potential sources of manpower.

Control of labor became a major issue in the Northeast and a bone of contention between landowners and leaders of the religious communes. Sometimes, political accommodations could be reached, whereby the communes served as employment brokers for the former. In Joaseiro, a formal agreement signed in 1911, the Pact of the Coronéis, assured landowners of access to the pilgrim labor that the community's patriarch, Padre Cícero, controlled. When such arrangements could not be made, however, the landowners and coronéis usually tried to destroy the communes. Canudos and the Contestado (on the border between Santa Catarina and Paraná) met this fate.[22]

A variety of factors played parts in the evolution of the communities. For example, Antônio Conselheiro, the founder of Canudos, had as a young man suffered personal tragedy in his married life, and this colored his outlook and ideology as leader of the religious commune. During the ten years preceding Conselheiro's arrival in the Bahia backlands (in 1876), the region had gone through a series of traumas: drought in 1866–68, election violence in 1868 and 1871, and economically devastating clan wars in Monte Santo, Itapicurú, and other areas.[23] Because of the demoralization of the masses, Conselheiro was able in just a few years to gain a following and to establish a commune to which the people went for refuge. By the 1890s Conselheiro had emerged as the savior of the rural masses, and the community of Canudos withdrew from the regional economy. For the next few years his following swelled into a major millenarian movement.

The formative years of Padre Cícero, founder of the Holy City of Joaseiro, were spent differently. Padre Cícero was inspired by the theosophy of social work while in a French Lazarist seminary. After ordination in 1870, he became active in charitable work in his native Carirí Valley. Watered by natural springs, the valley became a refuge for victims of periodic droughts as well as for those who had lost land and jobs because of the spread of capitalistic agriculture. The founder of the lay charitable houses throughout the valley was a lawyer-turned-priest, José Maria Ibiapina, whose philosophy and work were inherited by Padre Cícero after the mentor's death in 1884.[24]

By 1890 Padre Cícero had emerged as the unchallenged leader of a socioreligious movement that combined devotion to the faith and a pragmatic welfarism. The timing was right: neither the national political leaders nor the local landlords were in a position to aid the dispossessed masses. The poor saw the Carirí Valley as an oasis in an economic desert. Padre Cícero came to be loved and revered by the rural poor, but this huge following also aroused suspicion among church officials and landowners alike.

Conselheiro and Cícero became political leaders because of the large numbers of pilgrims who flocked to their communities. This was due in part to the enormous organizational tasks of building dwellings, supplying food, protecting the inhabitants, and providing necessary infrastructure. The socioeconomic tribulations did not diminish with time, for the late 1880s saw the demise of slavery and the fall of monarchical government, and the 1890s brought another agricultural depression and political turmoil. Displaced rural workers, cut off from their traditional livelihood, drifted increasingly to Canudos and Joaseiro: in the mid-1890s the former had eight thousand inhabitants, and by 1911 the latter had over fifteen thousand.[25]

Canudos had an autarkic or isolated economy that depended little on the outside world. Indeed, a dispute over an unfilled order for building materials helped spark the official military attack on the commune in 1896. Joaseiro, on the other hand, was a major emporium of the backlands, specializing in mining and sugar. As noted, it also supplied labor for the surrounding region and became an electoral redoubt of some importance. The experience of Canudos set it up for conflict with the surrounding regional forces; that of Joaseiro headed off conflict and indeed made the community a key element in the regional power network. The Pact of the Coronéis, mentioned above, allied the bosses of the region (including Padre Cícero) with the dominant clan in the state capital, the Acióli family, and helped end the endemic backlands wars.

In Bahia, the dominant party of the future governor, Luís Viana, courted Antônio Conselheiro for his support. Not as astute as Padre Cícero, Conselheiro managed only to alienate the regional bosses and eventually brought down the federal army on his community.[26] Enemies of Conselheiro branded him a monarchist, while church officials called him an antichrist. Such exaggerated accusations raised alarm throughout the country. At that point a series of military expeditions was dispatched to eliminate the commune. The tragic Canudos War (1896–97) was graphically chronicled by Euclides da Cunha's classic *Rebellion in the Backlands*, and recently it was adopted for the story line of *La guerra del fin del mundo*, by Peruvian novelist Mario Vargas Llosa.

In sum, Padre Cícero integrated his community into the outside world and managed to parlay his career into one of great power and wealth by the 1930s without losing the reverence of his followers. Even today hundreds of thousands travel to his shrine in Joaseiro. Conselheiro, on the contrary, refused to manipulate his flock for his own benefit, and hence the outside world turned against him. Canudos was the more orthodox messianic movement, Joaseiro a syncretic one.

Conclusion

Both banditry and messianism grew out of the agrarian crisis of the Northeast in the late nineteenth century, at a time when the Brazilian economy became more deeply engaged in international trade and capitalism. The two forms of rural protest experienced different trajectories, however, involving conflict, accommodation, and integration with the larger political system. Both were responses to the material progress generated by modernization of plantation agriculture and to the eclipse of the local patriarchy by a centralized state. But these processes did not occur in a vacuum. The Center-South of Brazil developed even more rapidly and enjoyed the lion's share of the benefits. This regional imbalance exacerbated the agrarian crisis, causing manpower and capital to migrate out of the Northeast. The economy and society of the nation became split between a modern urban-industrial core and a depressed agrarian periphery.

Because political power also migrated south after the turn of the century, the coffee plantocracy held the reins of government. The traditional elites and even the modern sugar industrialists of the Northeast became clients of their southern masters. Still, they sought to retain control over land and people despite the cataclysmic changes going on. They succeeded to some extent, but they lost control over large numbers of the rural poor, who became dispossessed and alienated. These masses became the clients of bandits and self-styled messiahs, who proliferated in the backlands in the late nineteenth and early twentieth centuries. The new power figures were not totally divorced from the regional power system, however, since arrangements like coiteirismo and the Pact of the Coronéis sprang up to keep society from fragmenting further. The Revolution of 1930 marked the beginning of the end for bandits and messiahs, for the Vargas regime intended to modernize and integrate the entire country, including the depressed Northeast. The old informal arrangements of governors, coronéis, and rural masses disappeared, and banditry and messianism became relics of the past, remembered only in folk literature and oral history.

Notes

1. A huge literature exists about the Northeast and its poor. A good starting point is Shepard Forman's *The Brazilian Peasantry* (New York: Columbia University Press, 1975). Messianism, briefly, refers to mass movements of the poor and uneducated, who abandon their homes and jobs to follow a putative religious leader in search of a "promised land." On banditry and messianism in Brazil, see Maria Isaura Pereira de Queiroz, *O messianismo no Brasil e no mundo*, 2d ed. (São Paulo: Alfa-Omega, 1977), and Duglas Teixeira Monteiro, "Um confronto entre Joazeiro, Canudos, e Contestado," in *História geral da*

civilização brasileira, ed. Boris Fausto (Rio de Janeiro and São Paulo: Difusão Européia do Livro, 1977), pp. 41–92. Another approach, that of Anthony F. C. Wallace, treats such movements as coming out of a struggle for identity that would result in an improved life. See his "Identity and the Nature of Revolution," in *Latin America: The Dynamics of Social Change*, ed. Stefan A. Halper and John R. Sterling (New York: St. Martins Press, 1972), pp. 172–86.

2. Eul-Soo Pang, "Modernization and Slavocracy in Nineteenth-Century Brazil," *Journal of Interdisciplinary History* 9, no. 4 (Spring 1979): 667–88; Peter L. Eisenberg, *The Sugar Industry in Pernambuco* (Berkeley and Los Angeles: University of California Press, 1974); Gadiel Perruci, *A república das usinas* (Rio de Janeiro: Paz e Terra, 1978); Nathaniel H. Leff, *Underdevelopment and Development in Brazil*, 2 vols. (London: George Allen and Unwin, 1982).

3. Eric J. Hobsbawm, *Primitive Rebels* (New York: W. W. Norton, 1959), pp. 13–29; Queiroz, *O messianismo*, pp. 330–31; and Maria Christina Russi da Matta Machado, "Aspectos do fenômeno do cangaço no nordeste brasileiro," *Revista de história* 46, no. 93 (1973): 139–45.

4. Billy Jaynes Chandler, *The Bandit King: Lampião of Brazil* (College Station: Texas A&M University Press, 1978), pp. 13–15.

5. Ralph Della Cava, *Miracle at Joaseiro* (New York: Columbia University Press, 1970), pp. 9–31 and especially 17–23.

6. *Guerreiros do sol: O banditismo no nordeste do Brasil* (Recife: Fundação Joaquim Nabuco, 1985), esp. pp. 76–77, 97–98.

7. Rui Facó, *Cangaceiros e fanáticos*, 2d ed. (Rio de Janeiro: Civilização Brasileira, 1969); Christina Matta Machado, *As táticas de guerra dos cangaceiros* (Rio de Janeiro: n.p., 1965); Amaury de Souza, "The Cangaço and the Politics of Violence in Northeast Brazil," in *Protest and Resistance in Angola and Brazil*, ed. Ronald H. Chilcote (Berkeley and Los Angeles: University of California Press, 1972), pp. 109–31.

8. Anton Blok, *The Mafia of a Sicilian Village, 1860–1960* (New York: Harper and Row, 1974), pp. 171–82, and Linda Lewin, "The Oligarchical Limitations of Social Banditry in Brazil: The Case of the 'Good' Thief Antônio Silvino," *Past and Present* 82 (February 1979): 116, 130–33, 145–46.

9. Lewin, "The 'Good' Thief," pp. 129–30.

10. Although the literature is large, many of the key issues may be sampled in Eric Wolf's *Peasant Wars of the Twentieth Century* (New York: Harper and Row, 1969).

11. On *coronelismo*, see Victor Nunes Leal, *Coronelismo: the Municipality and Representative Government in Brazil*, trans. June Henfrey (Cambridge: Cambridge University Press, 1977), and a revisionist treatment, Eul-Soo Pang, *Bahia in the First Brazilian Republic: Coronelismo and Oligarchies, 1889–1934* (Gainesville: University Presses of Florida, 1979).

12. Neill Macaulay, *The Prestes Column: Revolution in Brazil* (New York: New Viewpoints, 1974).

13. Lewin, "The 'Good' Thief,"; Billy Jaynes Chandler, *The Feitosas and the Sertão dos Inhamuns* (Gainesville: University of Florida Press, 1972).

14. In addition to Chandler's *Bandit King*, see Algae Lima de Oliveira, *Lampião: Cangaço e Nordeste* (Rio de Janeiro: Edições e Cruzeiro, 1970), and Rodrigues de Carvalho, *Lampião e a sociologia do cangaço* (Rio de Janeiro: n.p., 1976).

15. Oliveira, *Lampião*, pp. 276–78, and Queiroz, *Os cangaceiros*, pp. 113–15, 185–93.

16. *Jornal do Brasil* (Rio de Janeiro), July 31, 1968; Optato Gueiros, *Lampeão: Memórias de um oficial ex-comandante de forças volantes*, 4th ed. (Salvador: Livraria Progresso, 1956), p. 16.

17. Blok, *Mafia*, pp. 171–82.

18. Leonardo Mota, *No tempo de Lampião*, 2d ed. (Fortaleza: Imprensa Universitária do Ceará, 1967), p. 191; Chandler, *Bandit King*, p. 87.

19. Facó, *Cangaceiros e fanáticos*, pp. 41–46.

20. See Pang, "Modernization and Slavocracy," and Eisenberg, *Sugar Industry*.

21. Norman Cohn, *The Pursuit of the Millennium*, 2d ed. (New York: Harper & Brothers, 1961), pp. 1–13; Kit Sims Taylor, *Sugar and the Underdevelopment of Northeastern Brazil, 1500–1970* (Gainesville: University Presses of Florida, 1978), pp. 63–65; Maria Isaura Pereira de Queiroz, "Messiahs in Brazil," *Past and Present* 31 (July 1965): 71–72.

22. Raimundo Girão, *História econômica do Ceará* (Fortaleza: Editôra "Instituto do Ceará," 1947), p. 393; and Ralph Della Cava, "Brazilian Messianism and National Institutions: A Reappraisal of Canudos and Joaseiro," *Hispanic American Historical Review* 48, no. 3 (August 1968): 402–20.

23. Azarias Sobreira, *O patriarca de Juázeiro* (Juaseiro: Vozes, 1969), pp. 14, 19; Della Cava, *Miracle*, pp. 15–19.

24. Roger Cunniff, "The Great Drought: Northeast Brazil, 1877–1880" (Ph.D. diss., University of Texas at Austin, 1970), ch. 3.

25. Della Cava, *Miracle*, pp. 115–28. Estimates of Canudos' population vary widely, from 5,000 to 25,000. Cf. Angelina Nobre Rolim Garcez, *Aspectos econômicos do episódio de Canudos* (Salvador: Centro de Estudios Baianos, 1977), and Ataliba Nogueira, *Antônio Conselheiro e Canudos* (São Paulo: Editôra Nacional, 1974).

26. Pang, *Bahia*, pp. 59–64; Della Cava, "Brazilian Messianism," pp. 412–13.

Thomas H. Holloway

Immigration in the Rural South

Since the last quarter of the nineteenth century, foreign immigration and internal migration have transformed the social composition of southern Brazil. The immigrants came initially from Germany and Italy, later from Spain and eastern Europe, and eventually from Japan, with arrivals from Portugal continuing in a steady, if less noticeable, stream. The millions of newcomers were added to the existing population of descendants of Portuguese settlers, African slaves, and native Indians; since the Great Depression, increasing numbers of migrants from the Brazilian Northeast have arrived as well. Because of the influx of people from outside the region in the relatively recent past, in the four southernmost states of Rio Grande do Sul, Santa Catarina, Paraná, and São Paulo the masses have been different from the rest of the country in terms of ethnic origin, cultural tradition, outlook, and opportunities.[1] Thus, many of the generalizations about elites, masses, and the relationship between them must be qualified when the historian turns toward the South.

Climate, geography, historical experience, and economic focus—each of which, of course, has its own specificity and distinctive subregions—are among the factors one might invoke to set this region apart from Amazonia, the Northeast, and the Center-West. Such factors also relate directly to the history of immigration to the rural south. To put that social history in context, we must briefly address these related themes.

The natural environment of southern Brazil has attractive features that set the region apart from much of the rest of the country. Rising from a narrow subtropical coastal strip, the interior plateau enjoys a temperate climate in most of the region. These uplands include many hilly areas and steep valleys in the transition zone between coast and interior, but also large areas of gently rolling plains, well suited for European-style agriculture, in São Paulo, Paraná, and Santa Catarina. These plains slope inland away from the coastal escarpment toward the Paraná and Uruguay rivers. In Rio Grande do Sul the hills of the north give way in the southern half of the state to rolling grasslands that geologically are part of the vast pampas centered on the La Plata estuary. Rainfall is for the most part adequate but not excessive. There is no drought zone here, and no tropical rain forest, although before the advent of extensive agriculture woodlands of greater or lesser density spread over much of the interior plateau, and they still cover the hillsides. Native trees range from the deciduous varieties dominant in São Paulo and the coastal forests to the distinctive flat-topped Paraná pine in higher elevations further south. Despite the mild climate, a distinct temperature change with the seasons facilitates the cultivation of most European crops, such as wheat and wine grapes. Corn, beans, and tobacco also thrive, as do most commercial varieties of vegetables. A definite, if variable, climatic divider in the interior is the line of normal frost, which runs roughly along the Tropic of Capricorn, which in turn intersects the northern suburbs of the city of São Paulo. Historically this has meant that frost-sensitive perennials, notably coffee and citrus fruits, cannot be grown south of São Paulo and northern Paraná.

If the natural environment offers much to attract European farmers, it also has some negative aspects. Soil conditions are often less than ideal, and hilly terrain limits the applicability of European farming techniques. Paramount, however, is the difficulty of communication, particularly the barrier of the coastal escarpment separating the fertile and productive hinterland from seaports. Similarly, the rough topography of many areas has made internal transportation difficult, even with the construction of major railroad lines in the late nineteenth century and highways in the post–World War II period. This has meant that many farming colonies have been cut off from sources of supplies and markets, forcing cultural isolation and hampering potential growth. The earliest and best solutions to the problems of transportation were devised by the Brazilian elites in the areas of large-scale export agriculture, particularly in the São Paulo coffee zone, where rail and then highway and truck transportation have accompanied economic growth.

Before the era of foreign immigration, the South was only sparsely and sporadically occupied by Portuguese colonists. The original east-west division between Portuguese and Spanish territory, set by the Treaty of Tordesillas in 1494, ran through the coast at the town of Laguna, in southern Santa Catarina. That left all of Rio Grande do Sul and most of the interior of modern Santa Catarina, Paraná, and São Paulo formally under Spanish jurisdiction. Portuguese claims, based on de facto occupation, were finally recognized in the Treaty of Madrid in 1750, but the region continued in dispute thereafter. It was a zone of considerable diplomatic and military activity, but compared with the coastal sugar zones in the seventeenth century or mining in the Center-West in the eighteenth century, the South held little of economic interest for the colonial power.

With the mining boom, the demand for livestock and livestock products increased, and the southern pampas became an important source for mules for transport and cattle products, notably salt beef and leather, for the mining complex. This development added to the region's strategic importance but did not result in much permanent settlement of the area. In socioeconomic terms it was an extension of the nomadic and extractive livestock activity that characterized the early development of the La Plata basin, associated with the social archetype of the proud and independent gaúcho plainsman. The image of the gaucho in the popular mind tends to obscure the fact that most of the labor around the *charqueadas*, the primitive establishments for processing dried beef and hides, was done by black slaves. Today the nickname for the people of Rio Grande do Sul is *gaúcho*, and in the interior of that state and Santa Catarina horsemen in flat-brimmed hats and baggy trousers, knives tucked into the back of their belts, still ride after cattle, congregate in periodic *rodeio* competitions, and appear on tourist posters. Although both had their origin in livestock herding, the sociocultural type of the gaúcho of the South contrasts sharply with the leather-clad *vaqueiro* of northeast Brazil.

After the founding of early outposts of the sixteenth century, deliberate attempts to settle the southern region date from the mid-eighteenth century, when the Portuguese government transported a few thousand peasants and other working people, primarily from the Azores and Madeira Islands, to the area around the town of Porto Alegre, in Rio Grande do Sul, and the island of Santa Catarina. These efforts might be seen as a prelude to the colonization policies of the Brazilian government in the nineteenth century.

São Paulo's preimmigration history differs somewhat from the three states to the south but still contrasts with northern Brazil. São Paulo became the center for the exploring and slave-raiding groups of the colonial era, known as the *bandeirantes,* who did much to spread Portuguese occupation to the hinterland beyond the Tordesillas line and who discovered major gold fields in the last years of the seventeenth century in the area that became known as Minas Gerais. São Paulo itself was little more than a launching point for these expeditions, with subsistence production sufficing for local needs, until it grew in conjunction with the mining boom. It then became a way station for the livestock trade from southern sources to the mining zone, and by the later eighteenth century a significant sugar industry emerged in the interior plateau. Paraná was literally an extension of São Paulo until 1857, when it became a separate province. It remained a sparsely populated marginal area until deliberate colonization began in the late nineteenth century.

São Paulo's major period of expansion came only in the midnineteenth century, as the coffee industry, formerly centered on Rio de Janeiro and the Paraíba River valley, spread into western São Paulo. After the completion of the railroad over the coastal escarpment in the 1860s, finally connecting the interior to the port of Santos, São Paulo's future as the center of the coffee industry was assured. A period of expansion into the western frontier followed, on the basis of large landholdings and black slave labor, concurrent with the gradual demise of slavery.[2] The transatlantic slave trade was effectively cut off about 1850, just as coffee was becoming established in São Paulo. There followed the law of 1871 freeing children born of slave mothers, the freeing of slaves over age 60 in 1885, and final abolition in 1888. By the time slavery ended, mass immigration had begun, and the Paulista coffee planters never looked back.

This historical experience meant that southern Brazil, despite early colonial beginnings, was still a "new" area in the nineteenth century. Considerable numbers of black slaves remained, and a subsistence-oriented peasantry developed early and persisted in the interstitial and marginal geographical areas. Much of the interior, however, despite having been traversed occasionally by Europeans from early colonial days, was inhabited only by seminomadic tribal Indians who maintained a traditional subsistence base in hunting, gathering, and indigenous horticulture. The descendants of slaves, marginal peasants of mixed ethnic origin, and Indian communities are still present but have been subordinated, in both the popular mind and the historical experience of the last century, to the presence of the immigrant.

In Brazilian social history, immigration is associated with three settings: agricultural colonies in the far south, the coffee-producing zone of western São Paulo state, and the urban environment of the major cities of the southeastern coast, particularly the city of São Paulo. The latter two are related, but the southern farm colonies are distinct historically as well as geographically from the rural and urban complexes of São Paulo.[3]

The first numerically significant transfers of immigrants after Brazil's independence were to the officially sanctioned semiautonomous farm colonies of the two southern states of Rio Grande do Sul and Santa Catarina. Colonization projects were carried out sporadically beginning in the late 1820s, and the number and scale of these efforts picked up after 1870. Similar attempts in São Paulo in the 1870s were largely unsuccessful, but in the same period Paraná became a center of such colonies.[4] For the Brazilian government, the motivation for these colonization efforts was primarily geopolitical. The rivalries of colonial South America continued between the independent nations, and Brazilian state builders were concerned that they had never established an effective demographic or economic presence in the region. Colonization seemed to offer a solution to the threat of the piecemeal incursion of Spanish speakers or, worse, territorial encroachment by Argentina. There was the complementary hope that European immigrants would improve the cultural level and racial composition of the Brazilian population.

For the Europeans and Brazilian promoters of such colonies, the incentive was primarily entrepreneurial. Official agencies in Brazil entered into agreements with private companies or individuals who promised to bring a stipulated number of hardy folk, perhaps 50 to 200 families initially, in return for land grants, tax exemptions, such infrastructure development as access roads, and the initial costs of farm tools and temporary housing. The colonists themselves were recruited by the contracting entrepreneur, using glowing reports of existing conditions and predicting prosperity for all. The colonies were usually located on public lands, often in remote and inaccessible areas, and many failed outright.

Today the three southern states comprehend demographically and culturally significant centers of German and Italian ethnic tradi-

Map 1: Southern Brazil

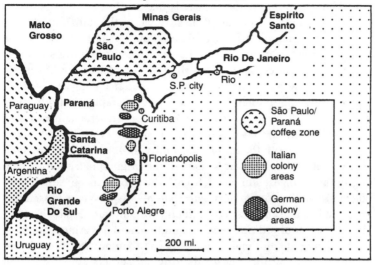

tions that trace their origin to the official colonization efforts of the nineteenth and early twentieth century. Other recognizable ethnic groups, notably Poles and Ukranians, live in Paraná (map 1).[5]

A common pattern of development began with the period of installation and adjustment, during which the successful colonies received new recruits from those nearby that failed and were disbanded. This was a time of hardship and recurring dislocation, with considerable adaptation required of those who came through the ordeal. There followed a much longer stage, lasting roughly from before World War I to the late 1940s, characterized by a predominantly subsistence orientation in which the earlier isolation was reinforced by economic stagnation and slow demographic growth. During this period of isolation the colonies developed a subculture that exhibited holdovers from the European background, adapted to the Brazilian environment. Domestic architecture and artisan techniques remained typically "German" or "Italian." Lutheranism in the German areas and festivals focusing on the local patron saint in the Italian colonies characterized the religious life of the communities. Until such practices were restricted by nationalistic measures at the beginning of World War II, most schooling continued to be conducted in the language of the old country. Even today many members of these communities are bilingual, and the Portuguese of the older generation remains heavily accented.

One custom that facilitated the survival in the Italian zones of a social and economic structure centered on the family farm was the informal practice of minority inheritance, contrary to Luso-Brazilian tradition. The colonies were originally situated on remote public lands, and new land remained to be occupied in territory adjacent to that already subdivided. Depending on topography and other factors, family plots ranged from 20 to 50 or even 70 hectares. When older sons married they customarily set up their own household on separate plots, with the remaining family unit providing a payment equivalent to the older son's share of the original patrimony. Eventually the youngest son was left with the "home place," often with the task of caring for the now aging parents. As the years passed this practice became increasingly difficult to maintain. Excessive subdivision of landholdings became common, and offspring were pressured to migrate and make their way in urban occupations.[6] Eventually the ethnic presence of the original settlers spread to other areas in the region, beyond the once-isolated original colonies.

Since the 1950s many of these "zones of colonization" have participated in the more general economic development of southern Brazil, becoming increasingly involved in production of agricultural commodities and such light manufactured goods as textiles and leather goods for the national market, shipped along the greatly improved highway system that has finally broken the isolation of the colonization zones. The descendants of the original immigrant groups predominate now in these areas, owning farms and significant commercial and manufacturing establishments, as well as participating in local politics, voluntary associations, education, services, and the usual institutions of the middle class. Pockets of the earlier "peasantized" existence remain, and one does not have to go very far into the hills to find rural poverty and stagnation. Even the peasant tradition, however, "just like Italy," has come to provide much of the attraction for a significant internal tourist industry in such areas as the hilly wine country of northern Rio Grande do Sul, centered on the city of Caxias do Sul. Distinctively "German" areas include São Leopoldo, the adjacent Sinos River valley in Rio Grande do Sul, and the region of the Itajaí River valley in Santa Catarina, including such towns as Joinville, Itajaí, and Blumenau. The last city, in particular, has become a mecca for tourists attracted by "chalet" style architecture, German cuisine, and factory outlet stores for the knit goods, crystal, and other products of local manufacturing firms founded by immigrants.

The southern agricultural colonies remain significant pockets of ethnic identity, are locally important, and form much of the popular image of the history of immigration in Brazil,[7] but they pale in comparison with the mass immigration to São Paulo state in the period from the 1880s to the 1920s, particularly from 1887 to 1914. In gross terms, total immigration to the farm colonies over the years numbered in the tens of thousands, and other immigrants to the three southernmost states stayed in the coastal cities rather than entering the sponsored settlements. For the same period the figure for São Paulo, rural and urban, exceeds 2.3 million people.[8] This was no matter of individual contracts for a few hundred families but a population transfer that puts Brazil in the league with Argentina, the United States, and Canada as a major recipient of immigrants.

An examination of the demographic evolution of southern Brazil reveals something of the distinctiveness of the region in the context of the nation as a whole and of São Paulo within the south. As shown in table 1, at the time of the first national census, in 1872, there were many more slaves than foreigners in Brazil, the latter constituting less than four percent of the population. Of the provinces under examination, only Santa Catarina had more immigrants than slaves, and in São Paulo slaves outnumbered foreigners by five to one—a reflection of the booming coffee economy based on slave labor. The four southern states together contained only 23 percent of the foreigners in Brazil in 1872. (The city of Rio de Janeiro alone had 31 percent, and the state of Rio another 12 percent.)

In 1872 slavery was beginning its long downward trajectory toward final abolition in 1888, while the small-scale immigration to Rio Grande do Sul, Santa Catarina, and Paraná was on the increase. Through the decline of slavery, the coffee industry of São Paulo was expanding rapidly, and during the 1880s the Paulista planters developed both the specific system of labor organization—the *colono* contract—and the program for recruiting and transporting immigrant workers that facilitated their "conversion" to the cause of abolition. From 1887 onward the São Paulo system was functioning to meet the rapidly expanding labor needs of the coffee industry.[9]

By 1920, as shown in table 2, the population of Brazil had tripled over the 1872 base. Comparable increases for the southern four

Table 1   Population of Southern Provinces and Brazil, 1872

Region	Free Brazilians		Slaves		Foreigners		Total
São Paulo	651,120	78%	156,612	19%	29,622	4%	837,354
Paraná	112,535	89%	10,560	8%	3,627	3%	126,722
Santa Catarina	128,844	81%	14,984	9%	15,974	10%	159,802
Rio Grande do Sul	325,297	75%	67,791	16%	41,725	10%	434,813
Total	1,217,796	78%	249,947	16%	90,948	6%	1,558,691
All Brazil	8,031,213	81%	1,510,806	15%	388,459	4%	9,930,478

Source: Brasil, Diretoria Geral de Estatística, *Recenseamento da população do Império do Brasil a que se procedeu no dia 1 de agosto de 1872* (Rio de Janeiro, 1873–76).

Table 2   Population of Southern States and Brazil, 1920

Region	Brazilians		Foreigners		Total
São Paulo	3,762,337	82%	829,851	18%	4,592,188
Paraná	622,958	91%	62,753	9%	685,711
Santa Catarina	637,500	95%	31,243	5%	668,743
Rio Grande do Sul	2,031,688	93%	151,025	7%	2,182,713
Total	7,054,483	87%	1,074,872	13%	8,129,355
All Brazil	29,069,644	95%	1,565,961	5%	30,635,605

Source: Brasil, Diretoria Geral de Estatística, *Recenseamento do Brasil realizado em 1 de setembro de 1920* (Rio de Janeiro, 1922–30).

states were 548 percent for São Paulo, 541 percent for Paraná, 418 percent for Santa Catarina, and 500 percent for Rio Grande do Sul. For all but Santa Catarina, the increase in the foreign-born population over 1872 was quite phenomenal, and the number of immigrants in the southern four states together had increased 1,182 percent since 1872. The southern four states had 23 percent of Brazil's foreign-born population in 1872 and 69 percent by 1920.

In the years between the censuses in tables 1 and 2 from 1872 to 1919, some 3.3 million immigrants were recorded as entering Brazil. São Paulo alone received over 1.7 million, or 54 percent of the national total. From 1893 through 1929, 1.3 million people were sent from São Paulo's immigrant receiving station directly to jobs in the western plateau coffee zone.[10]

The Paulista coffee planter elite had set up the program for recruiting and transporting immigrant families to provide a labor force for the plantations of the interior plateau of the state—first to replace slaves and then to make possible expansion on the western frontier. To understand the fate of immigrants on the plantations and their contribution to the agricultural development of São Paulo, it is necessary to examine the unique system of labor organization that the Paulista planters developed by trial and error between the 1850s and the late 1880s and that became standard in western São Paulo until the dislocation and retrenchment of the Great Depression. The workers in this system were called *colonos*, but the term has its origin in the *colonus*, the farm laborer of ancient Rome, rather than in the colonization of New World territories. Thus the colono of the São Paulo coffee plantation should not be confused with the immigrant smallholder of the southern three states. There is little evidence of significant internal migration of foreigners within Brazil between São Paulo and the farm colonies of the far south. The socioeconomic environments and the historical legacies of the two are quite distinct.

Variations in the details of the colono labor system from region to region and over time responded to changes in the labor market, the world coffee market, and natural conditions, but the essential features of the colono contract were similar. Each colono family agreed to keep a certain number of coffee plants free of weeds through the year, ranging from a minimum of two thousand if only one worker was available to perhaps as many as fifteen thousand if several members of the family were of working age. Contemporary studies calculated an average of some five thousand plants per family. Wages varied considerably and were calculated in proportion to other forms of income. Colonos might be allowed to use more plantation land to raise subsistence crops, for example, and might receive lower cultivation wages than on a neighboring plantation where less free land was provided. The annual cultivation wage made up approximately half of the colono family's income, and it did not depend on the size of the crop or the eventual sale price of the coffee harvested.

The other half of the money income came from harvest piecework paid per fifty-liter *alqueire* of coffee berries picked. The harvest period, from May through August, was a slack time in the production cycle of such food crops as corn and beans, and the colono families mobilized all available labor power to pick coffee. Unlike the income from cultivation, the harvest portion of the colono family's income fluctuated considerably from year to year as a result of variations in the total yield. By paying for the harvest at a piece rate, the planters kept their per unit harvest costs fixed and built maximum incentive into the system. A third but much less important source of money was miscellaneous day labor around the plantation.

Essential parts of the total income "package" of the colono contract were housing, often including space for a vegetable garden; permission to plant subsistence crops either between the rows of coffee or in separate plots; and the use of plantation land as a common pasture for domestic animals. It should be emphasized that the immigrant family paid no rent—in money, produce, or labor—in return for these nonmonetary provisions of the colono contract. The house, plot, and pasture were considered separate from and in addition to the money payments from cultivation and harvesting. Land was an abundant resource in the coffee complex of São Paulo, and the plots allotted to colonos were usually in the valley bottoms of the rolling terrain of the plateau, where coffee did poorly. By using his land in this way the coffee planter could offer incentives to workers and keep his monetary wage bill lower than it otherwise might have been. On a regional level, this system solved the potential problem of how to supply and what to feed the labor force while allowing the planter elite to concentrate on coffee production for export.

The contracts were renegotiated annually, at the end of the coffee production cycle in November or December. At that time the colono could contract to care for more or fewer trees, or he could move on. Many did move—further toward the frontier, to the city of São Paulo, or back to their homeland. An Italian journalist in 1891 summed up the colono's attitude in the following way: "Your employer does not satisfy you, or you don't like the plantation? Change employers. The employer is satisfactory and you recognize the plantation is a good one? Go in search of a better one."[11] The "nomadism" of the immigrant labor force was a constant preoccupation of the coffee planters, but as long as immigration continued and they could hire newly arrived families at the receiving station, the high rate of labor turnover did not seriously disrupt the coffee industry as a whole.

Because the colono families were allowed to keep the production of the food plots, in many cases the sale of surplus cereals and livestock products in regional markets provided an important source of cash. Such extra income could be added to savings or used to buy the items not produced on the plantation, such as wheat flour, salt, sugar, kerosene, clothing, and tools. As an example of the significance the immigrants themselves attached to the nonmonetary portions of the labor contract, a French analyst noted in 1909 that "what really enables the colonists to make both ends meet is the crops they have the right to raise on their own account. . . . They often think more of the clauses in their contract which relate to these crops than to those which determine their wages in currency.[12] A Paulista expert noted in 1902 that coffee work, from the colono's point of view, symbolized "meager, disputed, and at times uncertain wages." Corn, on the other hand, symbolized abundance and well-being. It meant polenta (the cornmeal staple of the Italian immigrant's diet), feed for chickens, plenty of eggs, fat pigs, and salt pork. From the sale of his excess food products he bought clothing, wine, and other needs.[13] Italian consular officials, often sharply critical of the negative aspects of the colono's existence, repeatedly noted the importance of the food crop and pasture provisions of the colono contract.

The potential advantages the colono contract offered the immigrant worker included the reasonable assurance of a minimum annual income, the reduction of living expenses through free housing and near self-sufficiency in food production, the possibility of accumulating savings through money income and low cash expenses, and the possibility of maximizing family income by pooling the labor of all members. The same combination of potential advantages was not to be found in other plantation labor systems. The coffee colono's lot contrasted clearly with that of the slave in earlier times and with that of the resident laborer—variously known as the *morador*, *agregado*, and *parceiro*—in other parts of rural Brazil in the post-slavery era. It also contrasts with the make-or-break self-sufficiency of the southern immigrant farm colonies.

The term "potential" is used advisedly. The inability or refusal of the planter to pay wages as contracted, the destruction of a harvest by frost, or a large debt to the employer could reduce or eliminate the colono's money income. An immigrant family with many mouths to feed and few able-bodied workers was at a considerable disadvantage. Prolonged illness might reduce the family's earning capacity, and professional medical care was either nonexistent or prohibitively expensive, particularly in isolated frontier areas. The historic lot of rural workers has been unenviable anywhere in the world, and immigrant coffee colonos suffered economic exploitation, misery, and the authoritarian whim of the landlord along with the meager opportunities provided by the specifics of the colono system and the mobile labor market of the São Paulo coffee zone.

The granting of "concessions" did not necessarily involve a reduction in the planter's potential profit or an increase in his wage bill. In establishing the provisions of the colono contract, the planters created incentives through an acceptable distribution of risk and a rational allocation of the resources at their disposal, particularly abundant land, rather than through a simple distribution of income in the workers' favor. No benevolent paternalism or altruism was involved, much less adherence to time-honored routine. The colono contract should not be confused with tenant farming, renting, or sharecropping. It was also not strictly a wage system, in the sense of a unit of pay per unit of time worked. In economic terms, the colono was a wage earner, a subsistence farmer, a producer of agricultural commodities, and a consumer all at the same time.[14]

It would be idealistic to conclude that all or even most immigrant workers in the São Paulo coffee zone achieved their dreams or were successful economically. Nevertheless, a clear conclusion from analyzing this historical complex is that a significant number of first-generation immigrants were able to acquire land and become coffee producers, albeit predominantly on a small and medium scale, in the heart of São Paulo's coffee-producing region. By 1905 immigrants owned more than 20 percent of the agricultural properties in the western plateau (some 6,500 of a total 31,000 farms). In 1920 they owned over 21,000 farms in São Paulo, or 28 percent of the rural properties in the entire state. In 1923 immigrants owned 42 percent of the coffee farms in the western plateau of São Paulo, or nearly 13,000 producing units, although the average size was about half that of Brazilian-owned coffee farms. By 1934 the foreign-born were numerically predominant in the ownership of small and medium-sized coffee farms in São Paulo, while Brazilians retained ownership of most large plantations.[15] By the last date, many "native Brazilian" landowners were in fact second-generation immigrants.

The period 1880–1920 was one of rapid frontier expansion and dynamic economic growth, and many immigrants could enjoy upward mobility without threatening the position of the native planter class. Upward mobility was hardly a universal phenomenon for immigrant coffee plantation workers, of course, nor does anyone expect it to have been. On the contrary, a common assumption has been that upward mobility in agriculture was blocked by the dominant Brazilian planters, with their supposed control over rural resources, particularly land. Land was abundant in the frontier environment, however, and immigrants with nest eggs could acquire farms without threatening the large holdings of the Paulista planter elite. The ex-slaves and native peasantry, it should be noted, were in large measure marginalized and excluded from the opportunities that some immigrant workers were able to take advantage of.

Unusual in the history of tropical export agriculture, there developed a middle stratum of producers, predominantly immigrants, many of whom had started out replacing slaves in the most menial of rural occupations—wielding a hoe.

The career of Geremia Lunardelli, the most phenomenal success among Italian plantation workers, illustrates the general change in São Paulo's rural social structure. Lunardelli arrived in São Paulo from Veneto in 1886, a child of one year. His family engaged in plantation work, and in 1904 he bought his first farm, in partnership with a brother and several other relatives. By 1927 he had become the "King of Coffee," owning more producing trees than anyone else in the world. He built his principal financial base during the second decade of this century not as a planter, however, but as a coffee middleman, buying small quantities from the many immigrants who had by that time become coffee producers but had no traditional links with established coffee brokerage houses.[16] Lunardelli's career can by no means be considered typical, but the economic "niche" he occupied—providing a necessary commercial service for his countrymen who had become coffee farmers—provides indirect evidence of emergence of a rural middle class of immigrant origins.

These results of a complex historical process were far from the original and continuing expectations of those Paulista planters and political leaders who promoted the immigration program and funded it through state subsidies. The São Paulo elite formulated no geopolitical strategy of populating border areas. While the native plantocracy saw most any European immigrant as better racial stock than the ex-slave or mixed-race peasant, they hardly considered Italians or other southern Europeans as much of an improvement. Germans came in some numbers over the decades, but other "preferred" groups of northern Europeans went primarily to North America.

The motivation for the entire immigration program of São Paulo, from its inception as a way to replace slaves in the abolition crisis of the 1880s to its demise with the Great Depression and the concurrent disruption of the coffee industry, was to provide a labor force for the plantations. Officials actively discouraged any deflection of the immigrant stream into other pursuits or any leak in the channels for transporting people from the ships in the port of Santos by train up to the city of São Paulo, where they were processed through the receiving station, contracted, and shipped out to the western coffee zone.

These efforts would not have been necessary had there been no opportunities for new arrivals other than employment in the coffee groves. In fact, the cities of São Paulo, particularly the state capital itself, boomed along with the coffee industry in these years.[17] As long as the overall labor needs of the plantations were satisfied by the system, however, no more stringent controls on the immigrants' freedom of action were imposed. From 1887 through 1900 some 80 percent of the immigrants to São Paulo had their passages subsidized by the state government. In the following decade the equivalent figure dropped to about one-third, and the proportion subsidized continued to decline slowly until the program ended in 1928. Immigration officials could closely regulate the first destinations of those sponsored by the state, but in March 1902 the Italian government prohibited emigration to Brazil under this program (the Prinetti Decree). Thus few of the Italians arriving in São Paulo after mid-1902 were subject to the restrictions that went with subsidized passage. Many continued to seek employment on coffee plantations, following the well-established pattern, but many others went directly into urban occupations.

In the period 1882–1930, for which data by nationality are reasonably consistent, just over one million Italians entered São Paulo. Following the Italians, in numbers and chronologically, were immigrants from Spain, with 388,000 in the same period. Little noticed in the historical literature and in the popular image of the "typical" immigrant, their history yet to be written, the Spaniards joined the Italians in the coffee zone, as well as in a variety of other occupations. Portuguese immigration also continued to be significant, although the Portuguese preferred such urban occupations as small commerce and artisan activities, and stevedoring in the port of Santos. Just over four hundred thousand Portuguese entered São Paulo from 1882 to 1930.

Another significant São Paulo group not usually identified with coffee plantation labor is the Syrian-Lebanese, who began arriving before World War I, when many were seeking an alternative to the oppression of Ottoman rule in their homelands. By the nationality of their passports they were labelled *turcos*, although very few immigrants from the Turkish Empire were ethnic Turks. The Syrian-Lebanese were identified historically with the figure of the itinerant peddler, or *mascate*, and later many entered the more sedentary dry-goods business. They are also credited with introducing the ethnic cuisine of their homelands into the cosmopolitan cultural mix of São Paulo. Nearly forty thousand of this group came in, primarily after 1910.

In 1908 an experiment began that makes it necessary to qualify all general references to "European" immigration. In that year 800 Japanese arrived, contracted to work the coffee plantations. This initial effort to bring Asians to Brazil was nearly a total disaster. "Culture shock" might be an appropriate general label for the problem, but more specifically there were misunderstandings about promised living and working conditions, compounded by a nearly impermeable language barrier and an inflexibility or unwillingness on the part of the Brazilian employers to ease the transition for the Japanese. Moreover, the first groups were composed primarily of single males, and the colono contract labor system functioned well only if families hired their labor power as a unit. Japanese immigration was sporadic until after the First World War. By the early 1930s more than one hundred thousand Japanese had arrived, creating the base for the largest concentration of people of Japanese descent outside the islands themselves.[18]

Japanese farmers popularized the system of renting farm plots from the landowner, rather than simply accepting the colono contract still dominant in the 1920s. Again, fundamental cultural differences played a role in their success. Landowners rented to the Japanese for a sum calculated from the return the Brazilian might hope to get from the plot, based on traditional extensive use of the land and rudimentary techniques inherited from the days of slavery. The Japanese, on the other hand, applied highly intensive techniques, often getting a considerably higher return for their effort than the rental fee. When after a few years the soil was exhausted by the intensive, Asian-style cultivation, the Japanese renter was able to repeat the operation in another location, usually in the direction of the frontier, leaving the hapless landowner with a few years of rent and exhausted land.

The rural labor force enjoyed considerable geographical mobility, including movement to the regional market towns of the western plateau and back to the state capital or to the country of origin. While a significant number of immigrants accumulated enough savings to set themselves up as small farmers, many others took their savings into urban occupations. Other former plantation workers opted for city life in economic desperation or to escape the isolation and monotony of a rural existence. In any case, the "nomadism" of the rural labor force was a constant complaint of the planters and their political representatives, and the state continued to import new workers to make up for the steady attrition due to migration.

The regional economy of São Paulo, fueled by the coffee export sector, was dynamic, flexible, changing. Change was not always for the better, either for planters or immigrant workers. Periods of boom and expansion were followed by times of low prices and dislocation, and by the first decade of the twentieth century chronic overproduction plagued the coffee industry. If a single term had to be chosen to characterize the coffee economy and the society built upon it, "mobility" would be the most appropriate. It would be an exaggeration to conjure up an image of a seething mass of humanity ebbing and flowing with the tides of the export economy, but relative to other regions of Brazil there was geographical mobility of both planters and workers in this frontier society. The immigrants so dominant in the coffee plantation labor force from the abolition of slavery to the depression of the 1930s were by definition mobile, on the make. Some made it and many did not, but upward mobility also became a significant feature of this system. An increasing number of immigrants who continued to arrive over the years became landowners. Thus there was a "demonstration effect," an illusion of opportunity and upward mobility perhaps as significant in the collective attitudes of immigrants as the already impressive reality.

As the agrarian society of São Paulo grew in size and complexity from 1888 to the depression, Paulista planters were supplemented rather than replaced by the entry of immigrants into the lower levels of the landholding group. To the extent that the acquisition of rural property by immigrants can be considered social mobility, then, they manifested structural mobility rather than exchange mobility. Instead of a revolutionary destruction of the old order, a process of accretion and evolutionary change took place over several decades.

The native planters adopted the colono system and developed a program for importing manpower, which facilitated the transition to free labor and the subsequent growth of the coffee industry. In so doing they helped ensure their own survival as an economic group and maintained political hegemony for several more decades. But as the twentieth century wore on, many immigrants moved into the proliferating niches in the socioeconomic system. The Paulista planters found themselves presiding over a transformation of agrarian society that few would have envisioned in the 1880s. Immigrants were essential human elements in that change. They were imported to replace slaves, and they established a place for themselves as landowners and independent farmers in São Paulo's western plateau.

The immigrant areas of southern Brazil contrast with the traditional rural society of the earlier slave era, and the backlands of the more northerly regions. In the former there has been much less time or historical precedent for the crust of social structure to dictate relations between elites and masses. In the specific subculture of the southern farm colonies, the inhabitants, although poor and isolated, did not owe their livelihood to the whim of the *patrão*, did not go hat in hand each season to reconfirm the exploitative relationship between those who ruled and those who obeyed. In political life the immigrants stuck to themselves, and very few members of the first generation became naturalized Brazilian citizens. Although political bossism characterized state level politics in the south as elsewhere, a complex of powerful political families did not dominate local regions generation after generation. The colonies were in new areas, where clientelistic politics and patriarchal social relations— dominant features of traditional rural life in Brazil—did not establish themselves quickly or completely.

In the plantations of São Paulo the colonos were certainly under the arbitrary authority of the landowner or his agents, but here an abundant, mobile work force and an active, expanding labor market gave individual workers some alternatives to continued submission and subservience. They had not left their homelands intending to sink roots in a specific locale or submit to an inflexible and demeaning relationship with the lord of the land. Immigrant workers had every reason to move from place to place, particularly in the expanding frontier and the fast-growing cities, in search for the best situation they could find.

Very few members of the immigrant masses joined the elites, but the remainder did not accept the idea that they were by nature and custom subordinate to the power of the elites. The capitalistic planters, for their part, achieved their general goal of obtaining an abundant and relatively inexpensive labor force by continuing to promote immigration. Like their workers, they had little motivation for creating a labor system that tied both them and their resident laborers into a patron-client relationship. The native elites also had little notion of the social and cultural changes their settlement and labor policies would bring to that part of Brazil. Immigrants in São Paulo were much more involved with the larger society than those in the southern colonies, and much less of an identifiable ethnic subculture developed and persisted after the first generation. Again, the exception was the Japanese, who arrived later and retained racial, linguistic, and cultural distinctiveness to a greater degree than the other large immigrant groups.

Since the watershed of the depression of the 1930s and the wartime disruption of the 1940s, southern Brazil has changed considerably. The agricultural complex has modernized rapidly, with wheat, soybeans, citrus and a new sugar boom surpassing the traditional emphasis on coffee for export and subsistence crops for local consumption. Northern Paraná saw a coffee boom in the 1950s that was a geographical extension of the earlier move into western São Paulo.[19] Many of the coffee farmers in this new era were the descendants of immigrant colonos, but the labor force, as in São Paulo in the postwar era, was made up increasingly of internal migrants from the Brazilian Northeast. Such workers now form a rural proletariat in the São Paulo/northern Paraná zone of commercial agriculture, unable to gain subsistence from plots they work themselves and forced to sell their labor in a fully monetized system of wage labor. Similarly, family farms in the southern colonial zones are much more dependent on external capital and markets, and the relative loss of self-sufficiency is the price of fuller participation in the general economic growth of southern Brazil.

Another major change of the postwar period has been industrialization and rural-urban migration, particularly in São Paulo but to some degree throughout the South. Economic development and the accompanying social change have made the region the destination of migrants from points north seeking opportunities that for many have proved illusory. These shifts have, in a sense, reintroduced "Brazilian" ethnic stock and cultural traditions into the South, after the high point of foreign immigration that lasted from the 1870s to the 1930s. The result is an even more complex society, where the descendants of native Americans, Africans, Asians, and people from many parts of Europe and the Mediterranean—with all degrees of admixture of recent and remote origin—form a society as ethnically diverse as one can find anywhere in the world.

Notes

1. Although the official scheme of regionalization of Brazil includes São Paulo in the Southeast along with Rio de Janeiro, Minas Gerais, and Espirito Santo, there is considerable rationale for including it with the South for the purpose of studying the historical impact of immigration.

2. The classic monograph on the coffee era in Rio de Janeiro province is Stanley J. Stein, *Vassouras: a Brazilian Coffee County, 1850–1900* (Cambridge, Mass.: Harvard University Press, 1957). A parallel study set in the São Paulo west is Warren Dean, *Rio Claro, A Brazilian Plantation System, 1820–1920* (Stanford: Stanford University Press, 1976).

3. Although colonization projects were attempted in other areas, few were successful outside the South. In Espirito Santo several hundred Europeans were settled during the period under consideration. Minas Gerais state tried to attract immigrants but largely failed. The only area outside the southern four states to attract demographically important numbers of immigrants was the city of Rio de Janeiro and its environs.

4. An analysis of the early São Paulo efforts is by José de Souza Martins, *A imigração e a crise do Brasil agrário* (São Paulo: Pioneira, 1973).

5. Altiva Pilatti Balhana, "Mudança na estrutura agrária dos Campos Gerais," *Boletim da Universidade do Paraná, Departamento de História* 3 (June 1963), 28–52.

6. Thales de Azevedo, *Italianos e gaúchos: Os anos pioneiros da colonização italiana no Rio Grande do Sul* (Porto Alegre: A Nação, 1975), p. 272; José Vicente Tavares dos Santos, *Colonos do vinho: Estudo sobre a subordinação do trabalho camponês ao capital* (São Paulo: Hucitec, 1978), pp. 51–54.

7. Altiva Pilatti Balhana, *Santa Felicidade, uma paróquia vêneta no Brasil* (Curitiba: Fundação Cultural, 1978); Instituto Superior Brasileiro-italiano de Estudos e Pesquisas, *Imigração italiana: Estudos* (Caxias do Sul: Escola

Superior de Teologia São Lourenço de Brindes, 1979); José Decanal and Sergius Gonzaga, eds., RS: Imigração e colonização (Porto Alegre: Mercado Aberto, 1980).

8. Thomas H. Holloway, Immigrants on the Land: Coffee and Society in São Paulo, 1886–1934 (Chapel Hill: University of North Carolina Press, 1980), p. 179. For an overview of Brazil's economic demography, including analysis of the impact of immigration and comparisons with Argentina and the U.S., see Thomas W. Merrick and Douglas H. Graham, Population and Economic Development in Brazil, 1800 to the Present (Baltimore: Johns Hopkins University Press, 1979), esp. chapter 5.

9. Thomas H. Holloway, "Immigration and Abolition: The Transition from Slave to Free Labor in the São Paulo Coffee Zone," in Essays Concerning the Socioeconomic History of Brazil and Portuguese India, ed. Dauril Alden and Warren Dean (Gainesville: University Presses of Florida, 1977), pp. 150–77.

10. For national data, see Arthur H. Neiva and J. Fernando Carneiro, "Ligeiras notas a respeito do quadro da imigração no Brasil a partir de 1820," Boletim Geográfico 8, no. 91 (October 1950): 845–46. For São Paulo, see Holloway, Immigrants on the Land, pp. 179–81.

11. Arrigo de Zettiry, "I coloni italiani dello stato di S. Paulo," Rassegna Nazionale 70 (March 1, 1893), p. 89.

12. Pierre Denis, Brazil, trans. Bernard Miall (New York: T. F. Unwin, 1911), pp. 202–3.

13. Augusto Ramos, "Questões agrícolas," Revista Agricola de São Paulo (1902), pp. 26–28.

14. Holloway, Immigrants on the Land, pp. 35–110 and passim.

15. Ibid., pp. 148–63.

16. L. V. Giovannetti, O "Rei do Café"—Geremia Lunardelli (São Paulo: n.p., 1951).

17. The most comprehensive study of São Paulo in this period, from the political, social, and economic perspectives, is Joseph Love, São Paulo in the Brazilian Federation, 1889–1937 (Stanford: Stanford University Press, 1980). See also Warren Dean, The Industrialization of São Paulo, 1880–1945 (Austin: University of Texas Press, 1969).

18. Also in the 1920s some 90,000 northern and eastern Europeans, including 20,000 each of Lithuanians and Rumanians and 28,500 Germans, arrived in São Paulo. The immigration data by principal nationality are collected in Thomas H. Holloway, "Migration and Mobility: Immigrants as Laborers and Landowners in the Coffee Zone of São Paulo, Brazil, 1886–1934" (Ph.D. diss., University of Wisconsin, Madison, 1974), pp. 185, 198.

19. Maxine L. Margolis, The Moving Frontier (Gainesville: University of Florida Press, 1973).

Michael M. Hall and Marco Aurélio Garcia

Urban Labor

Urban workers emerged as an important force in Brazilian life toward the end of the nineteenth century. Although the country remained overwhelmingly rural, several cities had attained considerable size. Rio de Janeiro, with a population of some 520,000 in 1890, was the second largest city in Latin America (and the fifth in the Western Hemisphere). Some craftsmen and skilled workers had established organizations to defend their interests rather early, and in 1858 the Rio de Janeiro typographers had even stopped work to demand higher wages. Large-scale strikes, trade unions, and a distinct working-class press, however, all date largely from the 1890s.

The Old Republic

The coffee export sector dominated the early economy, though overproduction in the mid-1890s provoked a marked decline in world coffee prices. Brazil's capacity to import fell sharply, and local industry began to produce a variety of goods previously supplied from abroad. During the First World War, with international trade difficult and the major manufacturinng nations otherwise occupied, Brazilian industrial production increased substantially.

The 1920 census reported 275,000 factory workers, though the average number per firm—21—indicated that many were employed in rather small workshops. Of the total, about half worked in the Federal District (Rio de Janeiro) or the state of São Paulo, with some 40 percent employed in the textile industry. The number working in

Michael Hall wrote the pre-1945 sections and Marco Aurélio Garcia those for the subsequent period.

enterprises too small to meet the census definition of factory (or in the construction and transport sectors) is difficult to determine, but a figure of slightly over one million urban workers is probably not far from the mark. The figure for those engaged in agriculture was 6.3 million.[1]

In addition to its vulnerability to world market fluctuations, another aspect of the Old Republic's economy should be mentioned. As the reader will recall from Thomas Holloway's chapter, the government maintained an extensive program to subsidize foreign immigration, initially from Italy but eventually from several other European countries and Japan, to provide cheap labor for the coffee plantations. In practice, many immigrants fled grim working conditions in the countryside and flooded the labor markets of São Paulo and other cities. The labor movement regarded the system of subsidized immigration, and the consequent ready supply of workers it provided, as an almost insurmountable obstacle to successful strikes and to the formation of strong trade unions. As the Italian-born journalist and anarchist militant Gigi Damiani put it in 1920 (after he had been expelled from the country): "Those who rule Brazil on behalf of the industrialists and their rural partners need always to fill the labor market with a plethora of workers. With this plethora they intend to be able to maintain starvation wages and prison hours and to destroy class organizations." Damiani concluded that the only way to improve the situation would be to interrupt immigration.[2] In fact, the periods of effective labor organization and greatest working-class activity before the 1920s coincided with declines or interruptions in large-scale immigration: 1906–08, 1911–12, 1917–19.

Workers faced uncompromising factory owners and businessmen. Although somewhat divided among themselves on account of divergent sectoral interests and varied national origins, business groups usually managed to present a common front in conflicts with their workers. Because wages usually represented a large part of total costs and because competition restricted the passing of higher labor costs along to consumers, industrialists generally were intransigent in dealing with workers' demands. Employers routinely fired workers for engaging in strikes or for joining trade unions. In addition, industrialists could call upon various forms of government repression against the labor movement.

In theory, the policy of the federal government before 1930 was to allow the free play of economic forces. In fact, it intervened in a number of areas. It controlled the labor supply by subsidizing immigration, effectively maintaining low wages and weakening the labor movement. And the federal government deported several hundred immigrant militants over the years on the grounds that foreign agitators were responsible for growing labor unrest.

Extensive state violence played an important role. While Brazil did not witness outright massacres of striking workers, such as occurred in Chile or Mexico during the first decades of the century, the savage and widespread employment of physical force impressed virtually all observers. As the Italian consul in São Paulo remarked in 1909, the police were "violent and aggressive, which is not surprising when one considers that their chief, and in general rather cultivated and calm people here, hardly distinguish between strikes and revolts."[3]

Even a conservative Brazilian writer, José Maria dos Santos, thought that "habits of grossness and unlimited brutality that particularly characterize our police in their relations with the poor" had become common by the early twentieth century. He observed that "police imprisonment, without legal charges, for an indeterminate period, made worse by the application of physical abuses, became the usual means of instilling good conduct. . . . The process of purging the proletarian milieu by deportations to distant locations was permitted as normal, even when there had been no disturbance of public order."[4] A famous phrase of the period noted that "the social question in Brazil is one for the police." While the attribution to President Washington Luíz (1926–30) may be apocryphal, the remark accurately describes state policy before the 1920s.

Divisions of various kinds within the working class also posed serious obstacles to effective and unified action. Workers employed in tasks essential to export agriculture, notably on the railroads and in the ports, enjoyed a stronger bargaining position than those in most other activities, although their strategic position in the economy also made them more subject to the full force of state control. Skilled craftsmen in construction and other trades could usually bargain more effectively than the easily replaceable women and children employed in the textile industry, and such segmentation made attempts at broader organization difficult.

The ethnic composition of the working class varied considerably from one part of the country to another. European immigrants, primarily from Italy, Spain, and Portugal, long dominated the São Paulo working class. In Santos and Rio de Janeiro, the foreign-born (principally Portuguese) formed a highly significant, though less overwhelming, part of the labor force. In both cities, as in much of the Northeast, African-born former slaves and their descendants also made up a very important contingent.

This ethnic diversity, which employers were quick to exploit, hindered cooperation among workers. The Italian-language newspaper *Il Pungolo* of São Paulo described the matter in 1909: "the great working-class collectivity is divided and subdivided . . . there is latent warfare in the very heart of the proletariat . . . whites, blacks, yellows. . . . Italy is united, free and independent, but I am Piedmontese, you are Tuscan, others are Sicilian, Calabrian, Venetian, Lombard, and so on and we don't even understand one another among ourselves."[5] For decades such ethnic hostilities, prejudices, and cultural differences caused strikes to be lost and labor organizations to be weakened or destroyed.

Observers described workers' living conditions with dismay. Public services lagged far behind the rapid population growth in the larger cities. Severe overcrowding, contaminated water supplies, and inadequate sanitation contributed to grave public health problems. Particularly in the 1890s, Rio de Janeiro became notorious throughout the world for its high incidence of yellow fever, smallpox, and malaria; Santos and the Northeastern coastal cities were hardly better. A very large part of the working class lived in sordid slum dwellings known as *cortiços* (literally, beehives). Rent for space in these crowded and unhealthy buildings absorbed a substantial part of the workers' pay.

Working conditions were also grim. The amount of arbitrary force and physical violence in the day-to-day operations of factories often provoked observers to describe them as places of punishment and confinement. "The textile factories are real prisons," a São Paulo labor newspaper commented. "Discipline in them is unbending and ferocious, no complaint from the workers is permitted. The supervisors of the factories are in general real bastards, very barbarous toward the workers." Another such newspaper pictured the factories as "[slave] galleys and some are worse." *Avanti!* said that conditions at one plant recalled "the regime of slavery."[6]

While a certain amount of rhetorical flourish may well be present in many such characterizations, the specific cases recounted are often quite poignant and persuasive: "You can't even exchange a few words, whistle, sing . . . especially at the Abílio Soares and Co. hat factory on the Rua Direito . . . the owners have sent a letter to those very humble ass-lickers, the foremen of the fulling and shaping section, recommending severity toward the workers and the imposition of silence, upon pain of a severe fine for the first offense and dismissal thereafter." Discharged workers could expect to be blacklisted with potential employers. Accounts of owners and foremen using physical violence and abuse against their workers also appeared quite regularly in the labor press. In a 1919 strike at a jute sack factory, the workers demanded an end to the beating of the children who worked there.[7] Physical violence against women, a majority of workers in the textile industry and clothing trades, often took the form of sexual abuse and accompanied other types of exploitation such as substantially lower pay than men for the same work.

The recentness of industrialization, combined with the newness and the predominantly foreign origins of the working class, made it difficult for industrialists to maintain control without high levels of overt violence. The fact that a substantial part of the labor force had been socialized in another culture deprived the factory owners of many of the customary Brazilian mechanisms of social domination. By emigrating, the foreigners had escaped the influence of their own countries' priests, landowners, and police. They had broken the cultural bonds that shaped and controlled their behavior. The establishment of other patterns of subjugation in Brazil—clientelistic or otherwise—proceeded neither rapidly nor smoothly.

The question extended beyond the gates of the factories. In other countries, the appeal to nationalism served to restrain class antagonisms, but in the Brazilian Old Republic, where both workers and employers were so often foreign-born, it was a rather ambiguous device at best. Neither the legal system nor the often farcial electoral process, in which few workers participated, served to legitimate the prevailing social and political order. Rulers, whose domination relies on so few sanctions beyond force and violence, open themselves to some rather brusque surprises.

The first collective attempts by craftsmen and others to protect themselves took the form of mutual aid societies, which sought to provide benefits in cases of accident, illness, or death. A few such

societies gradually came to take on recognizable trade union functions, but most of the emerging unions ("resistance societies," in the
terminology of the era) grew out of specific struggles and strikes.
Quite often in Brazil, unions adopted some ideas and tactics associated with anarcho-syndicalism. Militant workers at the turn of the
century in various parts of the world had developed these notions in
reaction to the growing reformism of the socialist parties. While
anarcho-syndicalism shared with anarchism the revolutionary ob-
jective of destroying the state, it rejected anarchist methods as ineffective and tended to appeal to industrial workers because it was
based on the trade union rather than on the utopia of small producers that characterized much early anarchist thought.

Anarcho-syndicalists emphasized above all the idea of direct action. By this, they meant that workers should rely on strikes, sabotage, boycotts, and similar weapons, rather than expecting gains
through laws or government favor. Anarcho-syndicalists argued that
political parties and voting could bring no significant improvements, a view which politics in the Old Republic only strengthened.
The trade union was to serve as both the main weapon in the
struggle to destroy the state and as the basis for a new society.

Anarcho-syndicalists said that they expected to destroy the existing order by means of a revolutionary general strike. For some this
was to take the form of a mass armed rising, while others envisioned
a relatively peaceful movement, so widespread as to be invulnerable
to repression. Although anarcho-syndicalists usually insisted that
strikes for limited economic objectives could not secure lasting
improvements, in practice they tended to support strikes of this sort
on the grounds that during such struggles workers could develop a
spirit of solidarity and militancy, and prepare themselves for future
revolutionary action.

The real influence of anarcho-syndicalism remains difficult to
evaluate. While a large number of unions, at least until the early
1920s, formally upheld such doctrines, only a small part of the
working class belonged to unions. In practice, leaders of anarcho-
syndicalist unions negotiated with the state or otherwise violated
movement doctrine on many occasions. Nevertheless, the anarcho-
syndicalist leadership clearly mobilized a substantial part of the
working class in the course of several general strikes and other
actions. The two national labor congresses in 1906 and 1913 endorsed anarcho-syndicalist positions, and the movement's news-

papers and other activities enjoyed wide working-class support. A large segment of the working class during the first two decades of the century, particularly in São Paulo, supported at least some anarcho-syndicalist theories, leaders, and organizations.

Reformist and conservative trade unions, which their enemies called "yellow unions," came to be the largest element in the labor movement of Rio de Janeiro. These unions, particularly strong among the city's transportation and dock workers, concentrated on securing immediate economic goals and had no qualms about collaboration with the government or politicians when this appeared to advance their interests. In other parts of the country, similar unions were also quite influential.

Unions in any case remained fragile, as workers organized and expanded them during favorable moments in the economic cycle only to see them disappear when unemployment (or persecution) grew. Early in the century, strikes tended to be largely spontaneous and defensive, as workers attempted to prevent wage cuts, firings, or abuses by foremen. Despite immense difficulties, some strikes spread beyond small groups with specific demands to mobilize impressive numbers of workers. In Rio de Janeiro, for example, a stoppage in 1903 among textile workers seeking increased pay and a shorter workday, spread to other trades and soon led to the country's first citywide general strike. The strikers, who numbered some forty thousand at the movement's peak, virtually paralyzed the capital for twenty days.

The first São Paulo general strike broke out in 1906, when employees of one of the major railroads stopped work to protest management abuses. As the strike spread, the state government moved to suppress it with notable brutality. Significantly, that year the São Paulo authorities concluded negotiations to hire French army officers to turn the state's militarized police into a small army.

In 1907, skilled workers in various São Paulo trades took advantage of an expanding economy and organized a successful general strike in which many secured an eight-hour day. When the economy took a downturn soon thereafter, however, owners were able to increase the workday once again, and most of the newly formed unions disappeared. Workers halted the port of Santos in 1905, 1908, and 1912 but secured few tangible gains in the face of government repression and the intransigence of the monopoly that ran the port. Despite renewed activity in many cities during 1912–13, the labor movement as a whole was able to begin expanding again only toward the end of the First World War.

The general strikes that swept the major Brazilian cities between 1917 and 1920 owed much to the specific economic dislocations of those years, but also more than a little to the inspiration that many workers drew from the revolutionary movements then underway in various parts of Europe. In the midst of severe economic hardship, a strike in São Paulo in July 1917 over a pay dispute at a textile factory soon spread to other firms. After the police killed a demonstrator, the passage of his funeral procession through the city, accompanied by 10,000 workers, set off a general strike. Over 50,000 people stopped work, and crowds looted warehouses, bakeries, and other stores. For several days workers virtually took control of the city, and various incidents raised the possibility of serious insubordination among the police and troops. Workers formed a Proletarian Defense Committee which presented a lengthy list of demands including pay increases, the eight-hour day, the prohibition of child labor, and measures to lower food prices and rents. The strike ended when most firms agreed to a twenty-percent pay raise and to take no reprisals against the strikers. The movement spread to the interior of the state and helped touch off a general strike in Rio de Janeiro. There workers won concessions and embarked on drives to unionize various sectors. Not only had the scope of the July 1917 strikes caught the various levels of government unawares, but the subsequent large-scale expansion of union activity seriously alarmed industrialists and their allies.

In August and September 1917, police broke up strikes and public meetings, with injury to workers, in Recife, Rio de Janeiro, and Porto Alegre. In the latter month, with the repressive apparatus reinforced, the police began to close unions, carry out extensive arrests, and deport a number of foreign-born militants. They also closed down most of the labor press and sacked union offices. A shadowy anarchist conspiracy in Rio de Janeiro in November 1918 heightened tension further, and a federal state-of-siege decree facilitated the persecution of the labor movement. General strikes in São Paulo and several other cities during 1919–20 mobilized large numbers of workers but met with increasingly effective and harsh repression.

There is little doubt that many politicians and industrialists had been deeply shaken. Ruy Barbosa, a veteran political figure hardly prone to shocks, confided to the British minister his alarm over the growing disaffection of the urban working classes. The minister reported to London that Ruy Barbosa "attributed the discontent to the spread and sustenance of those doctrines which are associated with the name of Bolshevism which were being fomented and stimulated by foreign anarchists, and unless the movement were controlled by a strong hand he thought it would end in a coalition between the working classes and the troops who were in anything but a state of discipline, in spite of the very large sums of money spent on the army." In 1919, the same diplomat, himself alarmed by the "spread of maximalist doctrines," reported—apparently in all seriousness—that the police had fortunately frustrated an anarchist conspiracy that "was combined with a dynamite plot to sack Petrópolis and carry off the young girls belonging to the best families who are educated at a College in this town."[8]

In general, the mobilizations of 1917–20 led both workers and their opponents to reformulate strategies and tactics. By 1920, the labor movement, in fact, entered a period of retreat that, despite a few isolated victories, lasted most of the decade. Not only had the movement lost many able foreign-born militants through deportations, but growing internal divisions over strategy and tactics left it in considerable disarray. In 1922, a group composed largely of former anarcho-syndicalist militants, dissatisfied with the results of the 1917–20 struggles and inspired by the success of the Bolsheviks, founded the Brazilian Communist Party (PCB). By the end of the decade, despite persecution and factional disputes, the party had begun to play a role of some importance in Rio de Janeiro, where it led several trade unions and succeeded in electing two of its members to the city council. The party also organized an electoral front, the Worker and Peasant Bloc, which enjoyed some success until 1928, when a shift in the Comintern line away from cooperation with noncommunists forced its abandonment.

As noted above, from 1917 onward, state and federal governments and industrial interests undertook a number of timid measures in the area of social reform at the same time that they attempted to strengthen and modernize the instruments of control. The major legislative measure of the period provided some pension and retirement benefits for railroad and dock workers. Laws on accidents, vacations, and child labor proved limited in their effects, however, because of lax enforcement.

The events of 1917 profoundly alarmed Roberto Simonsen, an

engineer and later an important spokesman for industrial interests, who sought another solution. In 1919, he published the first extended Brazilian discussion of Taylorism and the "scientific organization of work" in a pamphlet entitled *Modern Work*. Simonsen hoped through the reorganization of the labor process to avoid "class warfare." He argued, for example, in favor of more widespread use of pay incentives to prevent workers from forming "a hostile mass seeking remedies for their dissatisfaction in political conquests that disturb production." Simonsen claimed that with a proper incentive system, "we will thus have individualized the worker, interesting him directly in production."[9]

During the 1920s the Catholic Church sought to deal with the urban proletariat, establishing a series of publications directed at workers and organizing the Young Catholic Workers, "where young workers learn to acquire an honest and Christian way of life." Without detailed studies, it is difficult to evaluate the effects of such church teachings as the following: "The worker, and principally the working-class home, need an effective example of virtue and labor. None is more appropriate than that offered by the Holy Family— Jesus, Mary, and Joseph. Workers that they were, always uncomplaining, they give to the great laboring class a magnificent example of conformity to the will of Providence, in pain and in happiness."[10]

Toward the end of the 1920s, church organizations, private charities, company-sponsored recreational institutions, and (particularly after 1930) government agencies all sought to establish a more direct influence over working-class life outside the factory. The rhetoric stressed the need to organize "healthier and more productive leisure" for workers; not the least of the objectives was to secure more control over autonomous working-class organizations.

Industrial management groups sought also to improve and extend their methods of planning and surveillance. The case of the leading sector, textiles, is particularly suggestive in this respect. During the 1920s the textile industry's trade association attempted to coordinate policies and practices among the various firms and develop more efficient instruments of control and persecution. The organization's circulars were filled with details concerning the maintenance of effective black lists, instructions on more efficient cooperation with the police in the arrest of militants, plans for common action in the event of strikes, and much more.[11]

Certainly the level of repression continued to attract the attention of foreign observers not usually accused of undue sympathy toward the labor movement. In 1927, Mussolini's consul in São Paulo wrote of the "absolute repression by the Brazilian authorities of any attempt at trade union organization, even the most peaceful." The United States military attaché described a 1929 meeting on the steps of the Municipal Theater in Rio de Janeiro that was addressed by two Communist Party leaders:

> The Rio police never seem to handle such a situation with calmness and moderation, and therefore started clubbing right and left and even used their pistols, although there was no really serious resistance on the part of the communists. Three men were later treated for pistol wounds at the emergency hospital, and numerous others were badly bruised in their enounter with the police. . . . Communism has made but little headway in Brazil and has little prospect of becoming a force to be reckoned with. Its supporters here understand really very little about communist doctrines, but only want to protest against the government.[12]

In short, while the state and industrial interests sought to develop nonviolent means of controlling the working class during the 1920s, for the most part such efforts remained halfhearted. Outright repression, modernized and intensified, still served as the major instrument for the maintenance of a regime whose narrow social base and fragile legitimacy led to its overthrow in the economic crisis of 1930. Following the deposition of Washington Luíz by a military movement under the leadership of dissident groups from the traditional political parties, alarmed at least to some extent by a resurgence of the labor movement in the late 1920s, a significant change occurred in the policy of the state toward labor and social legislation.

Controlled Unionism and the Vargas Era

The incoming regime, led by Getúlio Vargas, embarked on a program that sought to destroy the existing unions and create a system of new ones under state control. Beginning in 1931, the new government set out to establish an elaborate legal and bureaucratic structure, of clearly fascist inspiration, for the working class. The labor system took its final form only in 1943, but its essential features were apparent from the first months of the Vargas government.

The regime quickly established the principle of federal recognition and control of unions. A 1931 decree defined a trade union as an "organ of collaboration" with the government and specified the broad powers to be enjoyed by the newly created Labor Ministry. Not only was the ministry to supervise internal union activities and finances, but it was also empowered to replace union officials with its own appointees and even to close unions for periods of up to six months. The measure further provided that only one union per category would be recognized.

(In 1934, under pressure from the church, which was interested in organizing Catholic unions, the Constituent Assembly, against Vargas's wishes, wrote a form of pluralism into the new constitution. In practice, this attempt at allowing more than one union per category had little success and was eliminated under the Estado Novo in 1939.)

The system provoked intense opposition from the existing unions. Despite considerable repression, as well as measures awarding various benefits solely to members of official unions, the regime encountered stubborn obstacles to imposing its control. The level of overt government violence continued high. In 1934, for instance, a long-time American observer described a police ransacking of a union headquarters and remarked that it was "a typical example of police excess. There was no justification for it, but there will be no redress. In Brazil, certainly in Rio de Janeiro, only the simple appeal for 'police protection'—unless it be protection from the police."[13] Repression even increased following popular mobilization against the regime in 1935. In November of that year, the Communist Party and some military sympathizers rose in a bizarre and easily suppressed revolt that served to justify persecutions.

With the establishment of the dictatorial Estado Novo in November 1937, the Vargas regime began to elaborate the final features of its labor policy. The government classified strikes as crimes, and control over the official unions restricted their functions to the point that they hardly existed at the factory level. Unions came to be grouped in several broad sectors (industry, commerce, overland transportation, etc.), and while each sector could form organizations on state and national levels, no links among the sectors—in the form of a national union federation—were allowed. The financing of the official unions was assured by means of the union tax (later called contribution) of one day's wages per year deducted automatically from each worker's pay. Finally, with the establishment of a system of labor courts, disputes became mere legal and technical questions that the government bureaucracy was to resolve. Strikes were to be not only illegal but theoretically unnecessary.

One of the livelier questions in Brazilian historiography is what workers gained in exchange for the loss of their ability to organize collectively and autonomously. The Vargas regime and its heirs always emphasized the social benefits accorded workers during the 1930–45 period. In the late 1930s, the government reorganized and expanded a rudimentary social security system, limited to certain categories of urban workers, by providing some retirement benefits and health care. The system proved precarious, however, because among other reasons, employers long managed to avoid paying their contribution. A number of the regime's other social measures remained largely on paper or were suspended during the Second World War. The establishment of a minimum wage for urban workers seems to have provided few concrete benefits. In 1939, the United States military attaché quoted members of the commission that had drawn up the minimum wage document to the effect that "a single individual could live with difficulty on this wage but that it is recognized as entirely inadequate for a laborer with even one dependent."[14]

The Vargas government, especially during the Estado Novo, sought to create other instruments of control, particularly ideological ones, by means of carefully orchestrated propaganda on behalf of the powerful notion of state paternalism and protection. One observer said that the Department of Press and Propaganda (DIP) was "the most potent political instrument of the regime, next to the armed forces." The DIP promoted the image of Vargas as the great benefactor of the working class, an "incomparable statesman with the heart to feel and to remedy the necessities of the weak and the unfortunate." It displayed his portrait in public places and staged highly choreographed spectacles in sports stadiums on May Day with ample radio and film coverage.[15]

Despite the long efforts to increase the legitimacy of the state and to widen its ability to intervene nonviolently in labor relations, repressive measures were never far below the surface, particularly as economic conditions worsened toward the end of the war. In January 1945, Euvaldo Lodi, president of the Confederation of Brazilian Industries, wrote to Roberto Simonsen, then president of the Federation of Industries of São Paulo:

It's a good idea to distribute the largest possible number of secret agents and have them in the factories with the largest number of workers. The instructions are always the same: the agent infiltrates the workers' circles, saying that he's a communist, against the government. Then the job is just to take down the names of those who are against us and against the government. The rest is in the hands of the police. . . . We are sitting on top of a volcano.[16]

Democratization and the Brazilian Communist Party

In October 1945, the crisis of the Estado Novo came to a head and the military ended the dictatorship. The chief justice of the Supreme Court occupied the presidency and, after an election, handed over power to Gen. Eurico Gaspar Dutra, war minister of the deposed regime.

The labor movement was involved in the events leading up to the coup d'état. The pretext for it was Vargas's removal of the police chief of the Federal District for prohibiting a large, union-sponsored demonstration that the communist-controlled Workers' Unification Movement (MUT, Movimento Unificador dos Trabalhadores) had organized in Rio de Janeiro. Late in the Estado Novo, some of Vargas's more zealous supporters worked with communists to stage pro-Vargas rallies (called the *queremista* campaign, from their slogan, "*queremos Getúlio*"). This led Vargas's critics to believe that he would seek to remain in power by calling a constituent assembly containing strong trade union representation.

The coup d'état removed Vargas, but the successor regime preserved the Estado Novo's legislation, maintained the corporatist trade union structure, and continued various restrictions on the right to strike.

The last months of the Estado Novo and the period that followed its overthrow witnessed an explosion of social struggles and displays of trade union vigor. This working-class mobilization cannot be attributed solely to the "redemocratization" of the country. Some contemporary observers and later analysts link the end of the Estado Novo to the defeat of Nazism-Fascism. The victory stimulated the liberal bourgeoisie to form an antiregime alliance with military officers who had been influenced in favor of democracy by the experience of fighting against Nazi Germany on the battlefields of Italy.

While this was the broad international and national situation, many pressures were at work. Beginning in 1942, struggles developed outside the official trade union structure in various factories. Stimulating worker unrest was a fall in real wages after the late 1930s; this had accelerated with the adoption of the minimum salary and particularly with the advent of war in 1939. Although Brazilian industry expanded greatly as a result of forced import substitution, the inflationary spiral accompanying it eroded real wages. Initially, the wartime industrial growth stemmed more from the utilization of unused capacity and increased pressure on labor to produce more than from the adoption of technological innovations. The government's labor authorities lengthened the workday (frequently to more than ten hours), abbreviated vacations, totally prohibited strikes, and imposed enormous restrictions—both legal and de facto—on trade union activity.

Nevertheless, working-class resistance to such measures increased after 1943, surely influencing Vargas's desire to use Labor Ministry cooptation of the unions as a means of maintaining his control of a reformed, albeit still corporatist, regime. The various government measures in favor of labor frightened the urban middle classes into approving the military coup d'état of October 1945.

After 1945, the Communist Party (PCB) influenced the direction the labor movement took. The party had emerged from its underground existence with its prestige enhanced, internationally by the Soviet Union's military victories and nationally by the romantic appeal of its secretary-general, *tenente*-turned-communist Luís Carlos Prestes, freed in 1945 after a decade in jail. Prestes's discourse, as well as that of unionists linked to the party, did not emphasize trade union autonomy. On the contrary, faithful to the orientation of the Soviet Union, accentuated in Latin America by Browderism, the PCB sought to include the labor movement in a coalition with what it termed the democratic bourgeoisie, for the democratization of the country.[17]

The communist leaders were so committed to the creation of a national unity alliance that they viewed with concern the increasing strikes and mobilization of workers. In Brazil, as in France and elsewhere at the time, the communists urged workers to tighten their belts.

If the relative freedom of the last months of the Estado Novo led to the outbreak of twelve strikes that would have been unthinkable a year earlier, the fall of Vargas opened the way to unprecedented levels of working-class mobilization, which would be duplicated only in the early 1960s. In the first two months of 1946 alone there were no fewer than sixty strikes, a particularly impressive number when one takes into account the hostile policy of the PCB, which accused strike leaders of a dangerous "adventurism" that they said favored the fascists.

A paradoxical situation developed in which union leaders tied to the PCB participated reluctantly in these strikes to maintain their hold over the rank and file, despite contrary appeals from the party leaders. The communists' difficulties in this period were particularly acute because the government and the conservative parties accused the PCB of duplicity for defending "national unity," while appearing to be sabotaging it with strikes and protest movements. As such occurrences increased, the communists found it impossible to avoid involvement, and, as a consequence, the government brought indiscriminate repression to bear against the party, the unions, and the MUT. While the Constituent Assembly discussed the new constitution, including clauses related to labor, the newly installed president, Eurico Dutra, made use of such instruments as the decree-law, a relic of the Estado Novo, to limit the right to strike. In reality, following Dutra's Decree 9070 the federal government regarded strikes less as a right than as an "inevitable evil" to be rigorously controlled. In 1946, a veteran politician of the Estado Novo era remarked that there was no place for strikes in countries that had appropriate legislation.

It did not take long for the limits of Brazil's postwar redemocratization to become visible. As in various countries of Europe and Spanish America, the winds of the Cold War reached Brazil and carried off the fragile national unity. As the economy adjusted to postwar trade conditions and as the rural-urban migration enlarged the labor pool, competition for jobs increased while living conditions deteriorated, provoking a steady increase in the number of strikes. The Dutra government responded with a wave of interventions in 143 unions (of a total of 944). And it moved against the Communist Party by lifting its legal registration and removing its deputies from Congress in 1947 and 1948.

At the same time, the PCB went through an exercise in self-criticism that resulted in its jettisoning the policy of class collaboration, assuming instead an insurrectionary line that came to be reflected in its trade union policy. Although until shortly before then the communists had urged nearly uncritical participation in the official unions, beginning in 1948 their policy became one of withdrawal from the official structure and creation of parallel unions.

Concretely this reorientation represented the breaking of the PCB's alliance with *trabalhista* groups in the trade unions.[18] One of the many paradoxes of Brazilian political reality during the period was Vargas's simultaneous founding of the Brazilian Labor Party (PTB, Partido Trabalhista Brasileiro) and the Social Democratic Party (PSD, Partido Social Democrático). Vargas sought to embrace in the PSD the conservative politicians, who had sustained the Estado Novo, and to employ the PTB as a barrier to keep the workers from being swept away by the PCB.

The communists' policy of class collaboration at the union level failed during the immediate postwar years because of the direction that labor conflicts took. A significant number of the 1946–47 strikes occurred without official trade union sanction but were organized instead by workers' commissions at the level of the factory or firm. These activities, although often undertaken by workers neutral or favorably disposed toward the communists, were at odds with the party's general orientation. Moreover, they demonstrated the weakness of the party's influence over workers.

The PCB's criticism of the government-controlled union structure was only rhetorical; the party did not seek a radical break with the existing system. Essentially the party wanted reform of the structure to permit more union freedom, to extend labor legislation to the countryside, and to improve the social welfare system. Its leaders became seriously interested in union autonomy and freedom only when the political system turned rigid and the government began systematic intervention in the unions. Such interventions might run from closure to replacing elected leaders with government appointees. Otherwise, communist trade unionists functioned within the existing structure of labor legislation and controls, trying to make the system work in their favor. For example, they sought to use the official unions as the basis for the creation of a national union confederation, even though such an organization was supposedly illegal. In September 1946, they worked in the Trade Union Congress of the Workers of Brazil to found the Confederation of Brazilian Workers (CTB, Confederação dos Trabalhadores Brasileiros).

The CTB occupied a key place in the PCB's strategy, which aimed at unifying and leading the labor movement, portraying the party as the representative of the working class, securing a role in the political process, and establishing an alliance with the trabalhista sectors of the union bureaucracy.

This so-called populist approach failed. The communists could not control the workers' spontaneous actions. The PCB found that it had to either join the strikes or be swept aside. Effectively the "national union" policy became a dead letter.

The alliance with the trabalhistas also failed to materialize, and this group used their positions in the government union apparatus to neutralize or repress the communists. Thus the communists did not, indeed could not, effectively press for trade union autonomy during the height of the social struggles immediately after the war. It became even more difficult to do so when the Dutra government repressed both the party and spontaneous worker-organized strikes.

The PCB became more isolated from the workers. The trend was in the direction of harder times for the latter and for hopes of organizing labor. As real wages fell, the disorganization of the workers was apparent in the parallel decline in the number of strikes and in the unionization of factories. The tide would not turn in labor's favor again until 1952.

Trabalhismo and Development

A decisive 1950 electoral victory returned Getúlio Vargas to the presidency the following January. The workers voted massively for him despite PCB attempts to convince unionists to annul their ballots. And Vargas, after several labor ministers failed to give his government a social base, named João Goulart, a young lawyer and neighboring rancher from Rio Grande do Sul, as minister of labor in 1953.

Goulart immediately made some important changes in the ministry's operation. He adopted a wage policy that resulted in considerable gains for workers. He also softened the application of labor laws, giving the unions greater freedom of action. He suspended government interventions and moderated restrictions against the communists, who took advantage of the situation and in 1952 began to ally themselves with the trabalhistas. Even so the communists suffered from the tension between their desire to form such alliances and their dislike of the Vargas government, regarded by the PCB as one of "national betrayal" that should be overthrown. The measures of "excessive liberty" that the government accorded unions caused opposition from the industrialists and the military and plunged the country into a grave political crisis in August 1954, provoking the president's suicide.

Earlier, in March 1953, a general strike involving three hundred thousand workers had shaken São Paulo. In the course of the strike, workers formed companywide committees to assure unity of action in multiple plants to prevent management from isolating or bargaining separately with company subdivisions. This strike also saw an intensification of communist action after some years of marginalization. This was taking place in a Brazil experiencing accelerated urbanization, particularly in São Paulo and Rio de Janeiro, where the working class reacted to the attendant decline in living standards by organizing neighborhood self-help associations or, more informally and violently, with frequent rioting and looting. Both nonviolent and violent working-class responses marked the 1950s, especially the first half of the decade.

In 1956, the inauguration of President Juscelino Kubitschek, who enjoyed great popularity among the workers, introduced new elements into the Brazilian labor movement. This was especially due to Kubitschek's launching of industrialization. His attraction of foreign capital to establish the automobile industry had rapid multiplier effects in the steel, machine tool, electrical, and related industries. His plan of "fifty years of progress in five" stimulated shipbuilding, home appliances, chemicals, and energy development, and, above all, caused a boom in the construction industry from government contracts for hydroelectric projects, highways, and the building of Brasília, the new capital city on the central plateau. The democratization of political life characterized Kubitschek's administration, which included former Labor Minister João Goulart as vice president. (American readers should recall that they belonged to different political parties and had been elected on separate tickets.) Not surprisingly, the unions' room to maneuver increased and they demonstrated their strength in huge strikes, such as those in 1957. During the Kubitschek administration, the minimum wage reached its highest real value for the 1940–88 period.

The reorganization of the labor movement in the Kubitschek era did not, however, include a change in or a struggle against the corporatist union structure. Rather than attack Labor Ministry controls, trade union leaders (including trabalhistas, communists, and others) preferred to get around the labor laws by organizing their unions into pacts, alliances, and so forth. These partly took the place of links among unions from the various categories, which continued to be illegal. The trade unionists also explored the possibilities in the officially sanctioned state and national federations of the different sectors. As a result, a coalition of trabalhistas, communists, Catholics, and independents gained control of the National Confederation of Industrial Workers (CNTI, Confederação Nacional dos Trabalhadores da Indústria), which government *pelegos* had previously dominated.[19] This victory had important effects during the agitated period from 1961 to the coup d'état of 1964.

Crisis of the Early 1960s

In September 1961, the union movement greeted as a major event João Goulart's assumption of the presidency following Jânio Quadros's startling resignation after only seven months in office.[20] Jango, as Goulart was known popularly, was well regarded in the working class. As Vargas's labor minister he had granted important wage increases and greater union freedom, for which the military forced him from office. This same image made business groups view him with suspicion.

A growing economic crisis marked the Goulart administration (1961–64) and produced constant political turmoil. The labor movement rapidly became politicized, in the sense that it participated more directly in the national debate over economic policy and the structure of the regime. This politicization was carried out against a backdrop of worsening recession, aggravated by the reluctance of Brazilian and foreign capitalists to invest and by an explosive inflationary spiral. Not surprisingly, labor conflicts multiplied, and the period witnessed the highest incidence of strikes up to that time.

Events of the era pushed the labor movement to define its political role more broadly. The movement's objectives appeared in the so-called Base Reforms Program, which sought to unite demands for income redistribution with proposals for structural change (such as agrarian reform). Labor's desired reforms were decidedly nationalist and statist. Although labor avoided criticizing, except indirectly, the government's domination of the unions, its leaders openly confronted federal labor legislation on one point: the prohibition of a national union federation, which they considered essential to carrying out their political platform.

In 1962 they openly challenged the system with the formation of the General Command of Workers (CGT, Comando Geral dos Trabalhadores), which even in its initials suggested the embryo of a future General Confederation of Workers (CGT, Confederação Geral de Trabalhadores). Between 1962 and 1964, the CGT called two general strikes, the first in support of San Tiago Dantas, then candidate for prime minister (during the brief period of parliamentary government instituted as a way to weaken Goulart's presidential powers) and identified with the Base Reforms, and the second to pressure Congress to call a referendum on restoring Goulart's full authority, as in fact happened. An attempted third strike, in opposition to the 1964 coup d'état, failed. In that instance the union power base crumbled in a few hours, resting as it did on a CGT composed mostly of high union officials who had not backed earlier autonomous worker initiatives. The CGT sought instead to organize "selective" working-class support for Goulart that could be mobilized in critical moments.

The excessive identification of the labor movement with the deposed government, and the clear hegemony of the PCB within the CGT, made the trade unions a principal military target after the officers took power in April 1964.

Workers and Soldiers

The obvious necessity for economic recovery led the government of Gen. Humberto de A. Castello Branco (1964–67) to open Brazil to foreign investment and to encourage domestic capitalists to keep their money in the country. In addition to repealing the law controlling foreign firms' profit remittances, the military adopted economic measures that harshly affected the working classes and required various forms of coercion to keep the unions under control. The monetarist policies of the new economic authorities, by restricting credit and public expenditures, increased unemployment. The rigid control over wages immediately restricted workers' buying power and eventually slowed demand, thereby worsening the recession and raising the level of joblessness.

At the institutional level, the Castello Branco government made use of two instruments to eliminate the unions' ability to resist its economic policies: the existing labor legislation, which allowed federal intervention and replacement of union leaders; and a new strike law, forced through the intimidated Congress, which made illegal practically all forms of work stoppage. If the strike had been a somewhat weak constitutional right before 1964, thereafter it all but disappeared, until the great strikes of 1978.

Aside from these legal instruments, the military-controlled government also relied extensively on police repression of any protest movement, no matter how mild, on the part of either political parties or unions attempting to capitalize on worker discontent. As the government installed controls on wages—the increases in pay usually fell below inflation rates—it also forced congressional approval of a law ending the existing job protection mechanisms. The congressional passage of the Guarantee Fund for Time of Service (FGTS, Fundo de Garantia por Tempo de Serviço) meant the end of job security for workers who previously had their positions guaranteed after ten years of employment, thus permitting greater labor turnover, with corresponding downward pressure on wages.

As long as the military governments, under Castello Branco and Gen. Artur Costa e Silva (1967–69), had not fully consolidated their positions, the labor movement managed—despite repression—to regroup by sectors, particularly around the banner of wage protection. This regrouping was distinctive in that it frequently occurred outside traditional union channels, thanks in large part to the efforts of young workers who, even when they held posts in the official union structure, maintained a critical attitude toward it. The 1968 strikes in Contagem (an industrial suburb of Belo Horizonte) and Osasco (a similar suburb of São Paulo), as well as the protests against the wage squeeze in the principal industrial centers, were attempts to reestablish trade union activity in new forms, since they were based on emerging sectors of the labor movement, quite distant from the pre-1964 trabalhista or communist leadership.

The Contagem strike, in April 1968, appeared spontaneous, coming from the seventeen hundred workers in the Belgo-Mineira steel mill, whose work stoppage and seizure of company managers as hostages caught the union leadership by surprise. Apparently, dissident leftists had been preparing for action and so were able to move quickly. Within a week, fifteen thousand workers had joined in, thereby paralyzing many of the principal industries of Minas Gerais. Since the Ministry of Labor already had planned to link wages to increases in the cost of living, it reacted to the workers' demand for a 25 percent increase with an offer of 10 percent, which the strikers immediately accepted. To head off others from following the Contagem example, the government issued a decree-law extending the 10 percent increase to all workers. But the same decree also made government control of salaries permanent.

The Osasco case was different. There the metal workers within factories, such as the Cobrasma company, formed "groups of ten" in each section to discuss work problems. These elected their own group and sectional leaders, who in turn elected a thirty-member factorywide committee. As early as 1965, the Cobrasma management recognized the legitimacy of the representative committee. Osasco was distinctive too, because many of its workers attended secondary school at night, which facilitated cooperation between the student movement and the workers. Indeed, the two groups had gained a strong voice in the municipality's government as a result of the elections of 1967. The union had worked to raise the level of the workers' political consciousness and formed strong links with committees in the various factories. In mid-1968, with a committee structure in a majority of the city's factories and a strike command of elected leaders in place, the union planned to call out its members in November. But by July, the workers refused to wait and pulled the union leadership along.

The government's repression was fierce and set an inhibiting example for the next decade. The ministry intervened, removing the elected leaders. The principal leader went into hiding, was arrested, and was one of the fourteen political prisoners exchanged for the kidnapped United States ambassador in 1969. At Cobrasma, as an illustration of what occurred, the workers who had staged a sit-down and taken over the plant found themselves attacked by mounted police, soldiers armed with machine guns, and two armored vehicles. Some one hundred twenty workers were detained and beaten, and many were tortured. Two of those arrested were Catholic priests, members of the worker-priest movement. Those who fled into the streets tried to enter their union hall but, finding it occupied by military police, gathered in a local church. This in turn was invaded and seriously damaged as those inside were dragged off to jail. The memory of Osasco made the unions extremely cautious over the next years.[21]

The coup within the coup of 1968, in which hard-line military leaders suspended constitutional guarantees, purged the Congress, and retired dissident military personnel and independent union leaders, was followed by even more authoritarian labor measures in 1969. The history of the labor movement during the dark period between 1968 and 1974 is not well known, for only recently have historians begun reconstructing the events and meaning of those years. Despite predictions from the left and the right of a capitalist collapse in Brazil, the country underwent an extraordinary industrial boom, beginning in 1969 and continuing intensely through 1974, with growth rates of over 10 percent a year.

The "Miracle" and Urbanization

The "Brazilian Miracle," as this period was called, witnessed increasing exploitation of the labor force, which suffered an unprecedented wage squeeze. Declining purchasing power was accompanied by deteriorating living conditions: housing, transportation, health care, and education worsened. Moreover, management pressure on workers to produce more for less occurred in an atmosphere where the unions were powerless, the press censored, and the political parties cowed. The workplace became less safe: during those years Brazil had the world's highest incidence of industrial accidents, which affected one worker in four. The social crisis in the countryside and the relative attractiveness that industrial growth gave to urban areas provoked the hypertrophy of dozens of Brazilian cities, whose lack of basic sanitation was responsible for a high incidence of disease. In 1975, some 70 percent of residences in São Paulo were not connected to sewer lines. The housing shortage stimulated the growth of shantytowns on the increasingly distant fringes of the cities.[22]

The factory and the neighborhood are crucial to understanding the development of the labor movement in the period. The factory served as the stage for resistance to the intense and growing discipline that management and government sought to impose on labor. Workers committed small acts of sabotage, organized slowdowns, and created information networks as replacements for the more dangerous strikes. The neighborhood became a virtual redoubt of the labor movement, in which a force rarely present before the 1970s, the Catholic Church, played an important part.

The 1964 closure of the political system, accentuated in 1968, had eliminated parties that represented urban labor. The regime, moreover, directed savage repression against the whole of the left, suppressing first the groups attempting armed resistance and then the more moderate PCB. This harsh repression disorganized the generation of labor leaders who emerged in 1968; the factory managers and security forces largely kept them out of the workplaces via blacklists.

Without political parties and with little room for maneuver in trade unions that were controlled by either government interventors or cowed moderates, the workers retreated to the distant fringes of the cities, where the parish church often served as a place of reflection and of organization. As groups such as the Ecclesiastical Base Communities arose, a profound change took place in the clergy, and eventually in the church hierarchy, which until the late 1960s had supported the military regime.

A succession of small events, plus the building of solidarity and resistance networks, gave the workers experience that contributed to the reemergence of the labor movement in 1974–75. As the economic growth rates declined from double to single digits and the inflationary rates rose more rapidly than the government was willing to admit, the social costs of the government's economic model became increasingly apparent.[23]

The government of Gen. Ernesto Geisel (1974–79) undertook to reform the dictatorship from within and acquiesced to a certain liberalization of the political system. In 1974, the tolerated opposition party, the Brazilian Democratic Movement (MDB, Movimento Democrático Brasileiro), won a surprising electoral victory. Coinciding with these economic and political changes were signs of a labor revival. In 1975, a strike of several hours at Volkswagen, which employed over thirty thousand workers, had a symbolic quality. In 1977, more militant unionists began a campaign for wage restitution, arguing that the Brazilian government had concocted artificially low inflation statistics at the beginning of the decade, thereby giving subsequent wage increases a false starting point. As foreign analysts confirmed this view, the matter became a rallying cry at public assemblies of workers who demanded payment of the wages that had been taken from them by such dishonest methods. This activity failed to secure such restitution but succeeded in unleashing trade union energies.

In those 1977 rallies, the workers paid close attention to the words of Luís Inácio da Silva (known as Lula), the president of the Metal Workers Unions of São Bernardo do Campo (the main industrial area of São Paulo). According to Lula, the factory owners would listen to the workers' voices only "when the noise of the machines stopped."

In 1978, workers at the Scandia plant in São Bernardo do Campo went out on strike, beginning an epidemic of stoppages that closed down all the factories of Brazil's major industrial center. The special characteristic of the 1978 movement, which took on the appearance of a general strike, was that workers' demands from inside the factory touched it off. The union, after the fact, took up the cry and linked the Scandia workers' specific demands to those of metal and automobile workers generally. In 1979 and 1980, more conflicts occurred in the Paulista industrial cities. The militant behavior of the metal workers set a standard for the other trade unions. Strikes spread to other categories of workers, including state employees and teachers, reaching distant parts of the country where little industrial or trade union tradition existed. The corporative union structure, meanwhile, showed itself incapable of containing labor's new dynamism.

The new unionism (or "authentic unionism" as it was also called) represented the joining of two new currents in the Brazilian labor movement. The first was the energized rank and file in neighborhoods and factories, who expressed resistance to their living and working conditions. Second, was the effort to secure union autonomy from both the government and the reviving political parties.

The government and the moderate opposition quickly lost whatever illusions they had about making the new unionism a functional element in a controlled democracy or having it form a tame basis for a Social Democratic alternative. With this clear, the government reacted strongly against the strikes and open union activity, once again utilizing the old labor legislation. Interventions and removals of officers proved fruitless, however, because the general membership continued to follow the ousted leaders. Neither this repression nor the recession that began in 1982 was sufficient to break the impetus of the new unionism.

The 1980s

In late 1979 and early 1980, representatives of this movement organized the Workers' Party (PT, Partido dos Trabalhadores), which attracted enthusiastic support from rank and file unionists, as well as participants in various grass roots urban movements, members of rural unions, participants in the Ecclesiastical Base Communities, significant numbers of intellectuals, particularly from the universities, human rights activists, and members of some small leftist groups.

In the 1980s this working-class and union movement has advanced to the point of being dominant among metal workers and has secured an important following among workers in chemical plants, other industries, and banking, as well as some influence among rural workers.

Another trend appeared among the remaining *pelegos*, however, who were allied with the now declining communist parties (the PCB, which adheres to a Moscow line, and the Communist Party of Brazil, PCDOB, which follows an Albanian model). The split in the trade unions was more than a dispute among political parties or a difference of opinion regarding support for, or opposition to, the New Republic, which peacefully replaced the military government in 1985. It involved two different and mutually exclusive concepts of trade unionism. One, identified with the Unified Workers' Central (CUT, Central Unica de Trabalhadores), emerged from the new unionism and emphasized the need to repeal the old, restrictive labor legislation. The CUT seeks total union autonomy, freedom from state control, and an end to the union tax, which the government collects and distributes to the unions to finance their activities. The CUT defends Brazilian ratification of Convention 87 of the International Labor Organization, which would mean government acceptance of such principles. While the CUT defends trade union unity, it implicitly accepts the end of the old Brazilian corporative structure of society and its replacement with a pluralist one. It emphasizes rank and file organization, and in the late 1980s negotiated with industry for the formation of dozens of factory and company commissions.

Second, the ideological tendencies that survive from pre-1964 unionism are found in the CGT. Among its components is one new and extremely dynamic sector made up of the majority of the rural unions affiliated with the National Confederation of Agricultural Workers. The CGT supports, but reserves the right to criticize, the New Republic, and it has opposed specific economic policies. It favors the controlled liberation of the unions but supports the union tax because its leaders fear that elimination would weaken or destroy the majority of organizations that make up the CGT.

In 1987 and 1988, real wages declined markedly, corroded by inflation which reached monthly rates of over 20 percent. The minimum wage fell to less than U.S.$50, the lowest level since its establishment during the Estado Novo. Workers reacted to the economic crisis with widespread strikes. Divisions within the union movement grew sharper as the CUT defended a policy of direct confrontation with employers and the government. Strikes led by its unions succeeded in several sectors, though its plans for a nationwide general strike did not. The impasses which the CUT faced in this period provided room for the emergence of a movement styling itself as "unionism based on results," supported by several São Paulo unions that urged accords with employers and the government. This avenue met with less success than expected, since it encountered little receptivity from business groups or the federal government.

The labor movement's attempts to pressure the Constituent Assembly have met with varying results but, in any case, have secured some important gains for workers. The most important were the recognition of the right to strike and a considerable loosening of state control over unions, in particular an end to the right of federal intervention. Despite the opposition of the CUT and the deputies of the Workers' Party, the Constituent Assembly voted to retain both the provision allowing only one union per category and the obligatory union tax levied on all workers regardless of whether they are union members or not. The continuation of this latter measure from the previous corporatist structure will permit the survival of unions which have little or no rank-and-file support. The two questions divided the labor movement, with the CGT defending the single union provision and the compulsory contribution, while the CUT opposed both measures.

The labor movement suffered a serious defeat on the agrarian question. The new constitution contains provisions that will make any project for agrarian reform extremely difficult and that are, in fact, more conservative than the legislation approved by the military after the coup d'état.

The labor movement won several other victories: the reduction of the work week to a maximum of 44 hours, better pay for overtime and vacations, job security guarantees, increased maternity leave (and even a provision for paternity leave), and social-security coverage for rural workers equal to that for urban workers.

Since many of these gains will require additional laws and decrees for their effective implementation, the labor movement will have to remain mobilized over the next few years so as not to lose in practice what was won in the new constitution. The other struggle will be to ensure the enforcement of the new provisions, since there is a considerable tradition of employers effectively ignoring the law in labor-relations matters. These circumstances should lead the labor movement to assign considerable importance to institutional questions over the next few years. The law and its application will become fundamental areas for union activity and, as in the struggle against the effects of inflation, will require the movement to join militancy with comprehensive and consistent proposals.

Notes

1. One should not expect too much from these census data because of, among other reasons, such enigmatic categories as "ill-defined occupations" (416,000), and the 5.6 million people over 21 years of age recorded as "undeclared or without occupation." Brazil, Directoria Geral de Estatística, *Recenseamento do Brazil realizado em 1 de septembro de 1920* (Rio de Janeiro: Typ. da Estatística, 1922–30), vol. 4, pt. 5, tomo 1, p. XII. See also vol. 5, pt. 1, tomo 1, pp. XX–XXI.

2. Gigi Damiani, *I paesi nei quali non si deve emigrare. La questione sociale nel Brasile* (Milan: Umanità Nova, 1920), pp. 8, 50.

3. Ser. Pol. 282, October 21, 1909, Archivio del Ministero degli Affari Esteri, Rome.

4. José Maria dos Santos, *A Política geral do Brasil* (São Paulo: J. Magalhaes, 1930), pp. 414–15.

5. *Il Pungolo* (São Paulo), May 1, 1909.

6. *La Battaglia* (São Paulo), March 4, 1906; *O Chapeleiro* (São Paulo), December 5, 1903; *Avanti!* (São Paulo), April 17, 1908.

7. *O Chapeleiro*, December 5, 1903; for some examples see *Terra Livre* (São Paulo), March 24, 1906; *Luta proletária*, February 8, 1908; *Avanti!*, May 7, 1908; *A Plebe* (Rio), April 26, 1919; the final quote is from *Combate*, July 5, 1919.

8. Peel to Balfour, Petrópolis, November 20, 1918, and Peel to Curzon, Petrópolis, January 14, 1919, Foreign Office 371, 1919–20, 3653, Public Record Office, London. The threat was presumably made more horrifying— if not more plausible—by the fact that Petrópolis was an upper-class resort where the government and diplomatic corps spent the summer.

9. Roberto Simonsen, *O trabalho moderno* (São Paulo: Secção de Obras do "Estado," 1919), pp. 38–39. Taylorism refers to the methods devised by Frederick W. Taylor to increase management control over the work process.

His system, known as scientific management, used standardization, time-and-motion studies, the increased division of labor, and other techniques to reduce the power of skilled craftsmen. Several São Paulo firms undertook to implement Taylor's principles during the 1920s.

10. *O Operário* (São Paulo), March 3, 1928, as quoted in Maria Auxiliadora Guzzo de Decca, *A vida fora das fábricas: Cotidiano operário em São Paulo, 1927–34* (São Paulo: Paz e Terra, 1987), p. 46; Sociedade Anônima Scarpa, *Lembrança do Cotonífico Scarpa e da sua organização social na Vila Scarpa* (São Paulo: n.p., n.d.), reprinted in *A classe operária no Brasil: Documentos, 1889–1930*, ed. Paulo Sérgio Pinheiro and Michael M. Hall, 2 vols (São Paulo: Alfa-Omega/Brasiliense, 1979–81), 2:214–19.

11. There is a selection of circulars in Pinheiro and Hall, *A classe operária*, 2:194–212.

12. Cerciai Alessandro, January 19, 1929, CPC, Archivio Centrale dello Stato, Rome; Lester Baker, "Communism in Brazil," November 8, 1929 (Department of State Microfilm 519, roll 8, frames 26–27), National Archives, Washington.

13. Harry W. Brown, Rio de Janeiro, October 11, 1934, 832.504/65, RG 59, NA, Washington.

14. Major Lawrence C. Mitchell, "Comments on Current Events," Rio de Janeiro, June 20, 1939, 832.5042/28, RG 59, NA, Washington.

15. Karl Loewenstein, *Brazil Under Vargas* (New York: Macmillan Co., 1942), p. 241; "Discurso do Ministro do Trabalho, Dr. Waldemar Falcão, saudando o Presidente Getúlio Vargas, em nome da massa trabalhadora," in Ministério do Trabalho, Indústria e Comércio, *Dez anos de legislação social* (Rio de Janeiro: Imprensa Oficial, 1940), p. xi. On the use of film, see Fundação Cinemateca Brasileira, *Cine jornal brasileiro, Departamento de Imprensa e Propaganda, 1939–1946* (São Paulo: Fundação Cinemateca Brasileira, 1982).

16. Included in U.S. Embassy report 832.00/4–945, RG 59, NA, Washington.

17. Browderism was the policy of class peace and national unity advocated by Earl Browder, head of the Communist Party of the United States. In 1944, Browder dissolved the U.S. party and replaced it with the Communist Political Association to facilitate wartime, and postwar, Soviet-American cooperation. The policy enjoyed considerable support in Latin America. The U.S. party abandoned it in mid-1945 and expelled Browder in 1946.

18. Literally "workerist." The term derives from the Partido Trabalhista Brasileira (PTB) and refers to a form of populism, identified with Vargas, nationalistic in tone, and associated with government concessions of social and welfare benefits to workers.

19. *Pelego* is the pejorative name applied to labor leaders who are subservient to the Ministry of Labor.

20. The reasons for Quadro's action are still debated; Amir Labaki, *1961: A crise da renúncia e a solução parlamentarista* (São Paulo: Editora Brasiliense, 1986), pp. 15–52.

21. Francisco Weffort, *Participação e conflito industrial: Contagem e Osasco, 1968* (São Paulo: CEBRAP, 1972); Cf. Maria Helena Moreira Alves, *State and Opposition in Military Brazil* (Austin: University of Texas Press, 1985); John Humphrey, *Capitalist Control and Workers' Struggle in the Brazilian Auto Industry* (Princeton: Princeton University Press, 1982).

22. Cândido Procópio Ferreira de Camargo et al., *São Paulo 1975: Crescimento e pobreza* (São Paulo: Edições Loyola, 1976).

23. *São Paulo 1975*, cited above, sponsored by the Archdiocese of São Paulo, was an influential denunciation of living and working conditions. That matters have hardly improved since then is indicated by the data in Hélio Jaguaribe et al., *Brasil 2000* (Rio de Janeiro: Paz e Terra, 1986).

Sam Adamo

Race and *Povo*

Blacks and mulattoes have played a central role in Brazil's history from the arrival of the first shipment of slaves in 1538 until the present. Reputed to enjoy harmonious race relations, Brazil appears to be a successful multiracial society that is rapidly escaping underdevelopment. Despite such appearances, however, powerful social forces continue to keep blacks and mulattoes at the bottom of the socioeconomic ladder. In fact, Brazil remains a country in which nonwhites face inferior opportunities. This chapter deals only with the city of Rio de Janeiro, but other studies suggest that the experience of blacks there was representative of what occurred in most cities.

Recent research has shown that blacks and mulattoes are caught in a "cycle of cumulative disadvantage" that prevents them from rising very far up the socioeconomic scale. For example, a disproportionate number live in the country's underdeveloped, agrarian regions where few educational and occupational opportunities exist. Nonwhites have difficulty gaining a basic education, the universal passport to higher socioeconomic status: the 1980 census revealed that nearly twice as many nonwhites as whites had less than two years of elementary schooling (48 percent, compared with 25 percent).[1] Social and economic deprivation went hand in hand with political disenfranchisement, since illiterates were not allowed to vote before 1985. Occupational analysis also reveals the extent to which nonwhites are at a disadvantage. They are heavily *over*represented in unskilled, low-paying jobs and *under*represented in white collar positions. Consequently, the income of different racial groups varies greatly: in 1980 nonwhite males earned half as much as white males. Since educational and occupational barriers to nonwhites' social mobility have not changed appreciably since slavery was abolished in 1888, it is logical to conclude that racism and discrimination play prominent roles in keeping blacks and mulattoes disproportionately represented among the lower classes.

The chapter examines the subtle and not-so-subtle forms of discrimination that plagued Brazilian blacks and mulattoes in the first two and a half generations after the abolition of slavery in 1888. The study is based on personnel records from four factories, two labor unions, the Brazilian navy, and the former federal penitentiary in Rio de Janeiro. It also draws on race-specific epidemiological data collected from the 1890s to the 1940s. The major categories of information are labor force participation, family and living conditions, nutrition, mortality, and crime.[2] These data are especially valuable because the country's official "color blind" attitude toward nonwhites prevented systematic investigation of race relations before the 1940 census. While blacks and mulattoes made limited social and economic advances after abolition, immigrants and native whites progressed more rapidly, so that differences between the races actually increased. This is prima facie evidence of powerful discriminatory forces at work in Brazilian society.

Demographic Characteristics and the Labor Market

White persons in Rio generally came from stable families and had higher levels of education than nonwhites or immigrants.[3] Whites converted these "assets" into the social and economic rewards that came with good jobs, for example as skilled technicians or administrators. This success story comes as no surprise, since it occurred in every society that had slavery.

The patterns of educational attainment, skills, and family background of white immigrants resembled those of Rio's blacks and mulattoes, yet the immigrants achieved greater upward social and economic mobility. They were promoted more quickly into better-paying jobs, and they used occupational advancement to enhance their social standing and assimilation into Brazilian life. By 1940 immigrants held a larger share of jobs in the industries sampled than their proportion in the overall population, indicating a hiring preference for foreigners.

A somewhat different pattern emerged among migrants from outside the city. Whereas whites made up a third of the internal migrants to Rio, they got from 43 to 47 percent of the jobs for which migrants were hired by factories in the sample, which suggests that white migrants enjoyed a hiring preference over nonwhite migrants. Such a preference could be due to whites migrants' greater literacy and skills levels. All the evidence points to highly selective employment of nonwhites: only the best qualified got jobs. The low proportion of black and mulatto workers is likely a consequence of racial prejudice on the part of employers who were reluctant to select nonwhites, whom they judged both poorly trained and "bumpkins" from the backlands.

Analysis of job categories (unskilled, skilled, and administrative) by level of education shows that native whites were best able to convert their educational assets into economic rewards and higher status jobs. Native whites were generally overrepresented in the skilled and administrative positions in all the industries examined. The same pattern emerged for other whites as well. Foreigners with little or no education were likelier to advance to skilled administrative positions than nonwhites with equivalent backgrounds. Nonwhites in the factories were generally better educated than immigrants, but they were at the bottom of the occupational pyramid and their level of literacy remained about the same at all job levels. The foreigners' greater probability of advancement suggests that nonwhites competed in a discriminatory labor market in which race played a major role.

The concentration of nonwhites of both sexes in unskilled positions was inevitably reflected in wage levels. Wage differentials between native whites, immigrants, and nonwhites appeared in all the businesses sampled. In addition, the starting salaries of native whites were higher than those of nonwhites and foreigners in all but one company.[4] Deviations in starting salaries may also be attributable to differences in experience, age, education, and the number of people in each job category.

It is important to note, however, that no overt wage discrimination was practiced. Native whites, immigrants, and nonwhites usually received equal pay for similar work. This was determined by comparing selected job categories in each business establishment. Though some variation by racial group occurred, it was not systematic and reflected different levels of skills and experience. Discrimination took place in society at large—inadequate education and training for the nonwhites—and in preferential hiring and promo-

tion of whites over nonwhites. The result was high under- and unemployment among the nonwhites and low wages for those fortunate enough to have jobs.

Housing and Nutrition

The lower wages earned by most blacks and mulattoes had important implications for their families' overall standards of living. Basically, they were priced out of decent housing in an urban market
saturated by migrants and immigrants, and their nutritional levels
suffered as well. Nonwhites were forced to live in unsanitary dwellings where contagious and epidemic diseases flourished. Poor nutrition sapped their natural defenses against illness. Unsanitary living
conditions, disease, and poor nutrition formed a debilitating and
often fatal alliance that undermined the city's lower class, especially
its blacks and mulattoes. Children under two suffered a particularly
high mortality rate.

Middle- and upper-class families usually occupied single family
dwellings, while the poor (among whom nonwhites were disproportionately represented) lived in tenements (most commonly *cortiços*
and *estalagens*) or shantytowns (*favelas*).[5] The former were cheap
structures designed to produce quick profits for their owners. Construction methods varied little: the main buildings were of un-
seasoned wood that rapidly dried and split. The resultant cracks
exposed the frame to humidity, which in turn accelerated rot. Ter-
mites took their toll. Most of the apartments lay along an extended
corridor, with a central patio and a single entry from the street. The
more spacious quarters had a small living room, a kitchen, and one
or two tiny bedrooms. At most, the rooms were several meters
square and had a single window, so that little air circulated. Often,
desperately poor people squeezed twenty or more people into quarters designed for no more than ten.[6]

Tenement residents shared common water supplies and latrines,
and hygiene suffered from lack of individual responsibility. Where
sewerage was available, service often broke down due to over-
crowded conditions. Animals kept in makeshift stalls in patio areas
contributed to deficient hygiene.[7]

Many chronically under- and unemployed blacks and mulattoes,
unable to afford even the rents charged in the cortiços and estalagens, built or rented shacks in the infamous favelas. These were

squatter settlements located on hills in and around the center of the city. They afforded cheap housing near major places of employment. The cost of building a shack was usually less than a month's rent in the tenements. The lower cost of favela living was offset by major disadvantages. The shacks were stifling in summer and bone chilling in winter. They had no running water or sewerage. The shanties quickly filled up with poor people, festering diseases that thrived in crowded quarters. The favelas gained a reputation for insalubrity.

The diets of the working class suffered due to low incomes and lack of information about the food values of proteins, minerals, vitamins, and fats. The diseases endemic to the city intensified the adverse effects of low caloric intake and poor nutrition, creating a frequently fatal cycle of malnutrition and illness. The handicap was passed on to subsequent generations.

Health officials themselves recognized the inadequate dietary habits of the poor. According to an 1860s study, the lower class ate light breakfasts consisting of coffee or tea with some bread. Lunch was a much heartier meal, at which time small portions of salted or dried beef were consumed, along with beans, manioc flour, bread, and fruit (usually oranges or bananas). Dinner was similar to lunch but had the addition of soup, vegetables, and more fruit. Fresh meat was a luxury that rarely appeared on the tables of Rio's working poor, who reserved its consumption for Sundays, holidays, or other special occasions. Codfish and sardines were available as sources of protein, but the poor rarely purchased them. Beans, among the most nutritious items in poor people's diets, were typically cooked with a variety of vegetables, including potatoes, yams, sweet cassava, squash, cabbage, turnips, and okra. The most popular beverages were coffee, tea, chocolate, and alcohol. Milk was not an important part of poor people's diets, partly because of the absence of refrigeration and transportation facilities.[8]

Modern studies of Brazilian dietary habits suggest that poor people have not improved their nutritional intake. A 1961 study found that the quality of people's diet had a strong correlation with their socioeconomic status. The average per capita consumption of meat and milk for the middle and upper strata was seven and fifteen times greater than for those at the bottom of the socioeconomic ladder.[9]

Even if the poor had been informed about nutritional values, they could hardly have afforded a good diet. Descriptions from newspapers and government officials indicate that all basic food prices were unusually high in the early twentieth century. The *Jornal do Brasil*, for example, called milk wholesalers "monopolists of commerce" who "extorted" money from the poor and made it impossible for them to provide adequate diets to their families. A 1930 study found that working class families spent from 50 to 75 percent of their wages on food.[10] Public authorities seemed powerless to combat speculation in fresh food, despite frequent public protests.

The quality of food available to poor people was low, reducing its dietary value and sometimes endangering consumers. Preserved foods, domestic or imported, were generally too expensive for the poor. Meat regularly arrived in marketplaces in a condition of decay. Preparation, preservation, and transport of meat were deficient. A local newspaper claimed that sanitation on the island of Sapucala, the city's garbage dump, was superior to that of the city's slaughterhouses. Meat was cut on wooden chopping blocks that could never be entirely cleaned; then it was wrapped in newspaper and shipped without refrigeration to retail outlets. Tubercular, cancerous, carbuncular, and rotten meats were regularly sold throughout the city.[11] Moreover, other fresh food—milk, fruit, and vegetables—was shipped irregularly and was subject to speculation by wholesalers. Once perishable food arrived in the city, it had to be retailed quickly, because few shops had refrigeration or other means of preservation. The scarity of good food contributed to such nutritional maladies as scurvy, rickets, ophthalmia, and xerophagia (caused by eating dry or desiccated food).[12] These various dietary deficiencies could not fail to affect adversely the mortality rates of the various social and racial groups in Rio.

Mortality

At the beginning of the Old Republic, mortality rates were extremely high for all groups living in Rio de Janeiro. The historical trend had been for nonwhites to have higher rates than whites. Over the next half-century, federal and local authorities made improvements in sanitation and health care that radically lowered mortality rates for all groups. The most famous episode was undoubtedly Dr. Oswaldo Cruz's campaign in the 1900s.[13] Despite such improvements, mortality rates for blacks and mulattoes fell less rapidly than those of whites, and indeed the gap between whites' and nonwhites' life expectancy actually grew. This was because environmental im-

Table 1　Infant Mortality in Rio de Janeiro
(per thousand)

Year	Whites	Mulattoes	Blacks
1890	397	407	497
1940	123	241	204

Sources: the 1890 census and Brasil, Instituto Brasileiro de Geografia e Estatística, "Retificação da taxa de natalidade, da quota de nascidos mortos, e das taxas de mortalidade infantil para o Distrito Federal," *Estatística Demográfica* 4 (Rio de Janeiro, 1948): 34. The 1940 rates were adjusted to correct for unregistered births, deaths, age, and additions made by migrants.

provements tended to concentrate in better neighborhoods, and the incomes of poor nonwhites did not allow them to overcome housing and nutritional handicaps.

Infant mortality, the most sensitive to poor environment, was alarmingly high in the 1890s: 397 per thousand for white babies, 407 per thousand for mulatto babies, and 497 per thousand for black babies. Given underreporting, the last statistic means that one-half of all black babies ever born died within their first year of life (see table 1).

Health and environmental improvements over the next half-century produced a marked decline in infant death rates, but more so for white babies than mulattoes and blacks: 1940 census data show rates, respectively, as 123, 241, and 204 deaths per thousand. So while all groups' rates fell, the difference *between* whites and nonwhites increased, so that the latter had mortality ratios between 40 and 49 percent higher than the former in 1940. Clearly, the benefits of progress were not shared equally.

The average overall death rates in Rio were of course much lower: 23 and 18 per thousand in 1901–20 and 1921–40, respectively.[14] (See figure 1.) As expected, white death rates were consistently lower than the nonwhite rates. Health authorities admitted that black and mulatto deaths were underreported, but even so, marked differentials appeared. (The rising levels of mortality before 1930 were not real trends but instead reflected better reporting for all racial groups.) Data reported after 1930 began to approximate the true mortality experience of all groups, and they resembled rates for counterpart populations in São Paulo as well.[15]

CRUDE DEATH RATES IN RIO DE JANEIRO, 1909–1939

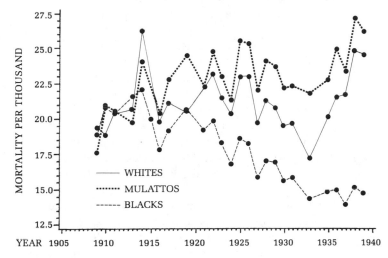

A stable population analysis of the 1940 census makes it possible to derive life expectancies for the several racial groups inhabiting Rio. A ten-year-old white male in 1940 could expect to live an average of 54 more years, whereas his black and mulatto counterparts could expect only 41 and 39 additional years of life. Even greater differentials existed among women: ten-year-old white women could expect to live an average of 60 more years, while black and mulatto women had only 39.

There can be no doubt, then, that the lower standards of living experienced by blacks and mulattoes—as a racial group and as the bulk of the working class—shortened their lives substantially.

Epidemic and contagious diseases proved to be especially lethal for Rio's poor blacks and mulattoes. In 1904, deaths from all infections and contagious diseases were 935 per 100,000 for whites, 1,133 for mulattoes, and 1,245 for blacks. By 1926 the rates had fallen sharply, to 594, 968, and 913, respectively. In other words, white mortality from these diseases declined by 35 percent, compared with only 15 and 27 percent for mulattoes and blacks.

Tuberculosis was especially lethal to poor blacks and mulattoes, and it resisted the public health department's efforts at eradication. It had long been known that slaves and blacks in general were highly susceptible to tuberculosis. By the 1930s it had become the foremost killer of nonwhites. The disease thrived on the heavy work regime, overcrowding, poor sanitation, and malnutrition that typified the lives of most nonwhites. Public health officials labeled tuberculosis an affliction of the "less favored classes" at the turn of the century, and the Brazilian League Against Tuberculosis recognized that the disease was more likely to strike blacks and mulattoes.[16] The rates in 1904 were 322 per 100,000 for whites, 394 for mulattoes, and 498 for blacks. Mortality from the disease more or less followed economic cycles, rising during periods of stress and hardship and falling in better times. For example, rates went up sharply during World War I and the depression of the 1930s, confirming a causal relationship between environmental conditions and mortality from tuberculosis.

Nutritional diseases were not a major cause of death, yet mortality from nonlethal afflictions like gastroenteritis, measles, whooping cough, and helminthic infections suggests that malnutrition was an important factor in the elevated mortality rates of nonwhites. Recent studies on nutrition show that antibiotics and immunizations played a much smaller role in the decline of infant mortality in less developed countries than originally surmised. Improved nutrition was a much stronger factor. Simply put, poorly fed babies died of such maladies as measles, gastroenteritis, and colitis because they were undernourished. Mortality from these diseases leveled off between 1915 and 1926, peaking at 467 per 100,000 for nonwhites in 1919. Whites had lower mortality rates for these diseases (385 in 1919).

Surprisingly, blacks had the lowest rates of mortality from these nonlethal diseases. Slaves in Rio often put together more nutritious meals than other Brazilians, and the women breast fed their children until the age of two or three. The low death rates of black children from nutritional-type diseases may be attributed to the survival of African nutritional and weaning practices.[17]

Crime and Cooption

Rio's nonwhite population living in poor neighborhoods faced high crime rates in addition to the problems described above. Prostitution and gambling throve in tenements and favelas. Crime's proximity to the poor raised the likelihood that they would become involved in criminal activities. Because the public at large stereotyped blacks and mulattoes as susceptible to criminal temptation, nonwhites were likelier subjects of police surveillance and sanctions than any other group in the city. Police had traditionally used violence and repression to keep poor people under control. Beginning in the 1930s, however, government agents increasingly relied on more subtle methods, including propaganda and cooption into organizations, discussed below, that could help ensure social control. Yet neither selective repression nor cooption fits the image of a people without racial prejudice.

Rio's experience with crime in this period was not unlike that in other developing nations: violent and property crimes accounted for the bulk of criminal activity.[18] Such offenses averaged 88 percent of the crimes between baseline averages in 1908–15 and 1942–47. A substantial body of literature suggests that such crimes correlate highly with a variety of socioeconomic problems, such as unemployment, slum residence, and low incomes.[19]

Violent crimes were far and away the most numerous for the period under consideration, constituting 66 percent in 1908–15 and 76 percent in 1942–47. On a per capita basis, nonwhite males and females were always likelier than whites to be arrested for violent offenses. This appears to have been a selective application of the law, because nonwhites did not always have unusually high crime rates. Sample data from late nineteenth century Rio suggest that the incidence of criminal activity was spread equally among the various racial groups. As time went on, however, nonwhites became more heavily represented among the criminal. Nonwhite males accounted for 37 percent of violent crimes in 1890 and 51 percent in 1940, while their share of the male population fell from 32 to 27 percent. The increase was corroborated in published statistics for the periods 1908–15 and 1942–47.

Statistics on crime involving property, about 15–20 percent of all violations, showed a similar increase in nonwhite perpetrators. Black males were arrested much more frequently than whites and even mulattoes, given their respective shares of the population.

The last crime category—public order violations—casts light on the real reasons for rising nonwhite rates of crime. Police surveillance and arrest were the principal methods the elite used to keep the masses under control. When other crimes could not be proven, police simply rounded up people for gambling, bearing arms, begging, drunkenness, disorderly behavior, and vagrancy. Poor people charged with these violations had little defense in the judicial system. Arrests for these crimes were actually used to keep city streets free of undesirable elements. They also created a law-and-order atmosphere in times of political instability. For example, public order violations made up 83 percent of all crimes recorded for males in 1890, the year following the overthrow of the monarchy.

Official and sample data concur that nonwhites bore the brunt of police enforcement for public order violations. Official reports of these arrests show that black males outnumbered white males by two or three to one. Incarceration of mulatto males exceeded that of white males in all years except 1913 and 1915. Racial differentials become even greater when females were tabulated. Sample data show that nonwhite males and females were overrepresented in public order crimes for all years, being charged with 65 and 85 percent of occurrences, respectively. Moreover, this trend grew over time.

The foregoing analysis suggests that whereas white migrants and foreign immigrants adapted rather quickly to life in the city after the turn of the century and thereby avoided police scrutiny, blacks and mulattoes did not. They lived at the fringes of urban life and suffered greater arrest and conviction rates than whites. To the extent that these rates reflected actual violations, they revealed the desperate plight of the poor and their inability to climb the socioeconomic ladder. Finally, the gradual reduction in public order crimes by nonwhites in the 1930s and 1940s reflected a new method of social control.

Beginning in the 1930s, during the long first Vargas regime, city officials gradually adopted new tactics for keeping the nonwhite masses in line. These tactics were most evident in their treatment of samba schools and Afro-Brazilian religious sects. Officials offered to end repression of such organizations on the condition that they register under government auspices and obey certain rules. This shift signaled changing attitudes on the part of Rio's elite and marked the beginning of a cooptive policy of social control.

"Blocos sujos," or raggedy parades of dancing poor people at Carnaval time, had long been discouraged and broken up by authorities. The dances, descended from African rites, were often lewd and provocative, and the police had instructions to keep them off the streets, if necessary by jailing the revellers. In 1933 and 1934, however, Rio's populist mayor, Pedro Ernesto Baptista, offered city support for the blocos, on the condition they curb their more disreputable features. The irregular groups organized themselves into "schools," and the mayor responded by subsidizing them with city funds. From that time on, the samba schools have been the lead tourist attraction of Rio's carnival.

By the late 1930s the federal government also endorsed this policy. The *Jornal da Polícia*, for example, ran an article praising the new cooperation between Carnaval groups and authorities.[20] One article in the official magazine, *Cultura Política*, portrayed black music and the samba as products of the Brazilian melting pot and played down their African origins; yet another found evidence of a work ethic in their lyrics.[21] Such interpretations, and the relaxation of repression that they signaled, eased tensions among the major racial groups in the city. Yet they also suggest that the elite had created new ways—bureaucratic and ideological—of controlling Rio's nonwhite masses.

Had the blocos preserved African religious practices, they might have evolved into authentic representatives of the masses. Now they became part of the official superstructure and even a symbol of the successful Brazilian melting pot![22]

The lower-class Afro-Brazilian religious sects, especially Candomblé and Macumba, underwent transformations similar to those of the blocos sujos. Before 1930, police had instructions to close down such religious centers and to jail the cult leaders. They sometimes used excessive zeal in rooting out the offenders. By the mid-1930s, however, authorities were content to allow the sects to exist and indeed began to register them through local agencies. The official rationale appeared in *Cultura Política* a few years later: *macumba* and *umbanda* were no longer black magic but rather represented a "spiritual symbiosis" of Catholicism and African religions.[23] The Afro-Brazilian sects now helped obscure race as a social issue and indeed contributed to the now-official myth of racial democracy.

In sum, blacks and mulattoes in Rio did make some social and economic progress in the half-century following abolition, but the gains were limited, especially when compared with those achieved by native whites and immigrants. Today's descendants of Brazil's slaves still find themselves locked into poor-paying, low-status jobs that offer little promise of upward mobility. Blacks and mulattoes live in the same favelas their predecessors erected at the turn of the century, and their children suffer the same handicaps of poor health and limited educational opportunity. Malnutrition, tuberculosis, diphtheria, measles, and whooping cough take their toll among black and mulatto youths. Worsening conditions in the big cities have led to a rise in crime rates, attracting international attention and inspiring at least one popular film, *Pixote* (1981). Luiz de Aguiar Costa Pinto's bitter assessment of nonwhite progress in 1950 seems equally apt a century after emancipation: blacks have gone no further than "from slave to proletarian."[24]

The Brazilian government still clings to the official myth of racial democracy, an ideology of social control that has proven effective for two generations now. But public acceptance of the myth is dwindling, and scholarly studies point conclusively to the existence of systematic discrimination. Several organizations fighting for Afro-Brazilian rights have been organized in the major cities, trying to create a general awareness of race problems. It may be that until a *tomada de conciência* or mobilization of public opinion occurs, Brazil's blacks and mulattoes can expect little progress. The selection of a black woman as Miss Brazil in 1986 may signify that change is in the air.

Notes

1. Carlos A. Hasenbalg, *Race Relations in Modern Brazil* (Albuquerque: University of New Mexico, Latin American Institute, 1985), p. 14.

2. The businesses sampled include América Fabril, the Companhia das Docas do Rio de Janeiro, and the Brazilian Traction, Light, and Power Company. Altogether I compiled records on 24,200 individuals, representing all racial and ethnic groups in the city. In addition, I processed some 10,000 health statistics.

3. For ease of expression I refer to racial categories at large, but the reader should remember that the conclusions refer to the specific data base.

4. In the exceptional case, foreigners earned more than native whites.

5. These and other foreign terms are defined in the glossary. *Favela*, which has come to mean slum, originally referred to a squatter settlement built in Rio by veterans of the Canudos campaign in the late 1890s. They named their shantytown after a cactus-covered hill in Bahia where they had bivouacked.

6. For an urban specialist's view, see Everardo Backheuser, *Habitações populares* (Rio de Janeiro: Imprensa Nacional, 1906). Aluízio de Azevedo's 1896 social protest novel, *O cortiço*, has been published as *A Brazilian Tenement*, trans. Harry W. Brown (New York: R. M. McBride, 1928).

7. Antônio Martins de Azevedo Pimentel, *Subsidios para o estudo de hygiene do Rio de Janeiro* (Rio de Janeiro: Carlos Gaspar da Silva, 1890), pp. 184–86.

8. Antônio Correa de Sousa Costa, *Alimentação que usa a classe pobre do Rio de Janeiro* (Rio de Janeiro: Typographia Perseverança, 1865), pp. 33–35; Pimentel, *Estudo de hygiene*, pp. 245–46.

9. Jacques M. May and Donna L. McLellan, *The Ecology of Malnutrition in Eastern South America* (New York: Hefner Press, 1974), pp. 299, 303–4.

10. *Jornal do Brasil*, June 2, 1920, p. 6; João de Barros, José de Castro, and Almir Castro, "Inquérito sobre condições de alimentação popular no Distrito Federal," *Arquivos de Hygiene* 4 (1930): 375.

11. See, for example, the *Gazeta de Notícias*, April 11, 1890; July 6, 1901; November 15, 1919; February 4, 1920.

12. Barros, Castro, and Castro, "Inquérito sobre condições," pp. 391, 396; Alvaro de Faria, "Alimentação e estado nutricional do escravo no Brasil," *Estudos Afro-Brasileiros* 1 (1935): 206–11.

13. Nancy Stepan, *The Beginnings of Brazilian Science* (New York: Science History Publications, 1976).

14. "Retificação das taxas," p. 34.

15. The 1937–39 death rates for whites were 15 per thousand in Rio and 16 per thousand in São Paulo; for blacks and mulattoes, 25 and 26 per thousand.

16. Mary C. Karasch, *Slave Life in Rio de Janeiro, 1808–1850* (Princeton: Princeton University Press, 1987), pp. 148–51; Edward E. Mays, "Pulmonary Diseases," *The Textbook of Black-Related Disease*, ed. Richard Allen Williams (New York: McGraw-Hill, 1975), pp. 417–18; and Kenneth F. Kiple and Virginia H. King, *Another Dimension to the Black Diaspora: Diet, Disease, and Racism* (Cambridge: Cambridge University Press, 1981), p. 146.

17. D. C. Morley, "Nutrition and Infectious Disease," in *Disease and Urbanization*, ed. E. J. Clegg and J. P. Garlick (London: Taylor and Francis, 1980), pp. 39–40; Karasch, *Slave Life in Rio*, pp. 138–40.

18. See Marshall B. Clinard and Daniel J. Abbott, *Crime in Developing Countries* (New York: John Wiley and Sons, 1973), pp. 17–18.

19. See, for example, Carl E. Pope and R. L. McNeely, "Socioeconomic and Racial Issues in the Measurement of Criminal Involvement," in *Race, Crime, and Criminal Justice*, ed. McNeely and Pope (Beverly Hills: Sage Publications, 1981), pp. 31–47.

20. *Jornal da Polícia* (Rio de Janeiro), February 1939, p. 1.

21. Ibid., February 1942, p. 280; December 1942, pp. 174–76.

22. Alison Raphael, "Samba and Social Control: Popular Culture and Racial Democracy in Rio de Janeiro" (Ph.D. diss., Dept. of History, Columbia University, 1981), ch. 3.

23. *Cultura Política* (Rio de Janeiro), October 1942, pp. 136, 155–60; March 1941, pp. 202–6; December 1942, pp. 54–70, 101–9.

24. Luiz de Aguiar Costa Pinto, *O negro no Rio de Janeiro* (São Paulo: Companhia Editôra Nacional, 1953), p. 99.

Part IV: Connections

Robert M. Levine

Elite Perceptions of the *Povo*

Brazilian historical scholarship traditionally sidestepped the existence of the lower classes except when authors spoke generically, as in the case of slaves under the Empire, or in imprecise terms (such as *povo*, for the people) that allowed the lower classes to be lumped together and held at arm's distance. Histories, written by members of the small urban elite trained in coastal capitals or in Europe, recorded events in such a manner that Brazil seemed to be progressing not as a result of collective labor, or men's sweat, but as the fulfillment of civilized Europeanizing ideology, the fruition of ideas about technological and material progress.

We know that Brazil's elites, those holding power or influencing it by virtue of their voices and perceptions, have long wrestled with ways of understanding, and dealing with, the impoverished and mostly nonwhite lower orders of the population. This chapter will examine the changing ways intellectuals and those wielding social and political power have viewed the status-less poor—the *povo* or the people. It is my contention that by the middle of the nineteenth century the *povo* posed a growing psychological threat to the affluent, who were bent on taming Brazil's wild and "uncivilized" reality. In this effort they conceived, partially overtly but mostly subconsciously, a dual set of images about the lower classes. Both portrayed things in the extreme. The first view romanticized the poor, emphasizing their docility and childlike state. The other characterized the poor as primitive malcontents, potentially disruptive and dangerous to social order. As time passed, a composite view, borrowing from both interpretations, captured the official imagination and became the basis for public policy.

Society reinforced the stereotypical views. Besides the military institutes, Brazil maintained only four university-level academies throughout the Empire: law schools in São Paulo and Recife and medical schools in Rio de Janeiro and Salvador. Graduates of these schools, never more than a few score each year, often practiced neither law nor medicine. Instead, the new *bacharéis* entered the imperial bureaucracy as officeholders, judges, and public prosecutors. A few others, usually from the highest echelons of the new urban elite, sought university training abroad and returned to exercise the craft of scholarship, which was often blended into journalism. After the explosion of cultural nationalism with the modernist movement rooted in cosmopolitan São Paulo in the early 1920s, a new generation of intellectuals attacked the Frenchified values of the Brazilian *belle epoque,* which had been characterized by a rigidly Comtean view of order and progress, one which blamed Brazil's lethargy on its racially mixed underclass and its tropical setting.

The modernists rejected the pessimism of the positivists, substituting lip service to indigenous culture for its own sake. The modernist movement embraced not only poets, essayists, and painters, but ethnohistorians (e.g., Gilberto Freyre), classical composers (e.g., Heitor Villa-Lobos), novelists seeking the substitution of Tupí language for official Portuguese, and others. Intellectuals rallied to the cause of the native Brazilian and championed the multihued rainbow of environmental texture and color. To some degree, this "valorization" of Brazil's tropical heritage followed logically from earlier literary depictions of the native, especially from the Indianist writers like José de Alencar, whose portrayal of godlike Indian nobility in his 1857 novel *Iracema* had fed the need of educated Brazilians for an idealized model to disguise the pathetic lives of the miserable and dwindling Amerindian population.

Euclides da Cunha's brilliant chronicle of the ill-fated Canudos campaign (*Os sertões,* 1901) excoriated the rebellious *jagunço* backlanders as regressive fanatics. But his elaborate descriptions of the "sub-human" rebels' tenacious resistance in the face of the Krupp cannons of the federal army conveyed deep-seated respect for the men and women whom he called "the bedrock of our race."[1] Da Cunha's epic so shocked the mentality of urban Brazil that da Cunha was hard-pressed to find a publisher for what ultimately came to be called a literary masterpiece of world scope and "the Bible of Brazilian nationality."[2] Taking arms against an era, *Os sertões* shattered the facade of Brazilian cosmopolitanism and revealed a hidden underworld of an alien and menacing lower-class culture.[3]

Narrowly circular despite its explosion of enthusiasm for new-found tropical virtues as the 1920s progressed, modernism nonetheless stretched the borders of Brazil's self-image by incorporating a mixed-race and lower-class perspective into its work. Mário de Andrade, the leading modernist celebrant, was himself a private man whose writings reflect a degree of disorientation about the themes of race and class. His major works, *Paulicéia desvairada* (1922) and *Macunaíma* (1928), shocked and astonished their readers not only for their stylistic chaos but also for their daring descent into the netherworld of race and national origins.[4]

As a private citizen, Andrade shed his cloak of flamboyance and studied Brazilian life as an amateur anthropologist. His diary fragments compiled during travels through the Amazon region and the coastal Northeast between 1927 and 1929 reveal how Andrade strained within himself to reverse da Cunha's apocalyptic vision of the hinterland and its population. Describing his reaction to the quality of life of the "lower orders" (*classes inferiores*), Andrade confessed that the physical conditions of the poor horrified him and brought on bouts of mental depression. But at the same time, he idealized the personality and character of the men and women of the countryside. People here, he remarked with relief, "greet you with smiles and hospitality. They are healthy and in excellent spirits. They rise in the morning singing. They sing leading their cows to pasture; their nights resound with their rustic choruses. From November to March the common folk immerse themselves in throbbing Carnaval rythms, deeply happy in their frenzied exhaustion."[5] These "proletarians," he observed, toil hard in the cane fields, shirtless under the torrid sun, but with an air of satisfaction nurtured by their "philosophy and patience." They take no solid nourishment at lunch, but drink *macororó*, a syrup of crude sugar, water, and lemons. "This kills hunger and thirst until their evening meal, which they consume at home after a full day on the land. Their wages are pitiful, but they seem contented. They are prolific. During the ten months of the drought they are idle except for producing children."[6]

Andrade's characterization of the childlike docility of the poor clashes with the stark reality of lower-class life in a region where eighty percent of a working family's entire wages had to be spent for food and where malnutrition and endemic disease afflicted large portions of the population. By the 1920s, other writers had begun to portray the dark side of rural life. José Américo de Almeida, for example, in his 1928 novel, *A bagaceira*, portrayed the harsh conditions of workers in the sugarcane fields of his native Alagoas. But on the whole, the nation's commitment to progress at any cost was reinforced by strong-arm measures to preserve social order. This was especially true after 1930, when the aftershock of the world depression brought down the federal republic. The so-called Revolution of 1930 apportioned centralized authority among civilian Getúlio Vargas, an eclectic coalition of politicians who had been relegated to the periphery of the First Republic, and military nationalists, at least at the beginning encompassing factions spanning the ideological spectrum from far right to far left.

New Worlds in the Tropics

Lacking comprehensive universities until well into the first third of the twentieth century, Brazilian intellectual life continued to find its expression in journalism and in the form of combative cultural movements exemplified by the rambunctious modernists. Only during the 1930s, when initiatives in education and to some degree in intellectual expression took on a more national orientation, did academicians, especially social scientists affiliated with the new universities in Rio de Janeiro and São Paulo, begin to look at Brazilian society in analytical ways. Under the influence of foreign, particularly French, social science, Brazilians in the 1930s produced essays and scholarly papers challenging existing interpretations of the past and examining the pathological social conditions among the povo.

Unlike the North American muckrakers earlier in the century, who probed social injustice to incite opinion on behalf of social change, Brazilian intellectuals shied away from social criticism. Indeed, some of them, led by Gilberto Freyre, scion of a long line of sugarcane patriarchs from Pernambuco's *zona da mata*, embellished the modernists' themes by extolling the virtues of Brazil's racially mixed population and proclaiming the mulatto and the *caboclo* the raw stock of a putative tropical civilization.

Reflecting the undercurrent of extreme conservatism that by 1935 had swept away most remnants of the preceding decade's mildly reformist efforts by politicians and educators, the new social scientists tended to define their subjects narrowly, describing conditions without offering measures to overcome them, much in the same manner as the abolitionists in the previous century. Or, like the wealthy industrialist (and Marxist) Caio Prado Júnior or the successful entrepreneur and economist, Roberto Simonsen, both from São Paulo, they presented new interpretations of the historical past in sweeping language, suggesting new periodizations and recognizing for the first time the impact of Brazil's economic dependence and conditions within its work force, but in neither case pointing to answers to Brazil's contemporary dilemmas.[7] Sérgio Buarque de Hollanda, another Paulista patrician schooled in Paris and Berlin during the early and mid-1930s, attempted to isolate the factors that had contributed to Brazil's unique national character. His *Raizes do Brasil* introduced the concept of the Brazilian as the *homem cordial*, pacific in nature and unwilling to employ violent solutions when conciliatory alternatives presented themselves.[8]

Of all the efforts to refocus historical emphasis and to recognize the contributions of lower-class culture and behavior, Freyre, the enfant terrible of his generation, went furthest toward challenging existing interpretations about Brazilian society. His *Casa grande e senzala* (1933), which described relations between masters and slaves on the sugar plantations of the Northeast throughout the periods of colonial rule and the Empire, utilized ethnohistory, folklore, and Freyre's own version of social psychology to substantiate the willingness of Portuguese men to mix sexually with native females and later with their own African slaves. Freyre shocked educated Brazilians by claiming that most elite families had widely practiced miscegenation. Arguing that the Portuguese lacked both the Catholic intensity of the Spanish and the repressed inhibitions of the Protestant English and Dutch, Freyre painted a sweeping canvas of benign paternalism and sexual license, richly documented with anecdotes from folklore and family histories, and in a way an academic version of Mário de Andrade's travel observations in the late 1920s. His writings captivated his readers with a certain adroit lasciviousness that titilated members of the educated classes, who normally expected history books to ignore the behavior of men and women after nightfall.

But the repressive mood of the Vargas regime by the mid-1930s, especially in Freyre's own Northeast, provided a convenient excuse for conservatives to run him out of town. Policemen padlocked the doors of the meeting of scholars he had organized in Recife in 1935—the First Afro-Brazilian Congress—because local families of good standing were scandalized by the scene of colorfully dressed black women selling Afro-Brazilian delicacies on the steps of the hallowed Teatro Isabel. Moreover, traditionalists were shocked to hear professors in academic sessions discussing such forbidden topics as the use of marijuana among manual laborers to stave off hunger.[9] Few noticed the irony that Joaquim Nabuco, scion of a white plantation family but also a leader in the abolition movement, had eloquently declaimed against the evils of slavery on those very steps. Freyre, who had just returned from foreign travels in 1934, took up residence in the South, where he emerged some decades later as a conservative and defender of the military regime. But if Freyre the young iconoclast was attacked as subversive, his message survived and was incorporated into the national mythology. It stood as an antidote to the traditional embarrassed pessimism that had suffused intellectual speculation about the human dimension of Brazil's past, present, and future.

Notwithstanding Freyre's undeserved label as a communist in the 1930s, his view of a new world in the tropics was especially appealing to nationalists who sought to combat what they considered the inherent weaknesses of Brazil's intellectual heritage. Freyre's outlook was molded by his educational experience, highly unusual for a Brazilian of the landed elite. As a boy, he was sent to the American Baptist School in Recife, and at the age of nineteen he was awarded a partial scholarship to study at Baptist-run Baylor University in Waco, Texas. After spending a couple of years there—his memoirs oddly skirt this period and he never talked of it later—he moved to New York City, where he took a Master's degree in history at Columbia University and attended, in the same class with Margaret Mead, lectures in anthropology by Franz Boas and other pioneers in the new discipline of group social behavior.

Freyre traveled to Europe before returning to Brazil with some avant garde notions that penetrated his thinking and were revealed in his growing interest in regionalism, folklore, and what today would be called popular culture. Although his 1930s writings in retrospect seem amateurish methodologically and fanciful in inspiration, his impact, publicly acknowledged only in the 1940s and beyond, was profound. Not only did Freyre invert popular wisdom

by accepting the notion of genetic improvement through race mixture, but he also declared the Brazilian product to be superior because of its pragmatic adaptability to the tropics. His clever and
elaborate impressionistic images of a tropical Eden forced scholars
to reexamine their own research and to deal with issues avoided by
polite traditional scholarship. His works were acclaimed as coura-
geous affirmations of national destiny; Freyre became a trophy on
the shelf of patriots seeking new myths to obscure social realities.
For at least twenty years after *Casa grande* appeared, novelists like
the regionalist writer Graciliano Ramos, who was jailed during the
1930s for his subversive views, carried the mantle of social consciousness. Most university scholars and social scientists remained
silent.[10]

Gradually, the 1930s saw increasing efforts to examine the social
fabric and to reform it. Deweyite educational innovation in the
states of São Paulo, Minas Gerais, Paraná, Pernambuco, and the
Federal District of Rio fell victim to conservatives like Cardinal
Sebastião Leme, who won official permission in 1934 to reintroduce
religious instruction in the schools in spite of the half-century-old
legal separation of church and state, and like Francisco Campos, the
nationalist author of the corporatist Estado Novo constitution and
Vargas's minister of education. The turn to the right politically did
not completely squelch academic research, although the government attempted, somewhat crudely, to manipulate public opinion
through its propaganda department and imposed some censorship.
Despite its authoritarian façade, the Estado Novo left most of the
universities alone. The late 1930s and early 1940s, in fact, saw a
limited flowering of social inquiry in some places, principally in
São Paulo, where a live-and-let-live attitude prevailed.

The record of the 1930s, then, was mixed. Some intellectuals
caught up in the anti-fascist popular front movements of the period
were arrested; educational reforms in the direction of mass literacy
campaigns and coeducation were suppressed; and the regime attempted to manipulate popular culture—even Carnaval samba lyrics—to instruct the unwashed masses in civic pride and the work
ethic.

In the Northeast, some social reformers and critics were dealt with
more harshly. Ulisses Pernambucano, a pioneer in the treatment of
mental illness (and a collaborator in Freyre's Afro-Brazilian Congress) was literally hounded to death by government agents who

kept him awake by sounding their automobile horns all night while the terminally ill physician, who had been fired from his posts, tried to sleep. Pernambucano had edited Recife's short-lived medical journal, *Neurobiologia*, which had examined such topics as the social causes of malnutrition and criminality. Others, including nutritionist and social critic Josué de Castro, fled into exile. On the other hand, some serious social science research was published, mostly under the sponsorship of the Arts and Letters Faculty of the University of São Paulo, established in 1934 with the help of foreign, mostly French, visiting professors.

A post-Freyre school of studies focusing on Brazil's social structure and on popular behavior slowly emerged. It was cautious and more restricted in scope but more sophisticated methodologically. Luís da Câmara Cascudo, a folklorist from Rio Grande do Norte, began to examine his region's African and caboclo heritage. René Ribeiro, a Recife anthropologist with training in psychology, embarked on studies of attitudes and deviance. But most studies in this vein continued to be descriptive, emphasizing the exotic. On the center right of the ideological spectrum, Catholics influenced by Jacques Maritain published essays and articles probing social responsibility. Likewise, Gustavo Barroso, a pro-Nazi member of the Integralist Party, published works of descriptive scholarship examining daily life in the backlands of his native Ceará, seeking new subjects worthy of nationalistic interest, as his mentor Plínio Salgado had done in the mid-1920s with second-rate modernist novels.

The Paulista school of sociology, the most lasting component of the gradual movement toward social self-examination, linked historians, anthropologists, and sociologists seeking to probe Brazilian life and to refute the contention that hierarchy in social organization was a desirable trait protected and reenforced by repressive authoritanism.[11] Its mentors included Roger Bastide, Claude Lévi-Strauss, Fernand Braudel, Pierre Monbieg, and T. Lynn Smith, who had been recruited from abroad during the middle and late 1930s to introduce university students to modern research techniques. Academic studies by the Paulista sociologists and anthropologists soon began to appear, as well as some pioneer work by the foreigners themselves, especially Bastide, whose work on blacks in São Paulo broke new ground in a number of areas. This new interest in social conditions was complemented by the work of economists on labor relations. But since the studies were aimed at academic audiences, they had little or no impact on policy making. For its part, the Estado Novo regime maintained its own roster of social scientists and journalists. Most worked for the Departamento de Imprensa e Propaganda (DIP), which produced a steady stream of articles and essays. Many of these appeared in the DIP's *Cultura política*, which for the most part extolled official efforts to examine social problems and remedy them. Real social reformism never flowed from scholars or from the universities, even after the 1950s, when Marxism became fashionable among many social scientists.

Defining the *Povo*

Society's views of the *povo* reflected the dreams and nightmares of the privileged. Usages of the term *povo* in modern Brazil constantly were built on pejorative images of laziness, weaknesses of character, and ignorance. Consider the slang term, *baile sifilítico* (syphilitic dance), defined in the dictionary as a "lower-class dance or festival of the *povo*, shabby and indecorous."[12] This contrasts strikingly with the Spanish term *pueblo*, which connotes, in neutral terms, the national population, or the German term *Volk*, which conjures up a folkloric image of people united by common roots.

In the political arena, the term povo evolved over time as a synonym for the electorate at large, with politicians dutifully paying rhetorical homage to the popular masses even though through the 1930s only a tiny percentage of the population—less than five percent—voted in elections. The first self-styled champion of the common man, Bahia's Ruy Barbosa, waged an unprecedented whistle stop campaign through the towns of Minas Gerais and São Paulo during his quixotic run for the presidency in 1910, yet by actual count Ruy delivered no more than a dozen speeches to public audiences, and in private he confessed that he preferred to remain in the presence of members of his own social class, whose civility he respected.[13] A half-century later, the incoming military president, Gen. João Baptista Figueiredo, stated to the press that he hated the charade of public appearances, because the povo smelled worse than his horse.

Over the years, the pejorative understanding of the term povo carried with it a clear connotation of cultural and social inferiority. Johann Moritz Rugendas, the famous Dutch painter of Brazilian scenes during the nineteenth century, wrote in 1835 that "if there is little difference between Lisbon and Rio de Janeiro, there is much more in the case of the lower classes, who may truly be called *povo*. Of the two nationalities, the Brazilian is by far the more shameless and crude."[14]

Some observers added a racial dimension to the distinction. Richard Burton, the British explorer, wrote in 1867, "Among the mestizo class, there are invariably some who are well behaved and proper. Boorishness increases proportionately with darkness of skin color."[15]

Imperial politicians who accepted the legal emancipation of slaves in the closing decades of the ninteenth century countered with new and stringent legislation promulgated immediately after slavery was outlawed. It defined vagrancy broadly and implemented repressive laws to limit the movement of indigents and gave authorities the right to expel any person not regularly employed. Even mestizos who themselves gained entrance into elite circles—elite is here intended to mean the upper, and part self-made, sections of Brazilian society—publicly gave to the povo attributes that, when identified with lower-class behavior, connoted degeneracy. Racist theories, introduced into Brazil in the late nineteenth century, fit with the prevailing positivist outlook, with its emphasis on Darwinian natural selection, and was taught in the medical schools even by mestizo professors such as Raimundo Nina Rodrigues in Salvador. Critics accepted at face value the theme of the infinite goodness of Brazil's landscape, but at the same time they accused its human inhabitants of despoiling the pastoral Eden. The nation, wrote novelist Octávio de Faria, is a "weak, poorly educated, and impertinent child, mediocre in all things; it has a few attractive features, but its body lacks regularity and proportion; it already has its vices, but does not yet have its virtues."[16]

The pejorative view reached a plateau of public acceptance with the ballyhooed publication in 1901 of Count Affonso Celso's *Porque me ufano do meu pais* (Why I boast of my country), a rhapsodic elegy to Brazil and the Brazilian character. To us today, the book seems a pompous testament of breathless patriotism. But for its public, still reeling from Canudos and insecure about Brazil's potential, it seemed to break new ground. In spite of his hyperbole, Celso damned the povo with faint praise, picturing the lower classes as a kind of national trophy, an essential ingredient in the tropical mix but a group to be treated with caution.

Celso's paean set the tone for generations of authors seeking simple, protective notions about Brazilian nationhood. Gilberto Freyre's works upheld this triumphalism, as did the writing of self-taught Mineiro writer Eduardo Frieiro, whose polemical *O brasileiro não é triste* (1931) refuted, point by point, the ringing pessimism of Paulo Prado. Prado, heir to the positivist natural selection argument, became a leading proponent of the more prevalent school, which held the povo in scorn. Such pessimistic viewpoints predated Canudos, however, appearing as early as the dour 1895 study by Pernambucano Sílvio Romero, *O caráter nacional e as origins do povo brasileiro*, and during the twentieth century tainted the writing of such diverse novelists as José Lins do Rêgo, Manoel de Oliveira Paiva, and Luís Martins.

The composite, or official, view of the povo borrowed equally from the triumphalist and the condemnatory ends of the spectrum. This view evolved as the years passed, sticking until the Second World War near the negative pole and afterward drifting closer to praise. What distinguished it from the other two was its pragmatism, rooted in the need to translate attitudes into policy.

The pragmatic strain was nurtured during the late nineteenth century, when Emperor Pedro II corresponded with the French diplomat Count Arthur Gobineau to personally refute some of the Frenchman's more extremist racist arguments. It crystalized in the early twentieth century writings of intellectuals Alberto Tôrres and Oliveira Vianna, both government ministers and archconservatives who speculated about the "problem" of the common people. Other officials, some with training as physicians or health care administrators, contributed to the view by offering medical explanations for the lassitude and dullness found among the lower classes. The armed forces invested considerable effort testing mental and physical fitness, as part of the larger modernization campaign during the 1910s and 1920s. The results usually confirmed existing prejudices, but although they offended liberal sensibilities, they were not necessarily inaccurate.

Grasping for euphemisms to describe the povo, writers and officials frequently chose terms like racial "substratum," barely hiding their distaste. "Of our rural population," a Paulista author wrote in 1924, reinforcing his argument with impressive (but unverified) census data, "15,200,000 are afflicted by endemic disease, including anchylosomiasis, malaria, grypanosomiasis, trachoma, leishmaniasis, leprosy, and alcoholism. Another 4,200,000 have syphilis or tuberculosis. Only 5,600,000 are relatively healthy." Cearenses, he continued, were thoroughly mixed racially and "patently reveal their physical and intellectual degeneracy. They are stunted, emaciated, and tend to have spinal defects." "Women, rarely attractive, are aged prematurely by excessive childbirth, frequently having fifteen or more children before turning emaciated at the age of forty. Naturally, this pauperized society produces an abnormally high percentage of dwarfs, cretins, deaf-mutes, blind, and victims of atrophied limbs." His solution? Inject "new and sanitary and honest elements" into the "Luso-Indian-African trinity" of the Brazilian population through immigration, a common theme in Brazil during the decade.[17]

After the 1930 revolution, critics turned to paternalistic models to deal with the problem of the masses. Prescriptions spanned the ideological spectrum. Left-wing nationalists, linked to the *tenente* forces that had come to power with Vargas, incited workers to mobilize, seeking a proletarian dictatorship and antifascist united front to rule for the benefit of all. Plínio Salgado's *integralistas* advocated corporatist discipline and vocational education for the underprivileged, a view not unlike the positivist notion or the prescriptions of the Mexican *científicos* under Porfirio Díaz. Vargas's provisional administration paid growing lip service to the povo, but it ignored the rural masses and the poorest elements in the cities, concentrating instead on skilled and semiskilled urban residents. With the advent of the Estado Novo in November 1937, the corporatist contention that the lower classes could be mobilized through planned action became official government policy. For the first time in Brazilian history, the government took an active role in teaching responsibility, the norms of acceptable behavior, the work ethic, and patriotic awareness to at least the urban masses. The DIP, in the planning stage since 1935 but formally inaugurated in 1939, directed nationwide efforts to shape public opinion and to reinforce family integrity and conservative values.

Underlying all this was the new official view of the povo as the undeveloped raw material of the future: passive, uncomplaining, in need of motivation, and potentially grateful to the helping hand of authority. This theme was revived almost intact after the 1964 revolution, when far more sophisticated vehicles, including government-controlled television, were employed to carry out necessary national guidance and instruction.

The political meaning of the term *povo* naturally took on more complexity as time passed. In the 1930s Vargas and other political figures adopted populist strategies designed to win the support of the growing urban vote, a good portion of which now included newly franchised members of lower income groups. The percentage of adults eligible to vote, determined by loose applications of literacy criteria by electoral officials, rose with each new election. This meant that politicians now had to provide rewards for urban voters, both in the form of personal recognition (hence the growing use of radio by Vargas and state-level politicians in the 1940s) as well as patronage and benefits. The creation of a national food-distribution agency, SUNAB, in 1938 represented to some degree a deliberate attempt by the government to keep prices of basic foods down by controlling competition and providing price subsidies when needed.

Thus the term *povo* in the political arena came to represent not the lowest elements of the population—the rural poor, and the most destitute urban residents, mostly migrants squatting in makeshift shantytowns—but the politically active (and economically mobile) urban lower classes. Politicians like Adhemar de Barros of São Paulo built their careers on their ability to speak to these Brazilians. Populism, revived in the 1950s during Vargas's second presidency (1951–54) and again under Juscelino Kubitschek (1956–61), championed the *povo* even if most of the benefits distributed by government went principally to the middle and upper classes. Under the even more populist regimes of Jânio Quadros and João Goulart, the definition of *povo* was stretched to incorporate rural as well as urban men and women, acquiring, at least at the end of the Goulart period, an image of an incipient proletariat, potential allies of the left-leaning regime against the forces of imperialism and internal privilege. The fall of Goulart in early 1964 ushered in the military and redefined the *povo* in the hierarchical terms of the 1930s.

Under the post-1964 military government, *povo* virtually disappeared from use. Gen. Emílio Garrastazu Médici's publicity advisors sought to exploit his well-known passion for soccer to emphasize his kinship with the common people, but the effort never succeeded in any meaningful way. It is noteworthy that since 1919 every civilian president elected to office was known publicly by his nickname or first name, except for those who governed under a state of siege (Artur Bernardes; Vargas at the outset of the 1930 revolution). Bernardes was derisively called "Seu Mé," and when samba composer Freyre Júnior in 1922 composed a *marchinha* entitled "Aí, Seu Mé," Bernardes ordered him arrested on three different occasions. Getúlio Vargas was known as "Gegê," but he permitted its use only during the later populist phase of his political career. The highly unpopular Paulo Maluf, official candidate for the presidential succession in 1985, was commonly known by a number of obscenities and mocking epithets, a measure of the degree to which the political process, in the streets, had come to deal with manipulated populist impulses.

Conclusion

Brazilian social history has typically been written in reaction to economic change and political policy. Even when protest wells up from below, it usually is dealt with in ways that preserve the status quo. One would like to examine laws and official policies in terms of their impact on society at large. But everyday events seem so mundane, so incoherent, and so lacking in internal continuity that they leave neither written records nor indications of motivations and perceptions.[18] It has been shown that whenever European artists attempted to grapple with the frustrations of the real world, they used social realism as a dominant cultural mode.[19] But in Brazil, the modernists sought a new kind of fantasy, rooted in the tropical earth but larger than life, distorted, profoundly removed from the daily conflicts and struggles of the people. A strain of social realism evolved among such writers on the left as Graciliano Ramos, but even Ramos and his fellow regionalists avoided obvious prescriptions for social change. The Cinema Novo of the early 1960s briefly riveted attention on the plight of the poor and on social injustice, but Brazilian audiences shied away, and the reappearance of cinema vérité in the late 1970s lacked the original intensity of its predecessor.

The tendency to evade the implications of endemic misery among the Brazilian povo has been compounded by the fact that the view embracing conformity and rejecting pluralism has dominated both official policy making and intellectual expression. This in turn has isolated centrifugal movements that promote group identity (e.g. black consciousness) or, oddly in a society proud of its multiethnic origins, that resist homogenization. It is not accidental that the modernists' prototypical folkloric hero, Mário de Andrade's Macunaíma, always is remembered for his "lack of identity and character."[20] From the modernists to the "tropicalists" of the 1960s, the theme has remained constant: fusion, not individuality; conformity, not idiosyncratic expression. The Brazilian national attitude, then, has withheld favor from assertive and combative elements within the population. This in turn has made the task of the social historian more difficult, since by definition the integrative thesis rejects nonconformity because it is anti-Brazilian.

Notes

1. Euclides da Cunha, *Rebellion in the Backlands*, trans. Samuel Putnam (Chicago: University of Chicago Press, 1944), p. 482.

2. The quote is from Olímpio de Souza Andrade, "Os sertões numa frase de Nabuco," *Planalto* 1, no. 14 (December 1, 1941), cited by Putnam in *Rebellion*, p. iii.

3. Braulio Sánchez-Saez, "Euclides da Cunha, constructor de nacionalidad," *Agonía* (Buenos Aires) 4 (October-December 1939): 50–56.

4. David T. Haberly, *Three Sad Races: Racial Identity and National Consciousness in Brazilian Literature* (Cambridge: Cambridge University Press, 1983), pp. 5, 136–42.

5. Mário de Andrade, *O turista aprendiz* (São Paulo: Livraria Duas Cidades, 1976), pp. 258–59.

6. Ibid., p. 295.

7. See Dante Moreira Leite, *O caráter nacional brasileiro* (São Paulo: Universidade de São Paulo, 1954), esp. p. 273; Carlos Guilherme Mota, *Ideologia da cultura brasileira, 1933–1974*, 4th ed. (São Paulo: Atica, 1978).

8. In 1975 he told me that his concept of the cordial man, when integrated with Freyre's view of a benign national character, seemed to have taken on a more romantic tone than he originally intended.

9. Robert M. Levine, "The First Afro-Brazilian Congress," *Race: A Journal of Race and Group Relations* 15, no. 2 (October 1973): 185–94.

10. See Graciliano Ramos's posthumous *Memórias da cárcere*, 4 vols. (Rio de Janeiro: José Olympio, 1954), which was made into a film with antimilitary overtones in 1984.

11. Interview with Florestan Fernandes, São Paulo, June 19, 1980.

12. Alexandre Passos, *A gíria baiana* (Rio de Janeiro: Livraria São José, 1973).

13. Courtesy of Washington Luis Neto, Fundação Casa Rui Barbosa, Rio de Janeiro. Cf. Gilberto Freyre, A condição humana e outros temas (Rio de Janeiro: Grifo Edições, 1972), pp. 138–39.

14. Johann Moritz Rugendas, Viagem pitoresca através do Brasil (São Paulo: Livraria Martins/Universidade de São Paulo, 1972), p. 78.

15. Richard Burton, Viagem de canoa de Sarará ao Oceano Atlântico (São Paulo: Universidade de São Paulo; Belo Horizonte: Editora Itatiaia, 1977), p. 161.

16. Haberly, Three Sad Races, pp. 167–73; quote from p. 168.

17. T. de Souza Lobo, São Paulo na federação (São Paulo: by author, 1924), pp. 153–57.

18. See, for example, Richard C. Cobb, The Police and the People: French Popular Protest, 1789–1820 (Oxford: Clarendon Press, 1970), pp. 3–4.

19. Carl E. Schorske, Fin-de-Siécle Vienna (New York: Knopf, 1979), p. 280.

20. Alfredo Bosi, "O nacional, artigo indefinido," Folha de São Paulo, May 10, 1981, p. 5.

Joseph Dean Straubhaar

Mass Communication and the Elites

Radio and, more recently, television have become the dominant forces in Brazilian mass culture and communication. The role of television may surprise those who are not familiar with recent Brazilian development. In the industrial countries, particularly the United States, Japan, and Western Europe, the major part played by television in shaping mass culture has long been recognized. In most developing countries, however, television has not had sufficient penetration among the lower social strata and in rural areas to make it such a powerful cultural force. In these societies, radio is still preeminent, and television and print media reach primarily the middle class and elites, who then pass on certain values and images to the lower strata in person, via extended personal networks or via more popular media.

In Brazil, at least two-thirds of the population are thought to have regular access to television. In 1980, television penetration of Brazilian households was 56 percent: 73 percent in urban areas and 15 percent in rural areas.[1] However, television is the most effectively national medium in that its major networks reach virtually the whole audience. For example, TV GLOBO's "Jornal Nacional" evening news program is by far the most widely shared source of information.[2] Radio is, by contrast, regional or local in Brazil, unlike Colombia or other countries where national radio networks have a significant reach and impact.

The only other truly national media, according to national surveys, are newsmagazines, whose readership tends to be limited to the middle class and elite. Daily newspapers have limited national circulation. While elite papers such as *Jornal do Brasil*, *O Globo*, *O Estado de São Paulo*, and *Folha de São Paulo* have some national reach, they are very limited in their actual readership outside their regions, even though they are influential in forming elite opinion and in setting news agendas for radio and television media.[3] The typical example might be a *Jornal do Brasil* story repeated in a Salvador, Bahia, newspaper that is then read over the air in a radio newscast in the interior of Bahia.

This central role of Brazilian television as the major mass medium is also attested by an analysis of the networks' size and industrial growth. Brazil's major television network, TV GLOBO, is currently considered the fourth largest commercial television network in the world (in terms of audience, production, and revenue), right behind the three major United States networks.[4] Brazil also has a vast system of radio stations, mostly commercial AM and FM stations, and a large number of regional and local newspapers. This chapter will focus on television and radio as the primary mass media in Brazil.

Although a substantial proportion of the entertainment and news programming broadcast on television and music radio is imported, chiefly from the United States, Brazilian stations create more of their own material than do most broadcasters in either the developed or less developed countries. The same is true of newspaper and news-magazine material. This national content and the industries that create it represent a thriving mass culture. The degree to which this Brazilian material represents an authentic popular culture depends on an industry structure and production process that is dominated by national elites, government, and multinational elites but is open to considerable assertion of local culture and interests.

This chapter concentrates on several types of elite uses or attempted uses of media to influence the mass audience and the ensuing effects on mass culture. First, the commercial pattern of the media industries represents the interests of business elites in creating a limited pattern of consumption among the populace. This reflects both national and foreign/multinational elite interests, but brings up a second separate question of foreign influence on the mass audience via elites and media. Third, military and other national elites have tried to use media content to create a perceived national identity, conducive to the model of the "economic miracle." Fourth, national elites now struggle to control mass media content on political, economic, and "moral" issues, with alternative political elites, as well as other interest groups such as feminists, influencing media content.

Masses, Elites, and the Broadcasting Industry

Some authors believe that an elite controls mass culture and ideology through ownership of the industry.[5] Others see the media as "ideological apparatuses" that tend to be dominated by the state but are the site of ideological struggle among elites and between elites and some mass groups.[6] Going a bit further, others argue that popular culture is sometimes successfully asserted and defended, despite elite control, even on a national level.[7]

Some definitions are in order. Popular culture usually signifies all forms of cultural expression by the general body of the people, as distinguished from those of artistic or commercial elites. Mass culture is a variation on that basic concept but entails a separation from both artistic high culture and traditional folk culture. Mass culture implies industrial-scale production and mass consumption of cultural artifacts.[8]

Brazilian scholars, in applying these ideas to their country's industrializing economy, tend to focus on the roles of the state and multinational corporations in asserting control over mass culture via this process of industrialization.[9] They analyze also the national commercial elites, which push for the development of a market economy in which culture is used to advertise a variety of consumer goods.[10]

The tendency toward commercialization of the media in different countries is interpreted in various ways. Until the development of the dependency critique, the focus in Brazil was on development of commercial media by powerful family or industrial groups. Dependency theorists tend to see a pattern of cultural imperialism, in which commercial media aid the penetration of the Third World by the capitalist system.[11] Others see a less concerted but still pervasive process of global homogenization of media systems brought about by importation of programming, transference of colonial powers' models to former colonies, adoption of advertising-based systems, and imitation of successful foreign models by local entrepreneurs.[12]

Most broadcast stations in Brazil (over 95 percent) operate on a commercial basis.[13] To attract advertiser revenue, they must draw an audience that the sponsor desires to reach and present programming that does not contradict the basic nature of the advertising message. The advertising itself carries a powerful, elite-determined message promoting certain goods. By offering an apparent chance for success in material terms within the system, advertisements also create an attitude of political conformism and acceptance of the existing social order.[14]

Both foreign and domestic commercial elites tend to create or reinforce commercialism and the basic acceptance of the economic and political system. Peter Evans's work on Brazil shows that dependence on external financial sources and technology is difficult to avoid and that many Brazilian industries operate within a tripod of support from multinationals, domestic firms, and public enterprises. This analysis fits broadcasting quite well, within some limits.[15] One difference is that direct foreign investment in broadcasting has ended, in Brazil and in most of Latin America. It was stopped by a combination of government intervention and buy-outs by local partners, as in the case of Time-Life and TV GLOBO in Brazil. Financial dependence on multinational advertising lingers, but as Sérgio Mattos has pointed out, local corporations and government have become relatively more powerful as competing sources of advertising revenue.[16]

In conflicts with multinational corporations, national personnel can and do assert their own interests and sometimes uphold local values, because they represent the national elites and can call on the government for support.[17] The case of TV GLOBO's 1962–70 joint venture agreement with Time-Life is illustrative. TV GLOBO executives used Time-Life capital and technical advice but rejected their programming suggestions. In 1968, just when the venture became profitable and gained dominance in the local market, the TV GLOBO owners again asserted their independence, using government pressure and subsidies to buy out Time-Life altogether.[18]

In a number of developing countries, where for years imported programs dominated the airwaves, more local initiative and autonomy have appeared, both for TV programming and for radio music. This has been especially true for television in Argentina, Brazil, Egypt, Hong Kong, India, Mexico, Taiwan, and Venezuela. Others, like Jamaica and the Dominican Republic, produce much of their radio programming.[19] Even with increasing national autonomy in production, however, the question of elite hegemony over content still stands. In fact, the opportunity to create national programming reveals most clearly the interplay between mass and elite cultures.

The relationship between the television industry and the military governments reveals a pattern of cooperation to cover Brazil's territory and audience with a "national" signal to reinforce a national identity. While striking, this is hardly unique to Brazil. A survey of Third-World broadcasting in the mid-1970s revealed such media-government interaction as a primary goal in most countries.[20] The pattern of censorship in both news and entertainment programming under the military governments and during the political transition or abertura does, however, reveal a struggle between elites for control of national media content. (These points will be further elaborated during the historical analysis below.)

Mass Audience Uses and Effects from Mass Communication

Both foreign content and national programming produced by elites affect the socioeconomic classes differentially. The upper and middle classes have the most contact with multinationals, have more disposable income with which to consume the manufactured products advertised, and have more contact with imported products.[21] Some scholars argue that the elite and middle class work with multinationals to create a dual economy in which income is concentrated to create a limited consumer economy for the select groups.[22]

Consumption of imported culture is also differentiated by class. In Brazil, the Dominican Republic, Mexico, and Venezuela, for example, audience surveys show that the upper and middle classes are more likely than lower class audiences to watch imported American television series when they compete with locally produced programs, such as the telenovelas (soap operas). This is consistent with the view that the bourgeoisie in a developing country has international tastes compared with those in rural and small town areas. Analysis of the 1963–77 period shows that Brazilian television programming has been nationalized increasingly as the audience has been extended to lower social classes and broader geographic areas.[23]

Many Brazilian scholars nevertheless believe that even those stations that feature domestically produced popular culture for a mass market are permeated and conditioned by an agenda and ideology set by elite groups and interests.[24] This corresponds to a debate in the United States and Western Europe about elite ideological hegemony, the determinism of economic class interests, and the role of the media. Some scholars, particularly those interested in political economy, have observed strong ideological control exercised through the media, based on economic determinism of media ownership and class interests.[25] Others, calling themselves post-structuralists, see media effects on audiences as fragmented and too inconclusive to support such a strong conclusion.[26] Finally, empirical audience research shows that audiences in Latin America, especially in Mexico, Brazil, and Venezuela, are active in selecting and thinking through media content depending on their own needs.[27]

Many United States, European, and Brazilian scholars now posit a complex interaction between classes, competing cultural ideas, and economic and other determining structures. Muniz Sodré, for example, observes that

mass culture has to be understood as a complex system that includes the following: (a.) consumer motivations oriented through advertising by the interests of domestic and foreign companies; (b.) government interests; (c.) a mythic level remnant and reincorporation of oral culture; (d.) the dilution and continuing creation within high culture; and (e.) the effect of the old mechanisms of the collective national conscience through which the powers of the communication system/structure project their elite ideas and training.[28]

Similarly, Carlos Eduardo Lins da Silva says we need to examine more carefully "how members of the subordinate class elaborate their own cultural production and select, interpret, reinterpret, absorb, and use the cultural production of the hegemonic classes." His observations derive from a study of how very differently workers' communities in southern and northern Brazil understand and interpret the main evening television news program, "Jornal Nacional," on TV GLOBO.[29]

History of Brazilian Radio Broadcasting

Brazilian media have been privately owned and commercially operated from the time of Portuguese colonization.[30] Most of the revenue for these media came from commercial advertising. At several times, however, major financial support has been provided by political parties, public agencies, and other interest groups.

Brazilian radio began with amateur, experimental clubs in the early 1920s. Stations soon began to take on paying sponsors and became commercially successful, even though early audiences were restricted to those with enough income to afford the new technology.

Most programming was live and emphasized news, but soon it shifted toward entertainment like variety programs and comedy with live audiences. The number of broadcasters and receivers grew dramatically in the 1930s and 1940s. As the audience expanded further into the middle and lower classes, more popular entertainment like recorded music and radio drama appeared.

Initial government involvement in mass media was minimal, but in the late 1930s President Getúlio Vargas found radio a useful tool for mobilizing popular support for his regime. He encouraged the development of commercial radio and used it extensively for propaganda between 1937 and 1945. He increased the power of the public Rádio Nacional, one of the most influential stations for several decades. He kept tight control over the political content of radio news through a censorship office, the Department of Press and Propaganda (DIP), setting a pattern for authoritarian uses of this medium.[31]

The presidents who served from 1945 until the late 1950s paid little regulatory attention to radio and television broadcasting, although both media were used in political campaigns. Commercialism continued to be the accepted form of financing, as private enterprise and consumption grew as a result of economic development. This period also saw rapid expansion in the manufacture of consumer goods that required advertising.[32] In this period, therefore, commercial elites probably had more direct influence over the direction and content of broadcasting than did political elites.

Brazilian radio networks followed a pattern common throughout Latin America in the 1940s and 1950s: ownership rested with a few newspaper magnates, usually based in key families and led by powerful figures like Francisco de Assis Chateaubriand (*Diários Associados*) and Roberto Marinho (*O Globo*). Networks developed as the commercial advantages of sharing program and news material among stations in different cities became clear. Networks also had a strong political motivation. Favors and patronage came more often to media owners, such as Assis Chateaubriand, who could provide geographically extensive multimedia coverage to politicians. This participation in electoral politics was strongest between 1945 and 1964, when Brazilian radio and television began to perform the mobilization role common to mass media in populist politics elsewhere. Partially in reaction to such mobilization of urban and rural masses, the military governments that took over after 1964 limited the electoral use of radio and television. In particular, the educational radio stations of the Catholic Church in the Northeast were dismantled or severely discouraged from mobilization efforts.[33]

The major radio network was Diários e Emissoras Associadas. As early as 1938 Assis Chateaubriand had acquired five radio stations, twelve newspapers, and a magazine. This group consciously played the political field to maximize profits. Nevertheless, hundreds of local stations emerged in the 1940s and 1950s that were not directly tied into national politics. AM stations increased from 440 in 1956 to 1130 in 1982, while FM stations rose from none to 398 in the same period. Furthermore, the largest numbers of stations developed in those states with many small and medium-sized towns beyond the broadcast range of major cities, i.e. Pernambuco, Minas Gerais, São Paulo, and Rio Grande do Sul.[34] Relatively few of these stations are now tied to national radio networks, although many are associated locally with other stations or media companies, educational groups, or even religious groups. In most cases, the basic message of these unaffiliated stations was and is commercial, with various forms of entertainment to draw an audience. These tie in to local political and commercial elites, as well as to national elites, via advertising agencies.

Elites and Mass Culture on Radio

Radio set patterns for broadcasting in Brazil: the pursuit of a mass audience; predominance of entertainment over educational or cultural programming; private over government ownership; advertiser support over government, public, or noncommercial financing; importation of program material; and a countervailing tendency to use a great deal of Brazilian music, drama, and comedy. Only a few stations, owned publicly or by religious groups, took a more educational, developmental, or even political approach. Where radio did not set a pattern for television was in its decentralization, which both reflected and reinforced a less central role for national elites in radio.

Although the emphasis on entertainment emerged fairly early in Brazil, the choice of regional, national, or foreign sources has never been uniform. For example, in a study of the cultural changes brought about by mass media in a small town in the state of São Paulo, Luis Augusto Milanesi noted that radio started out being popular for its rapid delivery of the news but then gradually became an entertainment medium. While broadcasting was still live, country or *caipira* and classical music prevailed. These forms were later replaced by recorded music from the big cities, sambas, Brazilian popular music (often called MPB), and foreign materials. Sports and talk shows also became popular on radio, as stations shifted to more limited or specialized audiences.[35]

The segmentation of audiences into special interest groups became most notable in the 1970s and in the larger cities, where competition between large numbers of radio stations led to more targeted appeals to certain groups. This was particularly true for FM stations, which sought middle- and even upper-class audiences. (Studies show that FM audiences do in fact have higher education and income levels and higher consumer aspirations.[36]) Elite audiences seemed to favor classical music, news, and talk shows focused on their interests. The mass audience tended more toward popular music, news, sports, talk shows pitched at them, variety, comedy, and soap operas.[37] The mass audience tended to use AM radio:

AM radio in Brazil seems to have escaped the massive infusion of North American materials. The programming tends to be more regional, with a predominance of Brazilian tunes. Newscasts, in general, emphasize local news related to politics, crime, and weather . . . [Our] results show that AM listeners tend to be less educated and have lower income levels. These audiences also seem to consume less food, appliances, and luxury items; a characteristic of most peripheral populations. Perhaps AM radio represents a hope for the revival of indigenous Brazilian culture, which has been gradually buried under the pressure of imported programming.[38]

Some overlap occurred, of course, so that radio audiences were not completely segmented by class; still, the proliferation of stations in major urban markets meant that only a few could hope to retain broad audience appeal. This proliferation and segmentation of radio stations and audiences seems to have resulted in a fractionalization of elite influence on the mass audience via radio; those elites not directly concerned with programming, advertising, and news on mass-oriented stations became less aware of what these broadcast, and commercial elites tended to be less concerned with broadcast content than with whether the desired audience was being attracted. Political elites retained an interest in content, as the elimination of some stations following the 1964 revolution indicates, but their ability to exercise direct control was strained by the proliferation of stations. The most obvious remaining control was censorship in the form of the list(s) of news items not to be covered; these were issued to stations by various political and military authorities from 1968 until the late 1970s.

In cultural material, radio seems to have emerged as a medium where lower-class interests are rather directly expressed, subject of course to elites' roles in the culture/music industry. Again, however, elite controls are diminished by the diffuse, decentralized nature of radio production.

Music programming at first depended on local culture and talent, since it was broadcast live. Even after recordings became available, radio continued to promote local forms, like samba, *frevo*, *baião*, and other folk music. These eventually became mass culture. For example, as internal migration from the Northeast to the Center-South occurred, rural music (*sertanejo* and *caipira*) became more broadly played. Radio accelerated the professionalization of music, allowing performers like Carmen Miranda national exposure.[39]

The soaps, known as *radionovelas*, derived from foreign sources, like serialized French novels popular during the 1880s and radio programs imported from Cuba, where the *novela* form was pioneered by the Colgate corporation. The soaps are a good example of a format or genre that was originally imported to serve elite commercial interests but that evolved into distictively national forms appealing to the middle and lower class. This is not to say that they no longer served a commercial elite interest: indeed, they became very effective ways to promote the Brazilian way of life developing in Rio de Janeiro and São Paulo, but they are a good example of the domestication by national elites of forms introduced by foreign elites for their own purposes.[40]

Many aspects of the American radio variety show were probably also copied by Brazilian programs. Charismatic hosts used live interviews, singers, games, audience participation, amateur performances, and games, for example. Nonetheless, writers and hosts inserted distinctly Brazilian characters and situations into these shows, with references to history, popular music, literature, and folklore. Such variety shows evolved into the *show de auditório*, which some analysts regard as the heir of several traditional oral culture entertainment forms, like story telling, circus patter, and popularized folk music. The military governments of the late 1960s and the 1970s censored the shows de auditório and even closed some down, due to morally and politically questionable content and to the inherent challenge of prior censorship for live discussion programs.

A good deal of political discussion occurs on radio talk and variety shows. At least during the 1964 revolution, this was within the limits set by censors, but this has changed since the late 1970s. Often local and national news serves as a vehicle for political commentary. Audience surveys suggest that the middle and upper classes listen to the radio primarily for music and prefer newspapers and television as a source of news. Lower-class audiences, on the other hand, tend to get their only news from radio, which seems to be one of the less directly elite-controlled media. Television, when it is available to them, is a source of entertainment.[41]

The History of Television

While radio still tends to be local and regional, television has emerged as the primary nationwide purveyor of news, information, and entertainment. Television and newsmagazines are the only media with truly national scope, and the latter are purchased only by the middle and upper classes. The national reach of television has been promoted by both private and public interests.

Due to the high production costs for television (roughly ten times those of radio), television stations are under greater pressure than are newspapers or radio stations to consolidate into networks of a few production stations and outlying affiliates. Some local television stations remain independent, but the most successful ones have often been bought out by larger chains. Even those that remain independent may affiliate with a network to obtain its programming and share its advertising. This centralization of television production makes elite control easier than in radio.

Assis Chateaubriand began television in Brazil when he created his TV TUPI network in 1950 to complement his media empire. Others started up stations, but revenues were too small to cover such proliferation. This was due to the small number of people who could afford televisions, limiting advertiser interest.[42]

By the early 1960s, however, the industrial situation changed for commercial television. The economy had grown rapidly as the government invested in infrastructure and basic industry, leading to the acceleration of a consumer goods market. Because of this economic incentive, the government stepped in to promote television, much more than it had radio. This process became even more pronounced following the 1964 coup. The government made available low interest loans for the purchase of television sets, built a microwave network that carried television shows to remote locations, and bought much advertising through its public corporations. More recently, the government launched a communications satellite and began building receiver stations in remote regions to make distribution less costly.

The development of a general telecommunications system was a high priority for the military governments. They saw it as vital for economic development, but also for national security and winning popular support. Broadcasting, especially in more remote regions, would help reinforce a sense of national identity by carrying news of government development efforts and other messages. The military governments also wanted a national television system to spur the market economy, coinciding with, if not driven by, commercial elite interests. This period of government sponsorship of television is probably the clearest case of elite intervention in mass media in Brazilian history.[43]

The television audience has grown enormously with such promotion by the government. Most members of the lower middle class in major cities have sets. Between 1960 and 1983 the number of sets in use went from three-quarters of a million to twenty-two million. Although television reaches over 70 percent of the Brazilian population, its coverage is still less than that of radio. The 1980 census revealed that about 55 percent of Brazilian households have TV sets: 73 percent in urban areas but only 15 percent in rural locations.[44] In the latter, bars, markets, and restaurants have public sets for their clients. Group viewing in a variety of places expands the rural television audience considerably.

The growth of a mass audience for consumer goods attracted major advertising revenues after the late 1960s. The share of advertising spent on television has risen from 6 percent in 1959 to 61 percent in 1983, largely at the expense of other media. (In 1983, newspapers took 15 percent, magazines 13, and radio 8.) Furthermore, these revenues have until recently been highly concentrated in TV GLOBO, which has usually drawn between 60 and 90 percent of the television audience.[45]

Several television networks—among them TV GLOBO, TV RIO, and

TV EXCELSIOR—revamped their programming to achieve more mass appeal. They began to create or import programs that would sell products like soap, tobacco, textiles, food, and electical appliances. Advertising for limited elite products began to shift to magazines and the few TV stations that targeted upper-class viewers. Unlike their radio counterparts, TV managers did not segment their audiences at first. Instead, they sought broad general audiences, like United States networks.

The commercial success of TV GLOBO in dominating the mass audience became evident in the late 1970s and early 1980s. Government officials seemed concerned about TV GLOBO's growing monopoly, so they encouraged the creation of two new networks, TV MANCHETE and TV SÍLVIO SANTOS, with licenses formerly belonging to TV TUPI. TV GLOBO continued to dominate, though, and competing networks began to seek more specialized audiences, even when they went national. TV BANDEIRANTES and TV MANCHETE program for the upper middle class, and TV SÍLVIO SANTOS (Sistema Brasileiro de Televisão—SBT) pursues the lower middle and lower classes. (A magazine advertisement for SBT says, "We cover popular themes and materials. . . . Our programming speaks to the people. This enormous mass of people who consume cigarettes, matches, drinks, who buy things and save . . . "[46])

TV GLOBO still dominates the market, despite tough competition in urban areas. In August/September 1987, TV GLOBO had 65 percent of the audience in the six major urban centers, compared with 23 percent for SBT, 3 for TV MANCHETE, 5 for TV BANDEIRANTES, and 4 for independent stations.[47] TV GLOBO is also often the only network available in rural areas. This makes TV GLOBO (and to a lesser degree the other networks) an excellent vehicle for transmitting culture, ideology, and propaganda. It also allows the network to charge high rates without driving out advertisers. This commercial success apparently had its political price: TV GLOBO seems to have worked very closely with government propaganda agencies and business elites.

Brazilian government influence in TV GLOBO and other networks has been extensive but far from complete. Between 1970 and 1984 the novelas and the news showed a pattern of censorship and self-censorship on critical economic and political issues. In addition, pro-government themes and announcements were frequently aired. A good example of government intervention was its insistence on national program production. In the early 1970s, several ministers pushed the networks to develop more Brazilian material and to reduce reliance on imports, especially those that contained violence. TV GLOBO pushed ahead in this direction, because its executives had discovered that general audiences preferred nationally produced musicals, comedies, and soaps over most imported programs.

Government censors in the 1970s closely monitored television for certain objectionable matter, and they sometimes cancelled novela episodes or required their refilming. Even TV GLOBO, which had fairly good relations with the government, sometimes had bitter exchanges with censors. During the 1970s and early 1980s, the production of TV programs was the outcome of a complicated dialectic among market demands, formal and informal censorship, and managers and writers.[48] This made for a complex interaction among elites, with cultural elites occasionally winning some battles with military and government elites over both "moral" and political content. Other elites, such as the church, national business interests, and multinational corporations, also affected the television content that the mass audience received.

Elite Mass Culture on Brazilian TV

Back in the 1950s, when television reached only the middle and upper classes in a few major cities, programming was necessarily elite. Theatre, ballet, classical music, and highbrow variety shows maintained levels of quality that have been called a "golden age." Moreover, technical problems kept out most foreign material. In the 1960s, however, the emergence of a mass audience led to shifts in programming. Imported shows became more common, and domestically produced programs tended toward the soap opera (novela), the variety show, game shows, popular music, and staged comedy.

The novelas provide a good illustration of this trend. They had been around since 1952 but had been somewhat limited in popularity, because of imported scripts and low production quality. Many of the technicians had been trained in radio. In the 1960s, however, the average length of a soap opera stretched out to nine months, they came to be aired daily, and quality was improved by using nationally recognized writers, directors, and actors. Scripts became more sophisticated and reflected Brazilian culture. A milestone in this process was the highly acclaimed 1968 novela, "Beto Rockefeller," which featured a singular Brazilian personality type who bridged mass and elite culture, the Rio de Janeiro bon vivant.[49]

Scriptwriters became especially good at building telenovelas into a distinctive genre by drawing on regional and historical themes. They also mined Rio's middle-̇ and lower-middle-class life, where the dominant themes tended to be upward mobility, consumption, and elegant life-styles. These messages not only appealed to their audiences—they also served the interests of economic and political elites by creating a climate favorable for advertisers and liberal spending.

Novelas have also been a major scene of elite conflict over culture, however. Conservative social and religious forces have reinforced government moral and political censorship, but have been opposed by commercial elites within the media and by other cultural and political elites. Multinationals and national business interests have pushed against controversial economic themes in some novelas. On the whole, novelas have reflected the political transition called abertura as much as the news, culminating according to some in "Roque Santeiro," a 1986 novela that showed politics in a small Brazilian town but so cleverly reflected the national political moment that its audience was often over 90 percent.[50] Other opposition points of view have also been expressed in novelas, even before the political transition. Feminist interests have also been reflected in "Malu Mulher" and ecologists' in "Sinal de Alerta," for example.

The variety show also made the transition from radio to television and became very popular among lower-middle- and lower-class viewers. Some, such as the "tropicalistas," even claimed that shows de auditório like Chacrinha's were the epitome of Brazilian popular culture, a genre where elite control over popular culture was lessened and where mass audience interests could really be expressed. Critics of the genre, however, decried the often vulgar behavior on the variety shows, and government censors, reflecting middle-class tastes and political fears about live talk shows, forced most of them off the air in the early 1970s. The relaxation of censorship in the late 1970s brought a resurgence in variety shows, the most popular of which was that of Sílvio Santos. Santos in fact founded a network oriented to such popular fare that, as noted earlier, gradually took second place behind TV GLOBO.

Variety shows have also specialized to meet the needs of particular groups, beyond the general "popular culture" audience. TV GLO-

BO had a weekday morning program called "TV MULHER," which had a variety of talk and discussion segments aimed at women, primarily those in the middle class.

Brazilian television, as a commercial medium, is clearly entertainment oriented. News also prospers, however, which is what ratings indicate the viewers prefer. Globo's evening news is very popular, even among working-class viewers.[51] News interview programs have also done well, especially in middle- and upper-class audiences. During the political transition, TV MANCHETE and TV BANDEIRANTES both promoted controversial interview formats and topics, and TV GLOBO followed suit. Such programs have enjoyed greater freedom in the early 1980s due to the relaxation of censorship, but self-imposed limits continue to exist. These programs also tend to appear at time slots and on networks that appeal more to the middle class and elite; while mass audiences could watch such programs, they do not seem to have been the primary targets for them.

Imported television programs, such as feature films, adventure series, and children's fare, flooded Brazil in the 1960s. They were cheap, slickly produced, and popular. Imports have gradually been replaced by domestic production, a trend definitely preferred by the mass audience. For example, in 1982 only 22 percent of viewing time was dedicated to foreign programs, down from 48 percent in 1965.[52] The principal mass audience demand for imports recently has been for an occasional action or adventure series on Globo's prime time. In general, though, imports are now relegated to non-prime-time slots as cheap filler and to smaller independent stations and networks that target middle-class or upper-class audiences. Many originally assumed that multinational advertisers would promote programming imports, but they seem to have accepted a market that is segmented by class but in which Brazilian programming probably predominates among all classes' viewing preferences.

Conclusion

Brazilian radio and television seem to be solidly established as major cultural industries, successful both commercially and esthetically. A great deal of news, sports, interviews, and music are produced for and by local radio, primarily for the mass middle- and lower-class audience. Extensive quantities of mass culture programming are also aired on Brazilian television. TV GLOBO, which enjoys around 70 percent of the market, produces 12–14 hours a day. Radio and television share a great deal, including ownership, genres, and material. Nevertheless, the implications for mass-elite communication are quite distinct in the two media, so I will treat them separately.

AM radio seems to be a more authentic purveyor of popular culture, while FM shows more penetration by foreign elite culture as expressed in imported music. The dispersion, independence, and diversity of radio stations tend to make them more responsive to local popular culture. Although nearly all stations are commercial; their intended audiences vary widely, as do their contents. Local talk shows, sports programs, and some musical fare continue to reflect local and regional cultures to a great degree. Even if they remain insulated from national elite control, however, these independent radio stations are closely tied to local elites, with their family, business, personal, and professional networks.

Most local radio stations have very low budgets, so they tend to use whatever prerecorded material is available and acceptable to their audience. This means that radio will use a great deal of imported music, in addition to Brazilian recordings. Media specialists using impressionistic evidence believe that radio uses more imported material than television.

Television, on the other hand, is more open to elite control because of its centralized network organization. A few key decision makers in government, in management, in advertising, and among the creative personnel exercise almost total control over the content of TV GLOBO, which reaches 50–90 percent of the audience. This potential for hegemony has not, however, become reality, due to internal debate within Globo and competition from other networks. It is particularly noteworthy that the audience Globo now loses most consistently to SBT (Sílvio Santos) comes from the lower middle and lower classes.

Competition is probably a mixed blessing in Brazilian television. TV SÍLVIO SANTOS and a few others opened up new audiences and experiment with new kinds of programming, especially featuring lower-class culture. This induced TV GLOBO to put more popular material on the air, but in sanitized or edited versions. They have

242 Joseph Dean Straubhaar

been very successful in this and have made a contribution to the creation of quality popular culture, particularly in the case of some novelas.

A tripartite alliance among local capital, foreign corporations, and government regulates broadcasting. The precise locus of control changes from sector to sector and over time. In the television industry, the preponderance of power had until recently been held by the government, a major source of advertising, capital, and censorship. Current trends, however, suggest a moderate swing back toward primary control by domestic economic and business elites; this continues to be the case with radio stations.

The civilian governments of the late 1980s promised to be less interventionist and ideological than their military predecessors, even though their economic influence will remain decisive. Although more manifest diversity of content will be available, if censorship declines, the latent and paramount message of both radio and television is still to promote the benefits of consumer culture to both mass and elite audiences.

Notes

1. Brazil, Secretaria de Imprensa e Divulgação, *Mercado brasileiro de comunicação* (Brasília, 1983), p. 86.

2. United States Information Agency (USIA), Office of Research, "Media Use by the Better-Educated in Four Major Brazilian Cities," 1982.

3. USIA Office of Research.

4. *Washington Post*, May 3, 1984.

5. Graham Murdock and Peter Golding, "Capitalism, Communication, and Class Relations," in *Mass Communication and Society*, ed. James Curran (London: Edward Arnold, 1977), pp. 12–43.

6. Louis Althusser, "Ideology and Ideological State Apparatuses," in his *Lenin and Philosophy, and other Essays*, trans. Ben Brewster (London: New Left Books, 1971); and Antonio Gramsci, *Selections from the Prison Notebooks of Antonio Gramsci*, ed. and trans. Quintin Hoare and Geoffrey Nowell Smith (London: Lawrence and Wishart, 1971).

7. Sérgio A. S. Mattos, "Domestic and Foreign Advertising in Television and Mass Media Growth: A Case Study of Brazil" (Ph.D. diss., Dept. of Mass Communications, University of Texas at Austin, 1982); Muniz Sodré, *A comunicação do grotesco* (Petrópolis: Vozes, 1971); and Joseph Dean Straubhaar, "The Transformation of Cultural Dependence: the Decline of American Influence on the Brazilian Television Industry" (Ph.D. diss., Dept. of Mass

Communications, Fletcher School of Law and Diplomacy, Tufts University, 1981).

8. T. W. Adorno, "Television and the Patterns of Mass Culture," in *Mass Culture*, ed. Bernard Rosenberg and David Manning White (Glencoe, Ill.: The Free Press, 1957), pp. 474–88.

9. Gabriel Cohn, *Comunicação e indústria cultural* (São Paulo: Companhia Editôra Nacional, 1971); Octávio Ianni, *Imperialismo e cultura*, 2d ed. (Petrópolis: Vozes, 1976).

10. Emile McAnany, "The Logic of Cultural Industries in Latin America: The Television Industry in Brazil," in *Changing Patterns of Communications Control*, ed. Vincent Mosco and Janet Wasko (Norwood, N.J.: Ablex, 1984).

11. Cees J. Hamelink, *Cultural Autonomy in Global Communications* (New York: Longman, 1983); Herbert I. Schiller, *Mass Communications and American Empire* (Boston: Beacon, 1969).

12. Jeremy Tunstall, *The Media are American* (New York: Columbia University Press, 1977); Elihu Katz and George Wedell, *Broadcasting in the Third World* (Cambridge: Harvard University Press, 1978).

13. In 1983, of 1818 Brazilian radio stations, 1784 were commercial. Of 118 television stations, 113 were commercial (*Latest Statistics on Radio and Television Broadcasting*, Statistical Reports and Studies, no. 29 [Paris: UNESCO, 1987], p. 42).

14. Luís Beltrán, "TV Etchings on the Mind of Latin Americans," *Gazette*, 1978; José Marques de Melo, "Escapismo e dependência na programação da TV brasileira," *Comunicação e sociedade* 5 (1981): 147–60.

15. Peter Evans, *Dependent Development: the Alliance of Multinational, State, and Local Capital in Brazil* (Princeton: Princeton University Press, 1979).

16. Sérgio Mattos, *The Impact of the 1964 Revolution on Brazilian Television* (San Antonio: V. Klingensmith, 1982) and "Advertising and Government Influences: The Case of Brazilian Television," *Communication Research* 11 (April 1984): 203–20.

17. Raquel Salinas and Leena Paldán, "Culture in the Process of Dependent Development: Theoretical Perspectives," in *National Sovereignty and International Communication*, ed. Kaarle Nordenstreng and Herbert I. Schiller (Norwood, N.J.: Ablex, 1979), pp. 82–98; and Ingrid Sarti, "Communication and Cultural Dependency: A Misconception," in *Communication and Social Structure*, ed. Emile G. McAnany, Jorge Schnitman, and Noreene Jonas (New York: Praeger, 1981), pp. 317–34.

18. Straubhaar, "Transformation of Cultural Dependence," pp. 121–77.

19. Tapio Varis, "The International Flow of Television Programs," *Journal of Communication* 34, no. 1 (Winter 1984): 143–52; Livia Antola and Everett M. Rogers, "Television Flows in Latin America," *Communication Research* 11, no. 2 (April 1984): 183–202.

20. Katz and Wedell, Broadcasting in the Third World.

21. Salinas and Paldán, "Culture in Dependent Development."

22. Antônio Dias, "Responsabilidade cultural da radiodifusão," paper presented at the Simpôsio Sobre Radiodifusão, Rio de Janeiro, August 1975; Teotônio dos Santos, "Brazil: The Origins of a Crisis," in Latin America: The Struggle with Dependency and Beyond, ed. Ronald H. Chilcote and Joel C. Edelstein (Cambridge, Mass.: Schenkman, 1974), pp. 415–86.

23. USIA, Office of Research, "Media Use by the Better-Educated in Four Mexican Cities," 1981, and "Media Use by the Better-Educated in Four Major Brazilian Cities," 1982.

24. Gabriel Cohn, "Televisão nos anos 1970," Folha de São Paulo, November 18, 1979; Ianni, Imperialismo e cultura; and Sodré, A comunicação do grotesco.

25. Graham Murdock and Peter Golding, "Capitalism, Communication, and Class Relations," in Mass Communication and Society, ed. James Curran (London: Edward Arnold, 1977), pp. 12–43.

26. Stuart Hall, "The Rediscovery of Ideology: Return of the Repressed in Media Studies," in Culture, Society and the Media, ed. Michael Gurevitch et al. (New York: Methuen Press, 1982), pp. 56–90.

27. Joseph Dean Straubhaar and Kwadwo Anokwa, "Information Seeking and Media Use by Elites on International Issues in Brazil, Mexico, and Nigeria," paper delivered at the International Communication Association, San Francisco, May 1984; John McNelly and Fausto Izcaray, "Selective Media Use by Venezuelans: The Passing of the Passive Audience in a Rapidly Developing Society," Studies in Latin American Popular Culture, forthcoming.

28. Sodré, A comunicação do grotesco, pp. 22–23.

29. Carlos Eduardo Lins da Silva, "Transnational Communication and Brazilian Culture," in Communication and Latin American Society: Trends in Critical Research, 1960–1985, ed. Rita Atwood and Emile G. McAnany (Madison: University of Wisconsin Press, 1986), pp. 89–111; Lins da Silva, Muito além do Jardim Botânico: Um estudo sobre a audiência do Jornal Nacional da Globo entre trabalhadores (Petrópolis: Vozes, 1982).

30. Nelly de Camargo, Communication Policies in Brazil (New York: UNESCO, 1975); Maria Elvira Bonavita Federico, História da comunicação: Rádio e TV no Brasil (Petrópolis: Vozes, 1982).

31. Miriam Goldfeder, Por trás das ondas da Rádio Nacional (Rio de Janeiro: Paz e Terra, 1981); Sérgio Caparelli, Comunicação de massa sem massa (São Paulo: Cortez Editora, 1980).

32. Mauro Salles, "Opinião pública, comunicações, marketing, e publicidade no processo brasileiro de desenvolvimento," speech at the Escola Superior de Guerra, Brasília, September 10, 1975.

33. Ralph Della Cava, "Catholicism and Society in Brazil," paper pre-

sented at the Conference on Popular Culture and Democratization in Brazil, University of Florida, April 1, 1985.

34. *Propaganda,* January 1983, p. 74.

35. Luís Augusto Milanesi, *O paraíso via* EMBRATEL (Rio de Janeiro: Paz e Terra, 1978), pp. 75–79.

36. Omar Souki de Oliveira, "Consumer Behavior and the Brazilian Media: Socio-Cultural Implications," paper prepared for the International Communication Association meeting in Belo Horizonte, Brazil, 1988.

37. José Silveira Raoul, "O desenvolvimento da televisão no Brasil," *Suplemento do Centenário do Estado de São Paulo* 4 (October 1975).

38. Omar Souki de Oliveira, "Consumer Behavior."

39. Robert M. Levine, "Elite Intervention in Urban Popular Culture in Modern Brazil," *Luso-Brazilian Review* 21, no. 2 (1984): 9–22; Federico, *História da comunicação,* pp. 52–55.

40. Tunstall, *The Media Are American;* Artur da Távola, *A liberdade do ver: Televisão em leitura crítica* (Rio de Janeiro: Nova Fronteira, 1984); Cohn, "Televisão nos anos 1970."

41. See the USIA's Brazilian and Mexican audience studies, as well as the various IBOPE surveys.

42. Grupo de Mídia, "Concentração econômica e mídia," paper presented at Congresso Brasileiro de Mídia, São Paulo, April 1978; Sérgio Mattos, "Advertising and Government Influences: The Case of Brazilian Television," *Communication Research* 11 (April 1984): 203–20.

43. Mattos, "Domestic and Foreign Advertising," pp. 25–62.

44. *Propaganda,* January 1983, p. 75; Brazil, Secretaria de Imprensa e Divulgação, *Mercado brasileiro de comunicação* (Brasília, 1983).

45. Grupo de Mídia, "Concentração econômica," p. 76.

46. "SBT: Líder absoluto da vice-liderança," *Veja,* November 10, 1987.

47. Ibid.

48. Távola, *A liberdade do ver,* pp. 76–78.

49. Joseph D. Straubhaar, "The Development of the telenovela as the Preeminent Form of Popular Culture in Brazil," *Studies in Latin American Popular Culture* 1 (1982): 138–50.

50. Joseph D. Straubhaar, "The Reflection of the Brazilian Political Opening in the Telenovela [Soap Opera], 1975–1985," and Randall Johnson, "Roque Santeiro," both forthcoming in *Studies in Latin American Popular Culture* 7 (1989).

51. Sarah Chucid da Via, *Televisão e consciência de classe* (Petrópolis: Vôzes, 1977).

52. Antola and Rogers, "Television Flows in Latin America."

Fred Gillette Sturm

Religion

The distinction between elites and masses becomes blurred when we consider the religious dimension of Brazilian society. This chapter defines elites and masses in terms of who possesses power and who does not, and separating the two in religious matters is often difficult. We can, however, identify some religious communities that consist largely of the elite or are controlled by elites, and others whose adherents are drawn largely from the masses.

In the internal power structures of religious institutions, the distinction between elites and masses refers to those who exercise authority and leadership within the community of faith, as opposed to simple adherents and practitioners of the faith. To be a member of a religious elite does not necessarily confer elite status in the larger society. Indeed, the religious community often provides an opportunity for those who have been disenfranchised in the secular world to rise to positions of authority. At the same time, some Brazilian religious institutions have provided avenues for social mobility and political expression for persons not born with the usual requisites for elite membership.

The chapter begins with a discussion of Catholicism, Brazil's oldest Western religion, as a connection between elites and masses. It then focuses on the religious movements that enjoy the most widespread popular support, Umbanda and other Afro-Brazilian religious communities. Finally, it examines Protestantism, which through educational institutions has had an impact on society far beyond what would be supposed based on membership size.

Catholicism

Roger Bastide wrote, "from the beginning of the colonial period [there have been] two Catholicisms that were different and often in opposition: the familial Catholicism of the colonists and the patriarch, and the more Roman and universalist Catholicism of the religious orders, especially that of the Jesuits."[1] It has become customary to refer to two Catholicisms existing side by side throughout Brazilian history. In terms of belief and practice, Brazilian Catholicism is often divided into a popular or folk religion side, and an official ecclesiastical side. Most recently, Leonardo Boff, the renowned Franciscan theologian of liberation, has described a church of the powerful standing opposite a church of the poor. The former is a capitalist church that owns the church and controls power, and the latter comprises the faithful, who are effectively disenfranchised.[2]

The true situation is far more complex, however, than either of the above views would suggest. First, the official church structure has never been a single monolith. Indeed, José Comblin insists that the Roman Catholicism defined by canon law and orthodox theology has never existed in Brazil, not even among the clergy and hierarchy.[3] In his study of the development of the church, Eduardo Hoornaert identified three major ecclesiastical strands that were woven into the unique syncretic Luso-Catholic fabric to which Brazil is heir.[4] First, he notes a medieval strand, with its accent on patriarchal organizational structure, an emphasis on other-worldliness, and the spirit of the militant crusades. Second, he finds a Counter-Reformation strand that stresses individualistic spirituality and sacramentalism, apologetics, and dogmatics. Third, he identifies a Catholicism of the Baroque, which shows an affinity for ceremonial pomp and drama, together with an emphasis on mystical spirituality tinged with emotion. The interweaving of these three strands produced something uniquely Luso-Catholic, rather than Roman and universalist, and had important implications for the development of both official and popular Brazilian Catholicism.

Two recent series of events reveal the unique nature of Brazilian Catholicism. First is its persistent opposition to the military government, from the mid-1960s to the return of civilians to power in 1985. The most vocal critics were Dom Hélder Câmara, archbishop of Olinda-Recife, and Dom Paulo Evaristo Arns, archbishop of São Paulo. Thomas Bruneau wrote in 1972 that "the Church is the only institutional opponent of the government, and the number of bishops, priests, nuns, and laymen who have suffered for their beliefs is legion."[5] This discord was only the most recent chapter in a long history of changing relations between the political and ecclesiastical elites of Brazil.

The second recent development reflecting the uniqueness of Brazilian Catholicism was the silencing of the leading theologian of liberation, Leonardo Boff, by the Vatican, followed by the unexpected lifting of the interdict. Although on the surface the issue seemed to be merely academic and theological, it really concerned the successes experienced by a grass roots movement within Brazilian Catholicism, the Ecclesiastical Base Communities, or CEBs. The Vatican viewed the CEBs as a threat to regularly constituted Church authority. Boff was seen as a spokesman for the masses who have no access to power in the traditional church and who are also socioeconomically disadvantaged in society as a whole. Boff's ordeal marked another chapter in a long struggle between the official ecclesiastical structure and popular or folk Catholicism.

The Church and the Political Elite

Cross and crown were intimately linked in Brazil from the moment its official discoverer, Pedro Alvares Cabral, anchored off the coast in 1500 and had his men go ashore to erect a wooden cross and hoist the flag of the Order of Christ. Even after Brazil's independence from Portugal in 1822, the church-state relationship remained intact, for Article 5 of the 1824 constitution declared that "the Roman Apostolic Catholic Church will continue to be the Religion of the Empire." For the next 65 years, the church remained tied and subordinate to the state, which carried out most of its administrative functions. Only one episode marred the usually amicable church-state relations: the Religious Question of 1872–76, when Bishop Dom Vital and a colleague went to prison for violating the constitution. More than any other event, the Religious Question proved that the church-state alliance was becoming untenable. Church and state were separated immediately after the overthrow of the empire in 1889.

Brazil's bishops soon published a pastoral letter celebrating the separation of church and state, calling it blessed independence from government control. They naively spoke of continued unity, since both church and state had the same followers. In fact, the liberated church of the 1890s was extremely weak, with reference to both the political elite and to the society at large. The intellectual elite of the late nineteenth century had rejected the faith as popularly practiced, viewing it as largely irrelevant superstition, and Brazil's high culture became increasingly secular. As Fernando de Azevedo observed, "There followed reciprocal indifference, if not practically a dissociation between the Church and the world, between religion and the living forces of society."[6] By the early twentieth century, the church appeared headed for gradual extinction in Brazil.

Beginning in 1916, several church leaders attempted to renew their contacts with the political elite, and these efforts gave rise to an informal collaboration known as the revitalization movement. Dom Sebastião Leme, Bishop of Olinda, is credited with beginning the process with his famous pastoral letter of 1916. In it he noted that although Brazil was nominally a Catholic country, the church wielded no influence in the nation's political life. He called on the faithful to act like the majority they were to influence the nation's destiny. This would be achieved in two ways: through popular education to raise the level of "religious literacy" and through recruitment of members of the secular elite to help broaden church influence in social and political affairs.

In the early 1920s, as Archbishop Coadjutor of Rio de Janeiro, Dom Leme took positive action to achieve the second goal. He created the Catholic Confederation, through which the many archdiocesan lay organizations could be coordinated. He also encouraged church leaders to become involved in journalism, education, labor unions, and social work. These efforts were eventually consolidated into the Brazilian Catholic Action, founded in 1935, which had subgroups for secondary students (JEC, or Catholic High School Youth), college students (JUC, or Catholic University Youth), and workers (JOC, or Young Catholic Workers). The latter groups provided much of the leadership for a growing progressive or reformist wing of the church.

In the 1920s, Dom Leme also sponsored a group of young intellectuals who began a veritable crusade to give the church a greater role in the nation's cultural life. At the time he began his work in Rio, Jackson de Figueiredo, a young and newly converted layman, had founded a journal, *A Ordem* [The order], and an organization, the Dom Vital Center, for the purpose of creating a Catholic intellectual elite. Although they sought rather broad bases, Jackson's overzealous approaches tinged the center's activities with partisanship, so that in the end its membership remained small. Jackson, for example, was a strong supporter of André Maurras's notion of a Catholic International that could fight godless communism and other enemies of the true church.

The direction of the Dom Vital Center changed sharply after Jackson's death in 1928. Its leadership passed to Alceu Amoroso Lima, a wealthy young writer and critic. Alceu (who wrote widely under the pen name Tristão de Ataíde) was an admirer of Jacques Maritain's neo-Thomism and integral humanism. In the 1930s he founded branches of the center in the major cities and managed to convert the movement into a liberal wing of the church. He sponsored conferences with leading authors, artists, and intellectuals, promising a veritable cultural renaissance. Following the tenets of the social encyclicals of Leo XIII and Pius XI, Amoroso Lima and his colleagues at the Dom Vital Center initiated a reform movement that addressed social, political, and economic problems.

Dom Leme supported the work of Amoroso Lima and of other Catholic lay leaders from 1930, when he was made Cardinal, until his death in 1942. He especially focused his efforts on Getúlio Vargas, who became provisional president in 1930 and managed to stay in power for the next fifteen years. Twice in his first year in office, for example, Vargas was presented with Catholic demands for policy reforms. In 1933 Leme formed the Catholic Electoral League, which gained political influence in several states. Using a pressure group strategy, Leme succeeded in having most of his policies accepted by Vargas and incorporated into the 1934 constitution.

Even after the replacement of the 1934 charter by the Constitution of 1937, which created the dictatorial Estado Novo, Leme and Vargas continued to relate dialectically with one another, the leader of the ecclesiastical elite attempting to influence the leader of the political elite and vice versa. Vargas, an agnostic, played along in order to gain more backing for his regime. This mutually supportive relationship, which Thomas Bruneau called Neo-Christendom, ended by the mid-1940s, with Leme's death and Vargas's ouster.[7]

In the absence of a leader of Cardinal Leme's stature, the ecclesiastical elite split sharply into two warring factions, the traditionalists and the progressives. The new church leadership came from the latter camp. In 1952, Dom Hélder Câmara, Archbishop of Olinda and Recife, organized the National Conference of Brazilian Bishops (CNBB) and served as its first general secretary. Except for the quinquennium 1965–70, the CNBB has since its formation been progressive and even radical in its social and political orientation. For example, it encouraged such initiatives as the MEB (Movement for Basic Education), CIM (Council for Indigenous Mission), and the

CEBs. It has encouraged grass roots activism in church as well as secular affairs.

The CNBB has been active since 1964 on a number of fronts, mostly in opposition to the military government. It may indeed be portrayed as an advocate for the disenfranchised and victims of oppression and injustice. Examples were its campaign for human rights and protests against political torture; its appointment of the Pastoral Land Commission to call for implementation by the government of agrarian reform legislation; and its defense of the sovereignty and rights of indigenous peoples in the Amazon basin.

Students of modern Brazilian church history disagree on whether or not 1964 marked the beginning of a new era, distinct from the earlier one dominated by Cardinal Leme and Amoroso Lima. Those who argue for continuity stress the relations between the church and secular elites. Both before and after 1964, the ecclesiastical elite came from the upper middle class and advocated social reforms in accordance with liberal Christian values. Those who emphasize change point out that the church's course of action is now directed toward politicization of the masses. Leaders at the grass roots are encouraging radical change from the bottom up, in accordance with a new reading of Christian scripture, history, and theology. Bruneau, speaking of the "substantial change in the Brazilian church's overall orientation," notes that "the new approach clearly favors the lower classes and other oppressed sectors and seeks to assist them by means of a variety of instruments and processes." His interviews in 1978 "indicated that politicians . . . are turning to the church for support . . . It may well be that this decade will witness a resurgent church."[8]

Popular Catholicism and the Organized Church

Until the appearance of a progressive faction of the ecclesiastical elite in the 1920s and 1930s, there had been little concern for the bulk of Catholic laity, which had for centuries lived on the margins of Brazilian society. This neglect had given rise to a popular or folk Catholicism that has taken on several different forms and has flourished despite the lack of pastoral leadership.

The first manifestations of popular Catholicism date to the early colonial period, when sugar dominated the economy and rural settlement patterns prevailed. It was the patriarchal or familial Catholicism of the plantation that Gilberto Freyre described so well.[9] Popular Catholicism also appeared in the urban centers of colonial Brazil. *Irmandades*, brotherhoods or voluntary lay associations loosely connected with the church hierarchy, were multipurpose organizations that served as religious fraternities, mutual aid societies, and service clubs. The irmandades provided a place where popular or folk Catholicism could flourish.[10]

By the early twentieth century, a class of lay holy men and women, called *beatos* and *beatas*, became associated with folk religion. They were usually very devout and pious people, uneducated and credulous, who responded to a sense of religious vocation. Most left no historical record, but a few—like Antônio Conselheiro of Canudos—founded messianic cults that became famous. Such lay-directed folk religious movements represented the popular Catholicism of the masses, a religious expression controlled by people who were not part of the church's hierarchy. These unofficial movements can be called the forerunners of today's CEBs and the *grupos da rua* (street groups), even though the latter have radically different beliefs and practices. Folk religion has been uninformed biblically and theologically and has concerned itself largely with festival celebration. The CEBs, on the other hand, have stressed Bible study and theological discussion of social action.

Cardinal Leme understood the need to transform traditional folk Catholicism through programs of adult education and the establishment of labor and peasant organizations that would work toward the improvement of living conditions for the masses. In 1922 he formed the first workers' circles in the industrial suburbs of Rio de Janeiro. These groups provided labor education and sponsored consumer cooperatives and medical clinics. In 1935 Leme incorporated the JOC (Young Catholic Workers) into his broad Catholic Action movement and extended its base of operations to include agricultural laborers. Through these and other societies affiliated with Catholic Action, Leme attempted to encourage widespread and active lay participation in the life of the official church.

Despite these efforts, he failed to generate a genuine Catholic mass movement, because the initial organization as well as continuing leadership tended to be provided either by the ecclesiastical elite or by laity associated with the Dom Vital Center. Amoroso Lima, for example, was committed to the development of a strong Catholic lay movement, yet his focus was on the intellectual and cultural elite, not the masses. Thus the center's membership was drawn almost exclusively from the upper and middle classes. As a result, Leme, Amoroso Lima, and others succeeded only in creating a Catholic lay elite that cooperated closely with the clerical elite in providing leadership in programs designed for the masses—a far remove from a genuinely grass roots movement.

Ironically, Dom Hélder Câmara and the CNBB—the top of the hierarchy—were most responsible for fostering the mass Catholic movements in the 1960s and 1970s: the MEB, which conducted Christian-oriented literacy programs, and the CEBs. MEB began in 1958 as a project initiated by the Bishop of Natal, using radio for a diocese-wide program of literacy and social education. Two years later the CNBB extended the project to include four dioceses. Shortly thereafter, a five-year federal grant arranged by President Jânio Quadros made it possible for MEB to encompass the whole nation. MEB guidelines came from the philosophy of adult education created by Paulo Freire in his literacy work in Recife in the 1950s. This approach utilized classroom dialogue that stimulated the participants' belief in their ability to transform the structures of the society that oppressed them, a process Freire called *concientização*, or consciousness raising.

The origins of the CEBs are more obscure. The earliest communities date from the late 1950s or early 1960s and may have been outgrowths of MEB literacy groups. Although many were initiated by parish priests or nuns, once established they continued to grow and function entirely under the direction of local leaders. Because these are true grass roots communities, their organization and functions vary widely. Most, however, engage in regular corporate prayer, Bible study, theological interpretation (the true locus of Liberation Theology), and discussion of practical communal concerns related to society and politics. As such, the CEBs are not just religious groups but also gatherings of poor peasants, factory workers, migrants, under- and unemployed persons: i.e., the socioeconomic masses.

Alvaro Barreiro describes CEBs thus:

Nearly all the CEBs in Brazil, located in the rural areas and, to a lesser extent, in the poor neighborhoods on the outskirts of cities, are communities of the poor. According to the study prepared by the [Brazilian Development Institute] . . . the locations of the CEBs . . . are as follows: 53.5 percent in rural areas, 10.9 percent in suburban areas, and 16.8 percent in urban areas. . . . The fact that virtually all the CEBs in Brazil are communities of the poor has been confirmed by the observations made at the General Assembly of Bishops of São Paulo, the wealthiest state in the nation.[11]

It is estimated that the number of CEBs rose from 40,000 to 80,000 between 1979 and 1981, partly due to encouragement of the CNBB. This support included convocation of annual Inter-Ecclesial Encounters of the CEBs, beginning in Vitória in 1975. Themes discussed in the six meetings held thus far reveal a radical bent: "A church that is born out of the people by the spirit of God"; "The church: A people on the move"; "The church: A people who are freeing themselves"; "The church: An oppressed people organized for liberation"; "CEBs: A united people, seed of a new society"; "CEBs: The church in search of the promised land."

Umbanda and Other Afro-Brazilian Religious Communities

This multifaceted religious movement continues to grow rapidly throughout Brazil.[12] The Afro-Brazilian sects began as exclusively African phenomena, efforts at cultural survival by peoples cut off from their heritages and thrust into slavery in an alien land. Although they have broadened their memberships greatly, they still represent religions of the masses.

The basic features of Umbanda, the most studied Afro-Brazilian sect, emerged as early as the seventeenth century. Slaves on plantations secretly recreated tribal leadership by annually selecting a king. Those fortunate enough to escape from slavery, to form *quilombos* or runaway camps, likewise selected their kings. In either case, they held ritual coronations called *congadas*, after the generic king of the Congo.[13] The congada ceremony called for at least two contingents of costumed persons to "dance the Congo." One represented the royal court, the other the retinue of a second nation on diplomatic mission to the coronation. Although the dates on which congadas were held varied, they usually coincided with a Catholic saint's day, to disguise the activities as Christian.

The most popular time of all for a congada was (and is) during the three days of pre-Lenten Carnaval celebrations. In many ways, modern Carnaval is a secular version of the congada. Rio de Janeiro's Rei Momo (King of the Carnaval) is none other than the king of the Congo. The competing lines of dancers in the samba schools replace the congada dancers. The samba itself derives from the rhythmic patterns that accompanied the dance movements of African ritual ceremonies. José Ribeiro reminds us, however, of a crucial transformation that has occurred: Rei Momo presides over three days and nights of carefree hilarity and symbolizes extreme social irresponsibility, whereas the king of the Congo represented restoration of authentic African political authority and provided both temporal and spiritual leadership to the underground community.[14]

Rossini Tavares de Lima, who studied congadas celebrated along the coast between Rio and São Paulo, discovered a variation in theme that pits two political elites (and two religious systems) against each other. Here the king of the Congo has been captured by Portuguese nobles and is being taken to celebrate mass in honor of São Benedito, patron saint of the blacks. The second line of dancers represents Congolese people who disrupt the mass, attempt to liberate their king, but ultimately fail. Tavares de Lima suggests that the congada "enlists 'sons of the earth,' who find themselves in an inferior status within society, socially and economically speaking, and in [the congada] they encounter the motivation to project themselves in confrontation with the external elements that have begun to exercise dominion within the same society. Remembering traditions, their components provide an outlet to the repressions of the social order."[15]

In traditional African societies, generations now dead (the "living dead") continue to play influential roles in behavior and policy. Therefore, continuity of historic community depends not only on annual reaffirmation of a king and his court but also on restoration of contacts with ancestral spirits. At first this presented a problem for Brazilian Umbanda leaders, who were forced to travel to Africa to complete the ritual. Gradually, however, Afro-Brazilians developed a sense of belonging to a community rooted in Brazilian soil, the place where their own living dead were buried. In this way, a new line of Brazilian spirits was added to the traditional natural and ancestral ones. Followers of Umbanda still must enter into contact with these spirits through mediums, who are usually called pretos velhos and pretas velhas, old black men and women who speak for the spirits by means of possession.

The mediums in Umbanda provide multiple links to the past— African origins, the slave experience, and former generations—and thus help preserve communal order. They are the culture bearers who maintain values of African life and community. In the repartee that occurs during the early part of their possession ritual (called theophany), they function as elders of the historic community and as a spiritual elite of the religiously restored African societies.

But what of the internal structure of the religious communities? Is there an elite that would correspond to the hierarchy of the Catholic church? On the surface, it would appear not, for the Afro-Brazilian leaders assert that *aquí todo o mundo é igual* (here everyone is equal). Admission to the centers and their ceremonies is open to anyone regardless of gender, racial or ethnic background, sex, or socioeconomic class. While one or another class may predominate among the faithful, considerable mixing of the working, middle, and upper classes occurs in Umbanda groups. Each center has a director (male or female) who exercises virtually absolute power with regard to religious and policy decisions. The mediums, drummers, and other ceremonial persons, because they are vehicles through which the spirits communicate, constitute a kind of clergy or religious elite. It is an open elite, however, so anyone who shows signs of talent or is capable of being possessed may become part of it. When compared with ecclesiastical elites in Brazilian Catholicism and Protestantism, the Afro-Brazilian communities provide far greater access to power by women and poor people.

Differences in accessibility are especially pronounced with respect to women. The official hierarchy of the Catholic Church has always been closed to women, of course. The sacrament of Holy Orders was restricted to male Catholics on the grounds that Jesus was a man who had selected twelve men (and no women) to be his disciples. Women have, to be sure, assumed positions of leadership in monastic orders. Yet while a mother superior exercises considerable power within her own order of nuns, and within the educational, medical, and social service institutions operated by her order, she has little power in the hierarchy of the church itself when it comes to policy decisions.

The situation was somewhat different within popular Catholicism. There have probably been as many beatas as beatos wandering in the *sertão*, and these folk heroines and heroes are treated with great respect by the faithful because of their healing powers. The CEBs, at the margin of both official and popular Catholicism, marked a new chapter in the history of feminine leadership of the Church. Just as nuns have been more active than priests in organizing these grass roots communities, women assumed lay leadership within them nearly as often as men.

Although the mother denominations of Brazilian Protestantism have witnessed increasing numbers of women entering the ordained ministry, their daughter churches in Brazil—Baptists, Methodists, and Presbyterians—have not encouraged the practice. Still, there is more opportunity for women to exercise roles of lay leadership within Protestantism than in Catholic parishes.

Finally, compared with Brazilian Catholicism and Protestantism, Afro-Brazilian communities of faith provide easy access to positions of leadership for women. While no accurate data are available, it is likely that more maes de santo preside over terreiros than paes de santo and that filhas de santo outnumber filhos de santo. Beyond local terreiros, however, males dominate the leadership at the level of federations and confederations.

With the transformation of Afro-Brazilian religious communities into multiracial congregations with membership drawn from all socioeconomic strata, leading to the commingling of elites and masses, interesting role reversals are possible. As Diana Brown comments,

The ritual corps' use of simple white outfits and the absence of such class indicators as jewelry and accessories do away with many visible indicators of socioeconomic status. And the importance of spirit possession skills as the basis of rank . . . permits many situations where poor mediums outrank more affluent ones, blacks outrank whites, and women outrank men. During the consulta period, as well, mediums may significantly outrank their clients. At this time, elegantly and expensively dressed white women from the professional sectors may be seen humbly asking advice of a Caboclo or Preto Velho spirit possessing a medium de consulta who is poor and black. . . . the reverse situation also occurs: many mediums de consulta are affluent whites attending to clients who are both poor and black.[16]

In recent years local centers have begun to federate at city, state, regional, and even national levels. This has resulted in an apparent hierarchy of officials that parallels that of the Catholic church. The presidents and founders of the federations are self-appointed, however, and they do not enjoy the religious authority invested in the office of Catholic bishop or archbishop, for example. Given the autonomy of local center directors, as well as the competition among federation leaders, it is doubtful that they will become a true hierarchy. They do, nonetheless, serve as power brokers. A major reason for the creation of federations was to defend the Afro-Bra-

zilian sects from control or harassment by local governments, and
they have been successful in this regard.

A recent study of the political involvement of the movement in
Paulista elections found that

> The 1960s marked a radical transformation in the relations of Umbanda
> with the military, civil, and religious powers. It could be said that after the
> 1964 coup, Umbanda ceased being persecuted and began to be coopted. . . .
> The Catholic church itself changed its position: the CNBB . . . approached the
> umbandistas . . . as separated brothers to be treated with tolerance and re-
> spect. . . . If earlier the police officials were the executioners, at present the
> secretary for security is the protector; if earlier the [center directors] were the
> transgressors, today the leaders of Umbanda are personalities honored by
> leading authorities.[17]

The rapid growth in membership and number of centers, and the
attraction of more and more middle and upper class followers, has
led candidates for city and state offices to seek the support of the
Afro-Brazilian communities in exchange for legislative and other
political favors. The presence of military officers in positions of
leadership within the centers and federations also helped prevent
possible conflict, such as what occurred between military authorities and the Catholic hierarchy.[18]

A second reason for the creation of Umbanda federations and
confederations was to standardize practices and to preserve traditions. Perhaps the most ambitious attempt at structuring an orthodox Umbanda was the 1955 legal incorporation of the National
Union of Afro-Brazilian Cults and the establishment of a Supreme
Afro-Brazilian Sacerdotal Council, as stipulated in the union's stat-
utes. The council was to oversee the creation of new centers, admin-
ister religious examinations to candidates for center director, award
diplomas to successful candidates, represent the movement before
civil authorities, and take measures to ensure the smooth conduct of
the movement. These efforts were not successful, however, and real
power in the movement remains vested in the directors of individual centers.

Protestantism, Pentecostalism, and Kardecist Spiritualism

These are minority movements on Brazil's religious scene and are of
relatively recent vintage. Brazilian Protestant denominations are
almost exclusively the products of foreign missionary activity that
began in the 1830s, while Kardecist *espiritismo* was introduced

from France in the 1850s. Pentecostalism seems to be strictly a twentieth-century movement. Although each of the three has experienced periods of rapid growth, Kardecism is now on the decline, and Protestantism is reaching a plateau.[19] Pentecostalism, however, has been growing at an annual rate of 8.2 percent, far faster than any other major religion.[20]

The history of Protestantism in Brazil provides good evidence for Max Weber's famous thesis linking the Protestant ethic to the spirit of capitalism. The German immigrants who brought Lutheranism with them, and the missionaries sent out by Baptist, Methodist, and Presbyterian churches in the United States, came largely from middle-class backgrounds. Although Baptist and Methodist missions attracted many members of Brazil's lower classes both in rural and urban areas, the general pattern followed by converts was to move up into the middle class within a generation. There are two main reasons for this: successful adoption of the moral attributes associated with the Protestant ethic, which have come to represent middle-class values; and the great emphasis placed on education by Protestant missions.

Protestant missionary strategy, especially that of Methodists and Presbyterians, sought to win the allegiance of the Brazilian elite. Included was the establishment of several high-quality schools, among them the Colégio Bennett in Rio, the Universidade Mackensie in São Paulo, and the Instituto Pôrto Alegre in Rio Grande do Sul. Because they tended to be model schools, they were patronized by the elite. Ironically, many of the missionaries who were committed to the recruitment of well-to-do members resisted turning over denominational and educational leadership to Brazilian colleagues, who were treated in a paternalistic fashion. During the 1930s, encouraged by the spirit of nationalism fomented by the Vargas government, many Brazilian members of Protestant sects revolted against their foreign superiors. The Methodist church became an autonomous body, and independent churches were organized by Presbyterians and Baptists. In this way, the foreign ecclesiastical elite was replaced by a Brazilian one in most denominations.

As the 1950s drew to a close, internal struggles occurred within the elite of each of the denominations. Older leaders who were both theologically and politically conservative were pitted against a younger generation that was theologically liberal and committed to church involvement in social movements.

This struggle for control was most clearly visible in the Presbyterian church. In his book, *Protestantism and Repression: A Brazilian Case Study*, Rubem Alves describes the process whereby defenders of Right-Doctrine Protestantism finally secured absolute control of that church and then "found a powerful ally in the political and ideological transformations that ensued."[21] The new church leaders silenced any protest against the military's repressive measures and thereby avoided problems with the government:

Two decades ago, the future of Brazil's Presbyterian Church seemed assured because it had produced an extraordinary new generation of ministers and lay men and women: intellectually gifted, socially concerned, and dedicated to the service of Church and country. . . . Ministers and lay persons of this new generation were acutely aware of their rootedness in their own culture and history, were deeply disturbed by the poverty and sufferings of their people, and were committed to working for social transformation. Their faith stance led them to enter various professions . . . and to become involved in political movements for change. Today, if they still continue to pursue these goals, they do so in isolation. The Presbyterian Church, rather than sustaining this quality of life, is identified with the most reactionary political developments and does its part to legitimize a repressive order.[22]

The military years, then, proved divisive and ultimately disorganizing for the mainstream Protestant sects.

Pentacostalism has enjoyed a meteoric rise in membership in recent decades. As Key Yuasa noted, "There was a time when the Baptists were the fastest growing evangelical group and succeeded in gathering together the largest number of persons from the lowest classes in Brazil. Today that description fits the Pentecostals . . ."[23] The Pentecostals are composed of four major and many lesser denominations, including Assembly of God, Brazil for Christ, Christian Congregation, and the Pentecostal Confederation.

As mainline Protestant churches, on the one hand, and the Afro-Brazilian religions, on the other, become more and more middle class in membership and appeal, Pentecostalism has replaced them as the religious movement of the masses. Typical services of worship combine the excitement of the old festivals of popular or folk Catholicism with the spirit possession of Afro-Brazilian religions. A higher degree of social democracy exists in Pentecostalism than in Umbanda, because the power of spirit possession is not exclusively held by the elite. In Pentecostalism each participant can, and usually does, receive direct divine power through immediate possession by the Holy Spirit. The only ecclesiastical elite, then, consists of professional pastors and lay deacons and elders. But, as René Ribeiro points out, "Access to the Pentecostal ministry is quick and easy. Individuals with leadership qualities, dedication, and sufficient motivation rise rapidly to positions in the hierarchy. . . . Pentecostalism recruits its deacons, elders, and pastors without formal training from persons with little education."[24]

There has been little concern to interact with, or influence, the secular elites, although some Pentecostal pastors, like Mário de Melo—who boasts that his Brazil for Christ temple in São Paulo is the largest church building in the world—are seeking legitimization within Protestant circles through ecumenical contacts. These leaders encourage qualified lay persons to enter the political and economic arenas for the purpose of spreading Pentecostal influence over legislation, policy making, and business.

The last major religion in Brazil is Kardecist Spiritualism, or *espiritismo* in Portuguese. This sect was founded by the Frenchman Alan Kardec in the mid-nineteenth century. Although it is sometimes held to be one of the parents of Umbanda, I believe that the two have developed independently, except for some linguistic borrowing. Leaders of the two spiritualist branches certainly emphasize their differences.[25]

Spiritualism draws its followers almost exclusively from the middle and upper classes. J. Parke Renshaw's definitive sociological study notes that it "requires an interest in study and in the intellectualization of beliefs. . . . Being a Spiritist is one way of being an intellectual."[26] Renshaw's fieldwork revealed that today's members are still drawn from professional ranks: they are physicians, attorneys, military officers, professors, and white collar employees.

Although from the beginning Spiritualists have evinced a strong interest in serving the needs of the poor through the establishment of clinics, dispensaries, food and clothing centers, and child care facilities, they make no effort to recruit members of the lower class into their religion. Indeed, the movement remains not only class conscious but also racist. Spirits of deceased Indians and blacks are barred from seances on grounds that non-Caucasians are disruptive because they are intellectually and culturally inferior. Mediums who make contact with such "inferior spirits" are automatically expelled from Spiritualist centers.[27] The attitude of the Spiritualists toward the Brazilian masses is the highly elitist one of noblesse oblige.

Conclusion

Spiritualism is clearly a religion of the elite, whereas Pentecostalism is a religion of the masses. Catholicism, Umbanda, and Protestantism are the religious communities where the elites and masses effectively commingle. Catholicism, however, still shows signs of being internally divided into two churches, one of which is *for* the masses, the other *by* the masses (e.g., the CEBS). Protestantism continues to be a religious community that attracts the masses, but it tends to transform those who join into members of the middle class. Perhaps the most ideal commingling occurs in the centers of Umbanda and the other Afro-Brazilian religions. If there is a melting pot in Brazilian society, it is to be found there.

Notes

1. Roger Bastide, "Religion and the Church in Brazil," in *Brazil: Portrait of Half a Continent*, ed. T. Lynn Smith and Alexander Marchant (New York: Dryden Press, 1951), p. 335.

2. Leonardo Boff, *Igreja, carisma e poder*, 3d ed. (Petrópolis: Vozes, 1981), ch. 8.

3. José Comblin, "Para uma tipologia do catolicismo no Brasil," *Revista eclesiástica brasileira* (March 1968).

4. Eduardo Hoornaert, *Formação do catolicismo brasileiro, 1550–1800* (Petrópolis: Vozes, 1974).

5. Thomas C. Bruneau, *The Political Transformation of the Brazilian Catholic Church* (New York: Cambridge University Press, 1974), p. x.

6. Fernando de Azevedo *A cultura brasileira: Introdução ao estudo da cultura no Brasil*, 2d ed. (São Paulo: Companhia Editôra Nacional, 1944), p. 162.

7. Bruneau, *Political Transformation*, p. 47.

8. Bruneau, *The Church in Brazil* (Austin: University of Texas Press, 1982), p. 92.

9. Gilberto Freyre, *New World in the Tropics* (New York: Knopf, 1959), p. 87.

10. Manoel S. Cardozo, "The Lay Brotherhoods of Colonial Brazil," *Catholic Historical Review* 33 (April 1947): 12–30.

11. Alvaro Barreiro, *Basic Ecclesial Communities: The Evangelization of the Poor* (Maryknoll, N.Y.: Orbis Books, 1982), pp. 8, 13.

12. Boaventura Kloppenburg, O.F.M., noted that during the decade of the 1940s, Brazil's population increased by 25 percent, Catholic membership by 24 percent, and "spiritism" by 78 percent (the latter term included a limited number of Kardecists in addition to the Afro-Brazilian sect members) (*A Umbanda no Brasil: Orientação para os católicos* [Petrópolis: Vozes, 1961], p. 26). The number of new Umbanda centers registered in the city of São Paulo has increased each decade since Kloppenburg's figures: 1,025 in the 1950s; 2,836 in the 1960s; 7,627 in the 1970s; and 1,389 between 1980 and 1982. See Diana Brown, "Uma história da Umbanda no Rio," in *Umbanda e política* (Rio de Janeiro: Editora Marco Zero, 1985)), p. 48.

13. Basil Davidson, *Which Way Africa?* (Baltimore: Penguin Books, 1964), p. 31. I say generic because slaves came from at least thirty different culture groups in Africa, in addition to that of the Congo. In the case of both Amerindian and African cultures, survival meant simplification and homogenization.

14. José Ribeíro, *Brasil no folclore* (Rio de Janeiro: Editôra Aurora, 1970), pp. 301 ff. Cf. Davidson, *Which Way Africa?*, p. 301.

15. Rossini Tavares de Lima, et al. *O folclore do litoral norte de São Paulo*, 2 vols. (Rio de Janeiro: Ministério da Educação e Cultura, 1969), 1:21.

16. Diana DeG. Brown, *Umbanda: Religion and Politics in Urban Brazil* (Ann Arbor: University of Michigan Research Press, 1986), p. 115.

17. Maria Helena Villas Boas Concone and Lísias Nogueira Negrao, "Umbanda: Da repressão à cooptação," in *Umbanda e política*, pp. 52, 58.

18. A good example of this is Hilton de Paiva Tupinambá, a lieutenant in the military police of São Paulo who was also founder and president of the Umbanda federation SOUCESP. Tupinambá actively supported Erasmo Dias and Paulo Maluf in the 1978 elections and later collaborated in their administrations, providing them with support from Umbandistas in exchange for official recognition as a legitimate religion. See *Umbanda e política*, pp. 57 ff.

19. Official figures show a decline in Kardecism followers from 760,000 to 633,000 between 1966 and 1969.

20. The census treats Pentecostals as Protestants. In 1960 authorities reported 1,527,000 Protestants, of whom 38.5 percent were Pentecostals. In 1970 the figure had risen to 2,623,550, with Pentecostals making up 49.2 percent.

21. Rubem A. Alves, ed., *Protestantism and Repression: A Brazilian Case Study*, trans. John Drury (Maryknoll, N.Y.: Orbis, 1985), p. xxii.

22. Dick Schaull, Foreword, in ibid., p. xi.

23. Key Yuasa, "Razões que justificam um estudo do Pentecostalismo no Brazil," *Boletim informativo da Associação de Seminários Teológicos Evangélicos* 2, no. 8 (March 1965): 6.

24. René Ribeiro, *Antropologia da religião e outros estudos* (Recife: Editora Massangana, 1982), pp. 278, 297.

25. The thesis of Umbanda deriving partially from Kardecism was stated by Roger Bastide, *The African Religions of Brazil*, trans. Helen Sebba (Baltimore: Johns Hopkins University Press, 1978) and by Brown, *Umbanda*.

26. J. Parke Renshaw, *A Sociological Analysis of Spiritism in Brazil* (Ann Arbor: University Microfilms, 1969), p. 89.

27. Renshaw, *Spiritism in Brazil*, p. 90.

Epilogue

This book has been designed to familiarize the reader with the broad sweep of Brazil's history in the twentieth century. Current events, therefore, have entered the narrative only occasionally. Still, two considerations recommend a brief epilogue focused on the late 1980s: the extraordinary pace of recent events and the working out of trends begun in earlier decades.

Elites

Politics registered amazing changes after the inauguration of the New Republic in March 1985. The entire world watched as President-elect Tancredo Neves suffered and then died on the operating table, unable to occupy the position he had fought so hard to win. The relatively unknown vice president, José Sarney, assumed the highest office and for a time enjoyed some of Tancredo's reflected popularity. By late 1987, however, Sarney found himself sliding down in opinion polls and losing control of the behemoth bureaucracy inherited from the military. Indecision regarding the length of Sarney's tenure spurred several presidential hopefuls to launch early election campaigns, among them Leonel Brizola, bête noire of the right.

The amnesty extended to political exiles in 1979 encouraged many former actors to reenter the public arena, and Congress became an unusually lively center of debate and activity. Most legislators were veteran office holders with moderate ideological positions, but they were joined by increasing numbers of newcomers, persons drawn from thinly represented sectors. The newly-invigorated unions, carrying the Labor Party (PT) banner, held sixteen seats by

1987. A women's caucus, made up of twenty-six deputies, debated feminist issues. Behind the scenes myriad lobbyists pressed for the special interests of their sponsors. And the army high command also watched developments, not always quietly.

The officer corps had not been of one mind about returning power to the civilian politicians. During the military years the corps had divided into those who saw the army's mission as external—defense against foreign aggression, which implied emphasis on traditional military training, operations, equipment, and organization—and those whose career choices had led them into internal intelligence and control of the regime's opponents. The former wanted the military to distance themselves from politics and to limit their internal involvements to maintaining order in extreme cases and to advising the government on defense matters. The latter functioned in an atmosphere that profoundly corrupted both them and the "system" (as it was called in Brazil) that they served.

For a military organization, mission and identity are tightly intertwined, the first shaping the second. In the post-World War II era the military suffered a severe identity crisis because the officers were uncertain of the institution's mission. This uncertainty had its origin, according to Edmundo Campos Coelho, in the identity crisis of the Brazilian state, which lacked a focal institution that everyone could accept as the "incorporation of national authority"; through the 1964 movement, the army leadership intended to impose its conception of the national state.[1] Though officers generally accepted the necessity to depose the João Goulart government, they voiced less of a consensus for maintaining military control thereafter. The army was not structured to rule the country. Two competing conceptions of military professionalism developed: one that Alfred Stepan has called the "new professionalism" of internal security; and another that sees conventional leadership of troops trained and equipped to fight foreign conventional forces as the essence of their profession.

The Serviço Nacional de Informações (SNI, National Intelligence Service), which was created in 1964 as a civilian agency of the executive branch, was militarized after the triumph of the hardliners in 1968. The SNI became the backbone of the system of control and repression. It may have employed as many as 50,000 persons. Unlike similar agencies in other countries, it enjoyed a near monopoly over intelligence operations and training, had a chief whose ministerial rank gave him a place in the president's cabinet, and installed an official in every government agency, state-owned business, and university to ensure conformity with national security goals. Most important, it was self-supervisory, even regarding finances.[2]

By the early 1970s the army, navy, and air force had set up their own intelligence services, which, while theoretically under the co-ordination and supervision of SNI, functioned with considerable independence. The army created its Centro de Informações do Exército (CIE), which in turn formed CODIS (Centros de Operações para Defesa Interna) and DOIS (Divisão de Operações e Informações) in each army command. The chief of staff of each command supposedly was responsible for the intelligence work in its territory, but in practice that officer was not necessarily informed of CIE (or CODI-DOI) activities, which followed a separate chain of command. The DOIs became centers of dirty tricks and torture. There is a cruel irony in that CODI sounds close to the Portuguese for code (código) and DOI means pain.

In the 1968–73 period this system combatted regime opponents, or supposed opponents, with secret arrest and detention, torture, and disappearances that masked outright murder.[3] With the coming to power of retired Gen. Ernesto Geisel in 1974 and of his successor in 1979, Gen. João Figueiredo, and with their consecutive policies of relaxing control (distenção) and then opening the political system (abertura), the CIE and sectors of the SNI turned against the government. Some of their personnel, fearing a return to a democratic regime that would hold them accountable for their actions, manufactured "incidents" that could be blamed on the Left or would intimidate the presidents to slow the pace of distenção-abertura. While their bombings failed to stop the inauguration of the New Republic, they were protected from prosecution under a general amnesty decree, and they prevented the Figueiredo government from punishing officers clearly involved in the 1981 attempt to bomb the RioCentro during a left-wing-sponsored concert. At times the intelligence community, as it began calling itself, was out of control.

Such activities undermined the officer corps' sense of unity and corrupted its hierarchical structure. The CIE irritated officers not involved in its work, because its personnel seemingly were favored with promotions and special pay. They cast a shadow of fear through the barracks.

As the military regime came to an end, officers associated with the SNI and CIE were uncomfortable. As late as August 1984, CIE personnel in Brasília tried to sabotage Tancredo Neves's campaign for the presidency by pasting up posters showing a cartoon of him with arms raised under Communist party symbols. In early 1985, before the New Republic began, SNI agents were reportedly racing about the country cleaning out files. Many of those whom they had been watching, and in some cases mistreated, were about to become the new government.

Though President Sarney sought to bring the SNI under closer control, it continued to have considerable freedom and to be run by military personnel. Minister of the Army Gen. Leônidas Pires Gonçalves cut the size of the CIE and placed some of his *homens de confiança* in charge at the SNI. These moves ensured the minister's control but did not provide institutional, let alone constitutional, safeguards against future abuses.

The scars of illegal repression and violence will mark the officer corps for years to come. In Italy in World War II, Brazilian officers in the expeditionary force prided themselves on the correct treatment that they accorded German prisoners under the Geneva Convention. Their successors, waging their war against subversion, were taught that international law did not apply in cases of internal security[4] and so used massive intimidation, kidnappings, beatings, secret arrest and incognito imprisonment, psychological and physical torture, murder, and secret burial. Much of this, carried on with sophisticated military planning and organization, reminds the historian of the throat slitting, shooting, and even beheading that were often the fate of prisoners in the civil war of the 1890s, at Canudos in 1897, and in the Contestado in 1912–15. In the past, rebels and criminals from the margins of society, and certainly working-class people, could expect brutal treatment from the forces of law and order; what the military years did was to bring that experience to the middle and upper classes. The "repressive apparatus" drew an invisible pale of fear through Brazilian society to dissuade the educated classes from crossing it. It also deterred opposition within the military itself.

The activities of the "system" prolonged the years of military dominance and disrupted military discipline. The slide from clandestine brutality, from secret orders and parallel chains of command to outright thievery and corruption is a short one. The press reported that intelligence personnel moved into hijacking drug and other contraband shipments, stealing cars, and appropriating property of victims. The full implications for military discipline of CODI/DOI units, such as Operation Bandeirantes (OBAN) in São Paulo, receiving financial backing from civilian businessmen have yet to be assessed. Of course, the extra per diems, an income fattened with business donations, and the obvious sense of power were not conducive to encouraging an eventual return to the routine of troop duty.

It is likely true, as General Leônidas asserted, that torture was never the "policy of the army." But he and his fellow generals were unwilling to condemn it because they did not want to admit that it had occurred.

In late 1987, dissatisfaction with their low salaries led captains at the Escola de Aperfeiçoamento de Oficiais (ESAO) to break discipline by deriding their commander's assurances that the government would improve salaries. In the same period a captain in a motorized infantry battalion in Apucarana, Paraná, seized the town hall to read a statement of protest. Meanwhile, an organization of retired hardline officers and civilian allies, called the Brazilian Association in Defense of Democracy (ABDD), which the CIE had originally formed in 1984 to destabilize Tancredo Neves's candidacy, was reactivated and held a well-publicized meeting in Rio de Janeiro. While Sarney wisely raised military salaries, the atmosphere of indiscipline could not help but worry the drafters of the new constitution. One of the principal matters they faced was the constitutional role of the military. It is ironic that the military are serving as a guarantor of the return to democracy and of constitutional reform, while remaining at least a latent threat to both.

The biggest show in Brasília was the Constitutional Assembly, convened in February 1987. Composed of all 559 senators and deputies, the assembly set about the huge task of writing a basic charter for the country. Faced with the choice of a short or long document, they opted for the latter—and some observers predicted it would run to thousands of pages. The process was remarkably open and efficient, so that citizens could mail in their suggestions, which were kept on a central computer, along with dozens of constitutions from other countries, used for reference. To many, the exercise called upon the highest talents of politicians and laymen alike.

The twenty-one years of military government had taken their toll, of course. Few politicians seemed to have the stature of leaders back in the democratic heyday, 1945–64. Had the best and brightest chosen different careers? Had politicians been so intimidated that they lacked courage? Would they be able to confront the whole gamut of problems facing the country? Social scientists and pundits, shifting their attention from abertura to redemocratization, grappled with these questions and often found discouraging answers. In its entire history, Brazil had had only about two decades of genuine democracy. Institutions, political culture, tradition, and even the economy seemed more suited to authoritarian than democratic rule.

Leaders of business and finance took a more active part in politics and policy formulation after 1985. Individuals and peak associations, like FIESP, stepped up lobbying efforts in Congress and various executive agencies. They formed especially close ties with powerful new government technocrats in the economic sectors. Their mutual aim was capitalist modernization of Brazil, yet they lacked a specific institutional program to achieve it.

Some business leaders went beyond lobbying, however, and actually attained appointive or elective offices in government. They included toy manufacturer Dilson Funaro, who as minister of finance commanded the 1986 Plano Cruzado and the 1987 debt moratorium; Northeastern industrialist Tasso Jeressaiti, elected governor of Ceará in 1986; and multimillionaire Antônio Emírio de Moraes, who came close to winning the governorship of São Paulo. About 32 percent of the delegates to the 1987 Constitutional Assembly were businessmen, and another 13 percent had close ties with the private sector. (In contrast, those identified with the labor movement accounted for no more than 12 percent.)

Despite the heterogeneity of Brazil's business community, its leaders in government leaned toward a neo-liberal philosophical stance. Their aims for the new constitution included: preeminence of the free market, preference for private enterprise over public, divestment of government industries, and noninterference in the economy. In general, they believed that a market economy, more efficient and profitable than a government-controlled one, should prevail.

Brazil's native ruling class is no longer as heterogeneous as it was under the Old Republic. The integration of the national commodities, financial, and labor markets as well as the advent of Paulista internal colonialism have brought greater uniformity. A change in the composition of the ruling class has occurred because industrialists and bankers are obviously much more important than formerly, and planters and merchants less so. The regional concentration of

wealth has remained and, if anything, been exacerbated. Multinationals play a much more important role now than they did before
1930, but the importance of foreign risk capital has declined vis-
a-vis native direct investment in the last two decades. Foreign
bankers and international agencies would seem to have even more
influence now, with a U.S.$120 billion debt, than under the Re-
public, but that is probably not the case. As the adage goes, if one
owes one hundred dollars, he is a debtor; if he owes one hundred
billion, he is a partner. Brazil has become too important and has
diversified its dependency too well for the international banking
community to succeed with threats of punishment.

The major innovation has been the rise of state capitalism. The
state's dominance of the economic elite grew after 1964 as the state's
role magnified. Today the state directs and paces the growth of the
economy through its regulations, fiscal and monetary policies, and
enormous state enterprises. Hence state officials not only oversee
the political system and international relations but also are themselves vital economic actors. Thus it is difficult for heavy manufacturers or bankers to successfully organize civil organizations to
influence the state when their largest members are themselves state
enterprises (Volta Redonda, Banco do Brasil, BNH, and state banks).
Also it is harder for them to have a common front when, as in the
construction industry, private companies are competing with each
other for government contracts. Many of the trade associations exist
almost more for the convenience of the state—to facilitate communication—than as weapons of the member firms.

Until the reestablishment of civilian democratic government in
1985, the economic elite had to appeal to technocrats who mandated
laws rather than to political parties that passed legislation. They
thus could not use the promise of votes in elections or contributions
to campaign chests to influence policy. The wealthy continued to
rely on friendship, kinship, and bribes as in the Old Republic. These
traditional networks have been modified, however, as the "state
bourgeoisie" is now drawn from the middle class more than from the
traditional oligarchy. Family ties, of course, remain important. Arguments about the economic impact of specific policies are much more
effective in the current planned economy than they were under the
laissez faire regime.

The advent of civilian government and truly competitive politics
may again strengthen civil associations. We have already seen a

growth in the power of the Paulista bourgeoisie, which the military had tried to marginalize. Two recent ministers of finance—Funaro and Bresser Pereira—were on the directorships of important private companies rather than just being technocrats. Moreover, the Paulistas' association with the dictatorship has led to calls for reduction of state authority. This has certainly been evident in the freeing of labor unions. Trade associations are probably becoming more assertive as well. But no matter how strong the pressure, the dependent nature of Brazil's bourgeoisie, overshadowed by foreign capitalists and state managers, will prevent the establishment of independent, strong trade associations. Individual firms will still rely on friendship and favors to gain state privileges.

With regard to labor relations, as legislated in the new constitution as well as enacted by the Ministry of Labor, the business elite opposed major alterations in the corporatist structure inherited from the past. Leaders proclaimed a preference for unregulated unionism yet balked at cancelling the union tax, by which the government has controlled unions since the 1940s. They favored the existing closed-shop, government-supervised system with compulsory dues check-off.

Despite this conservative stance in the halls of government, businessmen were a good deal more flexible when it came to settling the many strikes that broke out after 1979. In the more modern industrial sectors—automobiles, steel, appliances, electronics, and capital goods—strikes were called on a company-by-company basis and settled through direct negotiations, without government tutelage. This new pattern of labor relations violated the principles of corporatism, which favors industry-wide standards.

Business leaders strengthened parallel or nonofficial professional associations while preserving the older, traditional ones. In addition, they advocated the creation of neo-corporatist councils and commissions that would bring together representatives of business, government, and labor to formulate industrial policies and regulate the economy.

Considerable talk of a "social pact" among labor, business, and government surfaced in 1987, reminiscent of the pact formulated by Argentina's Juan Perón in 1973. Private sector leaders, recognizing that they could not determine the broad lines of policy by themselves, hoped to find compromise positions on which the major parties could agree. Such a pact would in turn strengthen the government's hand to carry out agreed-upon policies, ending several years of ineffectual drift in this area and helping to consolidate democratic processes. The centralization that occurred recently among business organizations should enhance the possibilities of a tripartite pact. Parallel associations have tended to unify their commands, and the traditional FIESP has assumed a position of recognized leadership in the private sector.

Still, major obstacles to a management-labor-government pact exist. Business leaders resisted labor's key demands: the right to strike, job stability, shorter work hours, and free unionism. In particular, serious reform of labor legislation proved elusive. While both sides paid lip service to eliminating the corporatist structure and the compulsory tax, incumbent labor leaders were reluctant to do so since they might lose their positions. For their part, political leaders, out of touch with the union movement, were unable to formulate social and economic compromises acceptable to the other parties. So chances for a social pact negotiated among business, labor, and political elites remained at best slim.

All elites tried to distance themselves from one thorny issue in 1987: the foreign debt. The total soared past U.S.$120 billion, kited by interest accrual and the decision in March to postpone payment. President Sarney froze accounts because foreign currency reserves had fallen so low the economy could not afford the payments. The measure won broad support, because everyone feared that raising the money would cripple the economy and hurt every sector. Still, few wanted the country to withdraw permanently from the international economy, so some accommodation with the commercial banks was necessary. The dilemma was how and when. In October, however, just when improved export performance made it possible to hold discussions with the creditors, the Wall Street crash further postponed talks.

Masses

The myth of a harmonious multi-racial and -ethnic society in Brazil continued to prevail through the 1970s, becoming virtual dogma during the military years. In 1970, for example, the census failed to tabulate race, in what many critics believed was an attempt to prevent empirical studies of prejudice and discrimination. Still, encouraged by the abertura, academics stirred up new debates and managed to convince the census bureau to include data on race in 1980. Racial discontent arose in that period and led to black political action. For example, the Unified Negro Movement, founded in São Paulo in 1978, soon became a national force. In other cities, black leaders created research centers to stimulate pride and awareness among members of their race. Black caucuses and working groups emerged in the leading opposition parties, and 1982 saw the election of a number of congressmen who campaigned as blacks. Discussions of discrimination and racial prejudice appear regularly in the scholarly and popular press, though a majority of Brazilians still cling to the old myth of racial harmony. It may take another generation before these problems gain widespread recognition and attention.

In the southern tier of states, which received a heavy influx of European immigrants, the postwar period has seen the steady decline of the "pioneer family farm," which is being replaced by large-scale agribusiness enterprises. This has been caused by changing production patterns, with a tremendous expansion in the past two decades of such crops as sugarcane (for methanol), citrus fruit (for juice concentrate exports), and soybeans (for livestock feed and export). Thus resources and economic power have become more concentrated in the hands of large firms, often with close ties to multinational companies and export markets. Even the wine industry of Rio Grande do Sul, developed originally for the local Italian immigrant colonies, has been penetrated by large foreign firms that are attempting to produce for middle-class consumers in Rio, São Paulo, and other big cities.

Descendants of the immigrant families who arrived around the turn of this century have generally done very well in Brazilian society, and indeed many are at the forefront of these new agricultural developments. They have been replaced at the bottom of the social ladder by more recent migrants from poorer regions.

These recent changes have had several effects on rural society in the South. Agricultural labor has become more proletarian, a process called the *boia fria*; rural workers have no access to subsistence land and must sell their labor in a fully monetized market to survive. A corollary is the voluntary migration or expulsion of workers from the southern rural zones when subsistence land is taken over by capital-intensive producers. The out-migrants generally go to the industrial suburbs of São Paulo or to the newly opened agricultural and ranching frontier of Rondônia and the Center-West in general.

Women, Marriage, and Fertility

The status of women in Brazil of the 1980s is different from that of a century ago. The steady urbanization and industrialization affected sex roles. While in the early nineteenth century upper-class women in rural areas were cloistered and poorly educated, in the cities, especially Rio de Janeiro, Recife, Salvador, and São Paulo they attended the theater, dances, and other public events. Foreign travelers commented on the sophisticated women that they met at the imperial court. Lower-class women faced a more difficult life but enjoyed greater freedom than did most upper-class women. Toward the end of the century it was more common to see middle- and upper-class women in public, there was a growing concern for education of women, and the early feminist and women's periodicals were launched. Despite talk of equal rights, however, these publications continued to stress women's "natural vocation" as mothers and wives.[5]

Throughout the Old Republic more women entered the work force and a feminist movement made its presence felt. Even so a social gap existed between these two segments of the female population. The feminists tended to be from middle- and upper-class backgrounds, and even though their rhetoric embraced their working-class sisters their organizations did not. Middle- and upper-class professional women preached liberating women through work and saw "women's economic emancipation" as a basic tenet of the movement. Their congresses discussed wages, hours, working conditions, and maternity leaves, all items of interest to workers, and feminists created associations of public employees, nurses, typists, etc., but not factory workers. The feminists did not facilitate their participation or seek to bridge the distance between them.[6]

The major victory of the movement was the securing of the right to vote in 1932. Women were enfranchised on the same basis as men, that is, illiterates were excluded. So while important, the acquisition of the vote benefited the female segment of the elite more than it did women generally. Debates during the Constitutional Convention of 1934 over a proposal to create a federal Women's Department showed that leaders of the women's movement were divided between those who wanted equal status with men and those who wanted special attention given to women's questions. It was integration versus separate status. The constitution's designers were concerned to maintain and strengthen family life, which placed the rights of individual women in a secondary position. Many of the reform proposals made then would take concrete form only after 1960.[7]

In the late 1940s females composed 14 percent of the economically active population; four decades later one in every three Brazilian workers was a woman. In the 1940s marriage offered young women the major way to leave their parents' homes, and it was not considered proper for married middle- and upper-class women to work outside the home. For such women the marriage either succeeded or they faced the social stigma of being a *desquitada* (legally separated). By 1977, so many couples had separated that an entire body of law had grown up to deal with problems of support, property, and children; and public opinion had shifted sufficiently to allow the Congress to pass a divorce law. Thousands of people took advantage of the opportunity to regularize their legal status. The numbers increased steadily from 29,000 divorced in 1980 to 76,000 in 1985. Of course, contested divorces require lawyers and court appearances, and due to the cost are not normally available to lower-class couples. Courts usually instruct the husband to pay a monthly alimony of about 30 percent of his income. Practically speaking, in the highly inflationary economy of Brazil, this means that both parties end up tightening their belts. Interestingly, the cost of divorce and the growing threat of AIDS has had the effect of increasing the number of marriages by 10 percent between 1983 and 1985, from 866,000 to 952,000.[8] Whether this increase represents a trend or a passing phenomenon is uncertain.

One thing that is certain, however, is that Brazil has experienced a fertility decline in recent decades. Elite and middle-class women used the pill as soon as it became available, and two- and three-children families became common in urban neighborhoods after the mid-1960s. Recent research has shown that a similar trend was underway among the rural masses.

Organizations such as the World Bank, which had tended to take an alarmist view of Brazil's supposed high fertility rates, attacked the unequal income distribution, the scarcity of social services, and the lack of an official national family planning program.[9] But research reports in 1985 by members of the Social Science Research Council and the American Council on Learned Societies, through their Joint Committee on Latin American Studies, showed that development in Brazil had in fact produced a decline in fertility rates. The change in the countryside from sharecropping to wage earning undermined the economic reasons field workers had large families. Before the late 1950s and early 1960s, most workers on the coffee lands of the Center-South and the sugar plantations of the Northeast were sharecroppers, whose contracts included housing, garden plots, and the opportunity for women and children to contribute to the support of the household. With increased mechanization and extension of labor legislation requiring social security coverage, landowners phased out sharecropping in favor of wages. The field workers discovered that having to pay cash for their housing and food increased the costs of maintaining their families and decreased the economic value of children.

The social changes that occurred in Brazil between 1950 and 1980 also influenced reproductive behavior. Large numbers of women had entered the work force. And while there was still much poverty, by the 1980s, consumerism had thoroughly penetrated what had become a mass society. As the Social Science Research Council's report observed, "The economic boom of the 1960s and 1970s was fueled by a transformation in the pattern of consumer expenditure, a transformation that was intensively promoted by the media. In addition to stimulating demand for items such as refrigerators and televisions, the media transmitted new notions concerning medicine, sexuality, women's roles, and family size."[10] As a result a major change in women's ideals and aspirations took place as they separated sexuality from reproduction and adopted new visions of self-fulfillment. This trend, together with increased employment opportunities, led women to take the initiative in controlling reproduction. Studies in São Paulo state found that 53 to 80 percent of married women were practicing contraception.

The gap separating elite women from those of the masses still existed. "The 'liberation' of upper- and middle-class women with their growing interests outside the family and home is partly based," June Hahner has observed, "on the labor of the lower-class women who cook for their families, clean their homes, run their errands, and take care of their children. Very few comfortably situated Brazilian women," she reminds us, "whether they pursue careers or not, can imagine life without their maids."[11] But Hahner also noted that feminist organizations are attempting to place "women's issues within the broader struggle for a democratic, just society and to give priority to the needs and demands of working-class and poor women."[12]

A significant trend of recent years has been growing concern and protest regarding male violence against women. This was a cross-class issue that generated front-page stories throughout the republic. Cases in which husbands and lovers murdered their partners and were then exonerated for "legitimate defense of their honor" drew demonstrations and in some instances retrial. Centers for battered wives were set up in various cities, and the São Paulo and Rio de Janeiro police created special sections staffed with women to deal with rape and violence against females.

Cartoons frequently capture a society's realities. Millions of Brazilian women could find easy identification with the character "Das Dores" (literally "of sorrows" as in Maria of Sorrows) in Miguel Paiva's "Happy Days," published weekly in *Isto É* magazine. Das Dores is a housewife of the impoverished middle class: plump, unkempt, with a perpetual scarf on her head and innumerable cockroaches swarming about her. She has an unsatisfactory sex life with a husband who is so tortured with financial difficulties that he cannot move himself to intimate contact. In one episode Das Dores revealed that "I had an orgasm once, but only after I obtained a writ of habeas corpus!" The effect on Das Dores of her husband's and her two children's criticisms is that she cannot even dream. While imagining herself being carried off by a prince on horseback, she is wondering if she turned off the black beans on the stove. Even though the portrayal is clearly stereotyped, it appeals to many women who thought that they alone suffered with such feelings and such treatment.[13]

As the 1980s drew to a close Brazilians could empathize with Das Dores's shattered dreams because their own dreams of economic security and physical well-being were also shattered. As the politicians struggled in 1987 and 1988 to write a new constitution, it seemed that private interests and ambitions counted more heavily than the national good. As President Sarney went through three finance ministers by the end of 1987, Brazilians wondered whether the economy would ever regain its lost footings. Had the dreams of national integration, of economic development, of great power status faded beyond recovery? Was optimism to be a lost Brazilian characteristic? Was the good God above still a Brazilian? Or was this a time of testing the nation's resolve prior to an age of prosperity?

Though the doubts were as grand as the problems, the long-term observer could say that Brazil and Brazilians had confounded doubters before and were likely to do so again. Brazilians could take some comfort in the knowledge that the nation's progress in the twentieth century had been remarkable and that the country stood in dynamic contrast to the stagnation that afflicted the rest of Latin America. With all its problems Brazil remained a complex, fascinating, and deceptive country.

Notes

1. Edmundo Campos Coelho, *Em busca de identidade: O exército e a política na sociedade brasileira* (Rio de Janeiro: Forense-Universitária, 1976), pp. 169–70.

2. Ana Lagôa, *SNI: Como nasceu, como funciona* (São Paulo: Brasiliense, 1983), pp. 19–21, 60–65; Alfred C. Stepan, *Os Militares: Da abertura à Nova República* (Rio de Janeiro: Paz e Terra, 1986), pp. 27–36. Neither the CIA nor the KGB enjoys the freedom of the SNI, and even the authoritarian regimes in Chile, Argentina, and Uruguay did not allow their intelligence services such free rein.

3. Archdiocese of São Paulo, *Torture in Brazil: A Report*, comp. Jaime Wright, trans. Joan Dassin (New York: Vantage, 1986).

4. A 1972 publication of the alumni association of the ESG recommended characterizing the opponent in an internal security situation as a belligerent "para evitar a aplicação dos princípios jurídicos internacionais" (to avoid applying international rules of justice) (Associação dos Diplomados da Escola Superior de Guerra [ADESG], *Segurança nacional e segurança interna* [Rio de Janeiro: Departamento de Ciclos de Estudos da ADESG, 1972], p. 39). A 1985 *Veja* story said that at least one pamphlet (*apostila*) of the ESG asserted that prisoners in a revolutionary war were beyond the reach of the Geneva Convention ("O tamanho do porão: O Regime de 1985 começa a exercitar uma difícil convivência com uma das heranças deixadas pelo Regime de 1964," *Veja*, September 10, 1986, p. 43).

5. Emilia Viotti da Costa, *The Brazilian Empire: Myths and Histories* (Chicago: University of Chicago Press, 1985), pp. 185–86, 193.

6. June E. Hahner, "Feminism, Women's Rights, and The Suffrage Movement in Brazil, 1850–1932," *Latin American Research Review* 15, no. 1 (1980): 65–111.

7. Rachel Soihet, "Bertha Lutz e a ascensão social da mulher, 1919–1937" (M.A. thesis, Universidade Federal Fluminense, 1974).

8. "A valsa das alianças," *Veja*, December 2, 1987, pp. 82–89.

9. See for example, the World Bank report, *Population Change and Economic Development* (Washington, D.C., 1984).

10. Joseph E. Potter, "Explanations of Fertility Decline in Latin America," *Social Science Research Council Items* 40, no. 2 (June 1986): 31–36. The quote is from p. 32. The ready availability of birth control pills in any pharmacy and the increased exposure to medical personnel thanks to the spread of social security programs and facilities have played a role in this trend. Scholars had not expected birth control technology to have such an immediate impact, partly because they underestimated the effects of mass media and economic change.

11. June E. Hahner, *Women in Brazil: Problems and Perspectives*, Brazil Curriculum Guide Specialized Bibliography, Latin American Institute, University of New Mexico (Albuquerque, [1984?]), pp. 9–10.

12. June E. Hahner, "Recent Research on Women in Brazil," *Latin American Research Review* 20, no. 3 (1985): 163–79. The quote is from p. 164.

13. "Melhores dias para um símbolo," *Isto É*, September 9, 1987, p. 50.

Glossary and Acronyms

ABDIB. Brazilian Association for the Development of Basic Industry.

Abertura. Gradual relaxation of dictatorship in the mid- and late 1970s.

ABIA. Brazilian Association for Food Industries.

ABIMEE. Brazilian Association for Electrical Materials and Electronics Industries.

Abolition (-ists). Slave emancipation movement and its supporters in the 1880s; culminated in the 1888 Lei Aurea, or emancipation act.

Adecista. Person who supported the Old Republic only after it came into existence.

Agregado. Hired hand, usually on a landed estate.

Alqueire. Measure of volume, similar to a bushel.

AMAN. Agulhas Negras Military Academy.

Anarcho-syndicalism. Political ideology calling for the end of government (anarchism) and its replacement by union committees (syndicalism).

ANFAVEA. National Association of Automobile Manufacturers.

ARENA. National Renovating Alliance. Government party from 1966 to 1982.

Aspirantes. First officer rank attained upon graduation from AMAN.

Bacharel (-ismo). Law school graduates, prominent in government service during the Second Empire and Old Republic.

Baião. A carnaval dance.

Bandeirantes. Colonial explorers and Indian slavers from São Paulo who charted the backlands and discovered gold.

Beatos (as). Lay holy men and women in popular Catholicism.

Biônicos. ARENA senators from several states in the late 1970s whose mandates were extended by the government in order to retain control of congress.

Blocos. Groups of several hundred to a thousand Carnaval street dancers.
-sujos. Unlicensed and formerly illegal blocos.

BNDE. National Bank for Economic Development created by Vargas in the early 1950s to promote heavy industry.

BNH. National Housing Bank, created in 1965.

BOC. Worker and Peasant Bloc.

Boia-frio. Rural day laborer (literally "cold lunch-pail").

Bucha. Secret society of São Paulo law school students and alumni.

Caboclo. Rural person, usually poor and uneducated. See *caipira.*

Café com Leite. Gentlemen's agreement between the Mineiro and Paulista elites in the Old Republic to alternate the presidency between them.

Caipira. A rural person, rustic and uneducated.

Candomblé. Afro-Brazilian religion, especially in and around Salvador da Bahia. Similar to Macumba, Umbanda, and Quimbanda.

Canoa. Military impressment. (Literally, canoe.)

Canudos. A messianic community in western Bahia in the 1890s, led by Antônio Conselheiro, finally eliminated by the army in 1897.

Capanga. A tough or hired gun, usually in rural areas; bodyguard for landowner.

Carnaval. Raucous pre-Lenten festivities celebrated throughout Brazil; like Mardi Gras.

Cassação. Removal of an individual's political rights, usually for ten years, under the Ato Institutional 1 of 1964.

CDE. Economic Development Council.

CEB. Ecclesiastical Base Communities, formed in the 1970s and 1980s by Catholics who wished to use the church to reform society and uplift the poor.

Central. A highly mechanized sugar refining factory.

CGT. General Confederation of Workers.

Chapas. Ballots or, by extension, alliances of parties or candidates in a given election.

Chapa única. Rule that voters have to choose candidates from a single party, i.e., vote a straight ticket.

Charqueadas. Establishments for processing dried meat and hides.

Científicos. Members of Mexican political elite who were followers of Comte's Positivism.

CIM. Council For Indigenous Mission.

Classes conservadoras. Propertied groups, economic elites.

CMN. National Monetary Council.

CNBB. National Conference of Brazilian Bishops.

CNTI. National Confederation of Industrial Workers.

Coiteiro (-ismo). A person of authority in the Northeast who protects rural gunmen in exchange for favors and loyalty.

Colégio. High school or prep school.

Colono. Tenant farmer who also works under contract.

Comissário. Coffee broker, esp. during the Old Republic.

Compadre. Coparent in ritual godfather kinship.

Conciliação. Tendency for Brazilian politicians to avoid conflict and to seek nonviolent resolution of problems.

Congada. Ritual coronation of African king in Afro-Brazilian communities.

Concientização. Consciousness raising.

CONSPLAN. National Planning Council.

Contestado. Violent dispute over lands bordering Santa Catarina and Paraná, finally ended by the army in 1915.

Continuismo. Efforts by incument politicians to stay in office beyond legal term.

Cordel. Folk versification, performed by troubadours, found in rural areas.

Coronel (-ismo). A rural landowner and boss who dominated local politics by force from the late nineteenth to the mid-twentieth century.

Cortiço. An urban tenement, built with so many small rooms that it resembled a beehive.

CPOR. Reserve Officer Training Units.

CTB. Confederation of Brazilian Workers (1946–).

CUT. Unified Workers' Central.

Degola. Fraudulent disqualification of elected official by political bosses.

Desquitado, -a. A person legally separated from his or her spouse, especially before divorce was legalized in 1977.

DIP. Press and Propaganda Department.

Distensão. General relaxation of dictatorship in the mid-1970s.

Do bico de pena. Fraudulent votes during the Old Republic, cast "from the tip of a pen" by the coronel.

Doutor. Urban political bosses during the Old Republic; often allied themselves with *coronóis*.

ECEME. Army Command and High Staff School.

ECLA. Economic Commission for Latin America.

Elitelore. Ethnographic technique for studying elites.

Empire. Period from independence (1822) to the Republic (1889–).

Encilhamento. Period of great inflation in 1890–91 (literally, saddling up).

Engenho. Sugar mill.

Escola Prática. Military school specializing in tactical training.

ESAO. Advanced officer Training School.

ESG. Superior War College.

Espiritismo. Spiritualism, or system of beliefs based on communication with spirits of the dead.

Estado de compromisso. Government sustained only by coalitions.

Estatização. Growing government ownership of business.

Favelas. Shantytowns in and around major cities, occupied by squatters.

Fazendeiros. Large landowners.

FEB. Brazilian Expeditionary Force; fought with the United States in Italy in World War II.

FGTS. Guarantee Fund for Time of Service.

FIESP. São Paulo Industrial Federation.

Filho(-a) de santo. Spiritualist medium, in African rites.

Frevo. A carnaval dance.

Gaúcho. Native of Rio Grande do Sul; also ranch hand.

GEIA. Executive Group, for advising President Kubitschek.

Homen cordial. A person of cool, affable disposition admired in Brazilian society.

Homens de confiança. Trusted colleagues.

IBGE. Brazilian Institute of Geography and Statistics.

IBOPE. Brazilian Institute of Public Opinion and Statistics.

Integralismo (-istas). Fascistic political movement in the 1930s, led by Plínio Salgado.

Interventor. Federal agent sent to take over a public agency or a union; appointed state governors during the Estado Novo.

Irmandade. Religious brotherhood in the Catholic Church.

ISEB. Advanced Institute for Brazilian Studies.

Jagunço. Backlands gunman, often in the hire of a coronel or landowner. See also *capanga.*

JEC. Young Catholic Students.

Jeito. Trick or clever maneuver to skirt obstacles.

JOC. Young Catholic Workers.

JUC. Catholic University Youth.

Legenda. Tabulations of votes by party, independently from those for candidates, for the purpose of allocating legislative seats proportionally.

Liberal Alliance. Coalition of opposition forces in the 1930 presidential election.

Liberation Theology. Body of Catholic thought favoring active church role in socioeconomic and political reform.

Macumba. Afro-Brazilian religion prevalent in Rio de Janeiro. See also *Candomblé* and *Umbanda.*

Mae or pai de santo. Spiritualist medium in African rites.

Marchinha. Popular song of the 1920s and 1930s.

Mascate. Itinerant peddler.

MDB. Brazilian Democratic Movement, opposition party from 1965 to 1982.

MEB. Grassroots Educational Movement.

Mestiço. Person of mixed racial heritage, usually Indian and white.

Mineiro. Native of Minas Gerais.

Morador. Resident or smallholder.

MPB. Brazilian popular music.

Mulatto. Person with Caucasian and Negroid heritage.

Município. A county-like administrative district.

MUT. Workers' Unification Movement.

Nação Armada. Nation in Arms. An army journal.

Novelas. Soap operas.

Old Republic. Period from 1889 to 1930.

Pacote. A "package" of political reforms, usually imposed with little warning and designed to thwart the opposition.

Panelinha. Informal group of colleagues who help one another in business and politics. Cf. *turma.*

Parceiro. Sharecropper.

Patrão. Employer.

Pátria. Fatherland, also Motherland.

Paulista. Native of São Paulo

PCB. Brazilian Communist Party (1922–).

PCdoB. The Communist Party of Brazil, ideologically opposed to the PCB.

Peixaria. Members of a *turma* who rise under the tutelage of someone from an older *turma.*

Pelego. Labor leader in the employment or under the influence of the Ministry of Labor, often open to corruption. Literally, saddle blanket.

Pernambucano. Native of Pernambuco.

Personalismo. Cult of the leader in politics.

Petrobras. Petroleos Brasileiros, the state-owned petroleum company.

Pistolão. Personal influence or leverage in politics.

Politics of the Governors. Tendency from 1900 to 1930 for the governors of the leading states to control national affairs.

Planalto, Palácio do. Presidential palace.

Positivism. School of philosophy, developed by Auguste Comte in the mid-19th century, stressing order and progress.

Povão. The unwashed masses.

Povo. The people, or the masses.

Povo fardado. The people in uniform, i.e. the army.

Prestes Column. Guerrilla force active from 1924 to 1927, led by future communist leader, Luís Carlos Prestes.

Preto (a) velho (a). A black elder who serves as counselor in an Afro-Brazilian community.

PSD. Social Democratic Party (1945–65), formed at Vargas's behest in 1945.

PT. Workers' Party.

PTB. Brazilian Labor Party (1945–65), formed at Vargas's behest.

Queremismo, -ista. 1945 campaign to nominate Getúlio Vargas for the presidential succession.

Quilombo. Camp founded by runaway slaves.

Revolution of 1930. Military movement that brought Getúlio Vargas to power.

Rodéio. Rodeo or roundup. Slang for evasion and subterfuge.

Salvações. Federal takeovers of state governments in the 1910s, often using the army, to influence local politics.

Samba school. Organization of several thousand persons to participate in Carnaval parades and activities.

Sertão, sertanejo. Backlands, backlanders.

Show de auditório. Television variety show.

SIMESP. São Paulo Machine and Tool Industry Association.

Sindicato. Labor union.

Situação. Incumbent political party or group.

SNI. National Intelligence Service.

SOUCESP. An Umbanda federation in São Paulo.

SUNAB. National Food Supply Agency.

Telenovelas. Television soap operas.

Tenentes. Radical military officers and cadets in the 1920s and 1930s who rebelled in order to force government reforms. See also *Prestes Column.*

Terreiro. Afro-Brazilian religious ceremonial ground or building.

Testa de ferro. Stalking horse.

Tiros. Target-shooting clubs, organized in the 1910s to train army reservists.

Trabalhismo. Labor doctrine devised by Vargas to win political support from workers. See PTB.

Tropeiro. Mule or cattle drover.

Turco. Turkish, or from any middle-eastern ethnic group.

Turma. Clique or informal group of professionals, especially military officers, who studied or graduated together. Cf. *panelinha.*

UDN. National Democratic Union (1945–65) formed to oppose Vargas.

Umbanda. Afro-Brazilian religion. See also *Macumba, Candomblé.*

Usina. Modern sugar mill.

Valorization. Coffee support programs organized by producing states from 1906 to 1925.

Voto distrital. Requirement that a party run candidates at all levels (i.e. at district as well as national levels) in order to qualify.

Zona da mata. Fertile and humid coastlands of the Northeast.

The Contributors

Sam Adamo holds a doctorate in history from the University of New Mexico and currently directs computer aspects of long-range planning for the city of Albuquerque. His publications include "Order and Progress for Some, Death and Disease for Others: Living Conditions of Nonwhites in Rio de Janeiro, 1890–1940," in *Investigating Natural Hazards in Latin America* (Atlanta, 1986).

Bert J. Barickman holds a Social Science Research Council grant to complete his Ph.D. dissertation at the University of Illinois, Urbana–Champaign. His research topic is slavery in Bahia between 1785 and 1888.

Michael L. Conniff is a professor of history at the University of New Mexico. His books include *Urban Politics in Brazil* (Pittsburgh, 1981); *Black Labor on a White Canal* (Pittsburgh, 1985), as well as an edition, *Latin American Populism in Comparative Perspective* (Albuquerque, 1982).

Eli Diniz is a professor of political science at the Instituto Universitário de Pesquisas do Rio de Janeiro. Her books include *Empresário, estado e capitalismo no Brasil, 1930–1945* (Rio, 1978), *Voto e máquina política* (Rio, 1982), and *Empresariado nacional e estado no Brasil* (Rio, 1978, with Renato Boschi).

Marco Aurélio Garcia is a professor of history at the State University of Campinas, Brazil, where he directs the Edgar Levenroth Social History Archive. He has published widely on Brazilian labor studies.

Michael M. Hall is a professor of history at the State University of Campinas, Brazil. He is coeditor of *A classe operária no Brasil: Documentos, 1889 a 1930* (2 vols; São Paulo, 1979–81) and author of "The Working Class and the Urban Labour Movement" in *The Cambridge History of Latin America*, vol. 4.

Thomas H. Holloway is a professor of history at Cornell University and past director of the Latin American Center there. His publications include *Immigrants on the Land* (Chapel Hill, 1980), *The Brazilian Coffee Valorization of 1906* (Madison, 1975) and numerous essays on social history.

Robert M. Levine chairs the Department of History at the University of Miami. He has written two monographs on Brazil, The Vargas Regime: The Critical Years, 1934–1938 (New York, 1970) and Pernambuco in the Brazilian Federation (Stanford, 1978), as well as several research guides, and is editor of and contributor to Windows on Latin America: Using Photographs to Understand Society (1987). He is past chair of the Columbia University Seminar on Brazil and of the Committee on Brazilian Studies of the Conference on Latin American History.

Joseph L. Love is a professor of history at the University of Illinois, Urbana–Champaign. His books include Rio Grande do Sul and Brazilian Regionalism, 1882–1930 (Stanford, 1971) and São Paulo in the Brazilian Federation, 1889–1937 (Stanford, 1980).

Frank D. McCann is a professor of history at the University of New Hampshire. His publications include The Brazilian-American Alliance, 1937–1945 (Princeton, 1973), winner of the Stuart L. Bernath Prize of the Society for Historians of American Foreign Relations, and A Nação Armada: Ensaios sobre a História do Exército Brasileiro (Recife, 1982). He is past president of the New England Council on Latin American Studies, past chair of the Committee on Brazilian Studies of the Conference on Latin American History, and current president of the Northeast Association of Brazilianists. In 1987 the Brazilian government gave him the rank of "Comendador" in the Order of Rio Branco in recognition of his efforts to improve scholarly relations between the two countries.

Eul-Soo Pang is director of the Latin American Center and history professor at the Colorado School of Mines. The author of Bahia in the First Brazilian Republic: Coronelismo and Oligarchies, 1889–1934 (Gainesville, 1979), and In Pursuit of Honor and Power: Noblemen of the Southern Cross in Nineteenth-Century Brazil (Tuscaloosa, 1988), he has for years contributed articles on Brazil for Current History and served as correspondent for the American Universities Field Staff.

Joseph Dean Straubhaar is a professor of telecommuncations at Michigan State University. He previously worked with the USIS office in Rio de Janeiro and in 1988 served as Fulbright-Hayes professor in the Dominican Republic.

Fred Gillette Sturm is a professor of philosophy at the University of New Mexico and past president of the Society for Ibero and Latin American Thought. His publications include numerous monographs, translations, encyclopedia entries, and journal articles about Brazilian philosophy.

Steven Topik is an associate professor of history at the University of California, Irvine, and the author of The Political Economy of the Brazilian State, 1889–1930 (Austin, 1987) as well as numerous articles.

Index

Other volumes in the Latin American Studies Series include: